Social Work Practice with
Children and Families

The book forms part of the SAGE Social Work in Action Series, edited by Steven M. Shardlow.

Social Work Practice with Children and Families

Carolyn Spray *and* Beverley Jowett

Los Angeles | London | New Delhi
Singapore | Washington DC

© Carolyn Spray and Beverley Jowett 2012

First published 2012

SAGE Publications Ltd
1 Oliver's Yard
55 City Road
London EC1Y 1SP

SAGE Publications Inc.
2455 Teller Road
Thousand Oaks, California 91320

SAGE Publications India Pvt Ltd
B 1/I 1 Mohan Cooperative Industrial Area
Mathura Road
New Delhi 110 044

SAGE Publications Asia-Pacific Pte Ltd
33 Pekin Street #02-01
Far East Square
Singapore 048763

Library of Congress Control Number: 2011922757

British Library Cataloguing in Publication data

A catalogue record for this book is available from the British Library

ISBN 978-1-4129-2178-7
ISBN 978-1-4129-2179-4 (pbk)

Typeset by C&M Digitals (P) Ltd, Chennai, India
Printed by MPG Books Group, Bodmin, Cornwall
Printed on paper from sustainable resources

Contents

List of Figures and Tables

About the Authors

Carolyn Spray is a service manager with responsibility for Service Improvement in Sheffield City Council's Children, Young People and Families Service. Improving the quality of children's social care in Sheffield is at the heart of her role and she also leads on recruitment, retention and the continuous professional development of social workers.

Carolyn has many years experience of social work practice and of managing operational services at different levels. Most of this is within local authority children's services. Carolyn is also an adoptive parent and has experience of being a service user of post-adoption support services. This has informed her perspective of how multiagency support for children and their family should work in practice.

Beverley Jowett is a University Teacher in the Department of Sociological Studies at the University of Sheffield. She teaches on the qualifying and post qualifying social work courses and is course leader for the MA in Professional Practice. Her teaching interests include Safeguarding Children, and law and policy relating to children and families.

Prior to moving to the University of Sheffield in 2008, Beverley had over 20 years experience as a local authority social worker, the majority of this being in children and families services. She has worked in a range of posts which have involved duty and access work to longer term involvement with children of all ages. Her most recent social work post was based in Sheffield's maternity hospital, undertaking pre-birth assessments.

Preface

This book is about what enables good and effective practice in local authority field social work delivered to children, young people and their families. Field social work provides an assessment and care planning service to Children in Need and their families. This includes child protection services for children at risk of harm and accommodation for children who cannot live with their own family or kinship network.

Our aim is to appeal to a range of people with an interest in social work with children/young people and their families. Student and newly qualified social workers will find that it provides a helpful introduction to local authority social work as it offers an overview of social work as it exists today, as well as discussion of what enables effective practice. It will also, however, appeal to experienced practitioners who want to explore action research or create the space for reflective practice as part of their continuous professional development. Managers will be interested in what the organisation can do to support evidence-informed practice. Other professionals involved in supporting children and young people will also find this book useful as it describes what social work is and what social workers do in a local authority setting.

This book is about social workers effecting change so that children can continue to live successfully with their families and within their communities. Key issues involved in the practice of social work, are reinforced through the use of learning points at the beginning of each chapter. Three detailed case studies are employed to assist the reader understand the process of assessment, planning, intervention and review (APIR) as applied by local authority children's field social work services. They describe how social workers assess and support Children in Need, children in need of protection and children who need to be looked after in public care. The case studies also consider what happens to these children and their families at different points of the APIR process, as change is effected. They are woven into Chapters 3–6 as case study exercises and can be found in their entirety after Chapter 7 towards the end of the book. Each chapter concludes with a list of recommended further reading to assist the reader to easily explore any area of particular interest.

Finally, two glossaries have been included: one that details the legislation that is relevant to working with children and their families and the other that explains acronyms and defines terminology often used in the world of children's social care. When taken all together, the reader will find that this book comprehensively describes and discusses both the context for and the reality of effective social work practice with children and their families.

Acknowledgements

The authors wish to express their appreciation to Vicki Bennetts and Ruth Mason for their support and contribution to the development of this book.

Chapter 1

Setting the Scene: The Historical, Policy and Legislative Basis of Local Authority Children and Families Social Work

Introducing local authority social work

The intention of this introductory chapter is to set the scene for social work practice in an English local authority. This will provide a brief résumé of the relationship between social policy and social work and the impact child deaths have had upon legislation concerned with safeguarding children.

Learning points

- The impact of the welfare state upon neglected and abused children
- Different trends in practice and their translation into legislation
- The impact of child deaths
- The cause and effect of the Every Child Matters initiative
- Baby Peter and Social Work Reform

First let us consider how one of the most remarkable characteristics of child welfare is that the same issues arise again and again. Questions such as

- What are parental rights and responsibilities?
- What rights do children have?
- Whose rights take precedence?

have been answered differently at different times. This is because people's opinions, beliefs and judgements change. Much of contemporary legislation and social work practice relating to children and families has come about as a consequence of how such questions were answered in the past.

For those social workers who choose to work with children and young people in a local authority setting, it is important to have an understanding of the history of children's social care and the social policy context. Both have impacted on the legislative framework and the way the profession has responded to some complex issues, such as the rights of parents when in conflict with the needs and rights of children. Lorraine Fox Harding (1997) in her seminal text *Perspectives in Child Care Policy* characterises the different values that permeate childcare policy at different times as

- *Laissez faire* and patriarchy – leaving the family largely free of state interference
- State paternalism and child protection – legitimising authoritarian state interference and minimising the rights of parents
- Defence of the birth family and parents' rights – state intervention is legitimate but has as its focus the preservation of the family unit
- Children's rights – child is an independent person with individual rights

From Children's to Social Services Departments (1948–1971)

Before the Second World War, child welfare had been the responsibility of the Poor Law Guardians, local education authorities and voluntary organisations. Post-war Britain, however, was a time of economic and social reconstruction that witnessed the creation of the welfare state. As new state welfare services were established, a whole new set of relationships between the state, the market economy and the family began to emerge (Parton 1999). In this context, and partly in response to the death of Dennis O'Neill in foster care in 1945, the 1948 Children Act established new local authority Children's Departments. These were designed to provide a service for children in public care deprived of 'normal' family life. During this post-war period the major institutions of work and family went largely unchallenged and it was accepted that the role of the welfare state was to ensure that anyone on the margins of these institutions was helped back into the main body of society (Parton 2006). Over the next two decades the emphasis within Children's Departments shifted towards keeping children out of care in the first place or, when not possible, to rehabilitate children back into the care of their natural families.

By 1970 it had became apparent that there would be considerable advantages in bringing the different branches of social work together to form one generic profession, based on a common training qualification (Stevenson 1999). The Seebohm Report (1968) concluded that by redrawing the boundaries between services, more effective family and community services could be provided. This led to the establishment of Social Services Departments in 1971 and the responsibility for childcare transferred from the Home Secretary to the Secretary of State for Social Services. The establishment of unified local authority Social Services Departments heralded a new era for social work as a profession and during the early 1970s personal social services came out of the policy debate shadows (Hill 2000). With the family as its focus, the profession confidently sought to deliver a personalised service based on preventative principles.

By 1973, however, it was becoming clear that the era described by Jock Young (1999) as the 'Golden Age', a period that was both consensual and inclusive, was coming to an end. Two major social changes were becoming evident: globalisation and individualism. Globalisation wrought changes in the labour market, which became increasingly characterised by stratification, mobility and the presence of women, particularly married women. The poorest and most deprived, with the least flexibility, were left in concentrated pockets of housing. It was these pockets that often had to absorb families arriving from other countries, seeking asylum or greater economic security.

Hobsbawm (1994) argued that one of the institutions most undermined by the new emphasis on individualism was the family. As individualism became more pronounced the structures that kept men, women and children together in families were to some extent dismantled. The family was now seen as constituting individuals and in this context children began to be viewed as autonomous beings with rights and interests distinct from the family unit itself (Parton 2006). The scene was being set for a more antagonistic and conflictual relationship between parents and social workers as the interests and rights of children and their parents were no longer viewed as one and the same.

As the impact of economic instability and recession during the 1970s began to be felt, the difficulties in sustaining the welfare state became a central focus of public and political debate. The consensus on which it was based was subjected to increasing questioning and criticism. In this context it is hardly surprising that by the mid 1970s this new professional confidence was severely dented, as an unremitting series of child death inquiries led to increasing public disquiet about social work practice.

The impact of child deaths and the Cleveland Affair (1973–1987)

The death of Maria Colwell in 1973 at the hands of her stepfather, together with the growing evidence that children were spending longer in care as they waited for reunification plans to take effect (Rowe and Lambert 1973), led to the 1975 Children Act and to the 1976 Adoption Act. This effected a shift away from parental rights towards the welfare of children (Daniel and Ivatts 1998) and introduced a new emphasis on fostering and adoption. The 1975 Act also made provision for an independent social worker to ensure the best interests of the child within court proceedings and thus established the new professional role of guardian ad item, now called the child's Guardian. The public inquiry into Maria's death published in September 1974 concluded that, although individuals had made mistakes, it was ultimately the system that had failed her. This led to the introduction of a new child abuse management system intended to ensure that all professionals involved in supporting children were familiar with signs of child abuse and that mechanisms were established for inter-agency communication and coordination (Parton 2006).

Parton and Thomas (1983) noted how, after the Maria Colwell Inquiry, social work practice was no longer seen as a private activity between social worker and client but as a legitimate arena for public scrutiny. Here the media took on a key role in raising issues previously mostly hidden from public view. Criticism of the nature of social work interventions reached new heights during the 1980s, with a succession of child abuse inquiries. The most well known of these are the inquiries concerning Jasmine Beckford (London Borough of Brent 1985), Kimberley Carlisle (London Borough of Greenwich 1987) and Tyra Henry (London Borough of Lambeth 1987). The emphases in the recommendations of the 30-plus inquiries published between 1973 and 1987 was on social workers using their legal powers more effectively to protect children, on improving their knowledge of the indicators of abuse and on the need to improve collaborative processes between all professionals involved with children (DHSS 1982; DH 1991b). The concept of 'child abuse' was defined, redefined and then enshrined in government guidance during the 1970s. By the 1980s it included physical, emotional, sexual abuse and neglect, focusing not just on very young children but on all children and young people up to 18 years of age (*Working Together under the Children Act 1989*, DH and the Home Office 1991).

The events in Cleveland in 1987 introduced a new dimension into the controversy surrounding the work of social workers with children and their families. This focused on the removal of more than 100 children from their families by social workers, subsequent to a diagnosis of sexual abuse by two paediatricians, based in a hospital in Middlesborough. For the first time the issue of abuse publicly impacted upon middle-class families, and disadvantaged and poor families could no longer be seen as the sole source of child abuse. However, the Cleveland Affair also appeared to demonstrate the failure of both social workers and paediatricians to protect the rights of parents, as well as the use of draconian powers to remove children prematurely from their families. Social workers were now routinely represented in the media as either '*fools and wimps*' or '*villains and bullies*' (Franklin and Parton 1991).

Social workers now seemed to represent all that was wrong with post-war welfarism. It was not therefore surprising that the third term of Margaret Thatcher's Conservative administration, which was centrally concerned with reforming welfare provision, turned its attention to reforming legislation pertaining to the welfare of children.

The Children Act 1989

Though the Children Act 1989 can be seen as the culmination of a period of controversy both about welfare policy and the role of social workers in the lives of children, drawn up at a time of 'New Right' dominance (Packman and Jordan 1991), it was in fact a further piece of consensus legislation.

> The Act was informed not just by child abuse public inquiries, but by research and a series of respected official reports during the 1980s, particularly the Short Report (Social Services Committee, 1984) and the Review of Child Care Law (DHSS, 1985) and was subject to careful civil service drafting and management and exhaustive consultation with a wide range of professional groups and interested parties. (Parton 1999: 15)

Those responsible for drawing up this Act were seeking not only to get the balance right between the families' right for privacy and autonomy but also between the responsibilities of all the agencies involved in supporting children and how they exercised those responsibilities.

The Act therefore had three primary aims. First, it set about forging a new set of balances between children, parents and the state. It introduced the concepts of parental responsibilities and working in partnership and gave a new emphasis to the views of the child. Secondly, it sought to unify public and private law relating to children. Thirdly, it aimed to bring together all services relating to children, including children with disabilities. This act also broadened the concept of prevention, from simply preventing children from entering public care, to one of preventing family breakdown through the duty to provide services whenever a child was deemed to be in need. Further information about some its key provisions can be found in the Legislation Glossary at the end of the book.

Problematically, the Act was implemented in 1991 in an economically, socially and politically hostile climate. The combination of Conservative government reforms in relation to health, housing, social security, education and community care and the impact of recession had a particular impact upon children. In 1979 1.4 million (10%) children lived in poverty. By 1993 this had increased to 4.3 million children (one-third) (DSS 1995). This was an increase far greater than the population as a whole.

During the early 1990s a number of other trends can be identified. Social work managers, as opposed to practitioners, became the brokers between the purchaser/provider relationship engendered by the Community Care legislation. The combination of both the Community Care Act 1990 and the Children Act 1989 resulted in the generic social worker increasingly being replaced by the specialist social worker. Moreover social workers working with children became almost exclusively involved in child protection and the management of risk.

The impact of institutional abuse

In 1997, Tony Blair's 'New Labour' Party swept the Conservatives out of power after 18 consecutive years of rule. Two months later Sir William Utting's Report *A Review of the Safeguards for Children Living Away from Home* commissioned following a series of scandals relating to the abuse of children in residential care, was published. Concern now began to focus on abuse that took place outside of the family and the need to protect society from 'the paedophile' became a source of increasing public anxiety and media attention. Utting's report, together with other publications such as the 1998 Social Services Inspectorate Report *Someone Else's Children* (Hoare et al. 1998) and Norman Warner's report *Choosing with Care* (1992), were hugely influential in formulating the new government's reform agenda for child welfare, as outlined in *Modernising Social Services* (DH 1998). This outlined the government's strategy for strengthening child protection systems, improving the quality of services and improving the life chances of children in need and looked after children. This led to the *Quality Protects* initiative, implemented in 2000, a five-year programme designed to transform the management and delivery of children's social services. Ronald Waterhouse's report: *Lost in Care, Report of the Tribunal of Inquiry into the Abuse of Children in Core in the Former County Council Areas of Gwynedd and Clwyd Since 1974* was published in 2000 and this informed the Care Standards Act 2000 which sought to reform the regulatory system for care services for vulnerable adults and children in England and Wales. In 2002 and 2003, National Minimum Standards were issued with regards to fostering, adoptive, and residential provision as well as to child minding, day care provision and boarding schools. All such providers had to register with either the National Care Standards Commission or the National Assembly for Wales and were subject to a new inspection regime.

At the same time the government introduced its *Best Value Performance Management Framework*, which set targets for all local authority services relating to quality and efficiency of services, and a new performance-focused regime for all social services departments was born. The emphasis was now on achieving performance targets, inspection and league tables. This shift towards managerialism and the manager's right to manage was the means by which the Labour government sought to achieve value for money and accountability both to the taxpayer and to the service user. However within children's social care it also served to force managers to become preoccupied with meeting performance targets and with inspection preparation. Decision making about children became a managerial function rather than something that should be based on the professional judgement of the social worker (Munro 2010).

Refocusing social work

During the 1990s considerable evidence had amassed that demonstrated that local authority social services were failing to develop family support services as envisioned by the Children Act 1989 (Aldgate and Tunstill 1995). An Audit Commission Report (1994) and a Department of Health publication called *Messages from Research* (1995) led to a major debate about the balance and relationship between child protection and family support. The view that prevailed concluded that, unless children's needs were assessed holistically, then intrusively focused social work investigative processes could only produce poor outcomes. Its proponents sought to eliminate the divide between protection and prevention and concluded that both were essential aims at every level of intervention. When New Labour came to power, the government sought not only to rebalance child protection and family support but to encourage all agencies involved in supporting children to develop accessible preventative services (Parton 2006). The role of early years provision was seen as particularly important in delivering this agenda. The government view was made clear in their Green Paper *Supporting Families: A Consultation Document* (Home Office 1998). Ensuring children, particularly poor children, were better supported by both supporting and penalising parents to make them parent more effectively was to be a key strategy in combating youth crime (Maclean 2002). For the Labour government it was also a key strategy in another policy priority, combating social exclusion.

At the same time as the government was issuing its revised child protection guidance *Working Together to Safeguard Children* (DH 1999), it was also setting up a pilot study to assess the development of a multi-agency approach to assessment.

This led to the *Framework for the Assessment of Children in Need and Their Families* (Assessment Framework), which was implemented in 2001. This now frames all assessments of children and their families undertaken by local authority social workers. It is also the basis of the Common Assessment Framework (CAF) introduced in 2005 to assist other professionals involved in supporting children identify and assess children with additional needs. Together with the Looking After Children materials implemented in 1995, the Assessment Framework forms the basis of the Integrated Childrens System (ICS), which was implemented during 2007. These will be discussed in more detail in Chapters 3 and 4.

The Labour government also brought in a whole swathe of legislation to frame how personal social services are delivered to children and their families and to promote the safeguarding of children. A brief description of the most significant can also be found in the Legislation Glossary.

The death of Victoria Climbié (2000) and Every Child Matters (2003)

Outcomes of inquiries into child deaths continued to impact upon social policy and guidance, notably Rikki Neave (Cambridge 1995), Lauren Wright (Norfolk 2000) and Ainlee Walker (Newham 2002). In 2002 the Joint Chief Inspectors Review Report was published. This found that whilst all agencies accepted their responsibilities in relation to child protection, this was not always reflected in practice. Agencies were not always willing to support or fund the work of Area Child Protection Committees. These were non-statutory partnerships that brought together agencies involved in child protection work to clarify roles and responsibilities, agree inter-agency protocols and oversee Part 8: Reviews of Child Deaths, as outlined by *Working Together* (DH 1999). Difficulties in recruiting and retaining professionals required to work in child protection were also reducing the effectiveness of procedures in place to safeguard children. This report, together with the report of the Inquiry by Lord Laming (2003), into the prolonged abuse and subsequent death of Victoria Climbié (London Borough of Haringey 2002), at the hands of her great aunt and her great aunt's partner, was to lead to profound changes in the arrangements for children's social services and, in effect, to herald the demise of the entity known as the Social Services Department:

> The death of Victoria Climbié exposed shameful failings in our ability to protect the most vulnerable children. On twelve occasions, over ten months, chances to save Victoria's life were not taken. Social services, the police and the NHS failed, as Lord Laming's report into Victoria's death made clear, to do the most basic things well to protect her. (DfES 2003: 5)

The immediate impact of the Laming Inquiry Report was the decision to move the responsibility for children's social services, family policy, teenage pregnancy, family law and the Children and Family Court Advisory Service (CAFCASS) from the Minister for Health to the Minister for Education and Skills (DfES). This brought the responsibility for all policy and legislative changes relating to children and young peoples under the jurisdiction of one ministry. This was with the notable exception of youth crime, which remained with the Home Office.

The longer-term and infinitely more profound impact was felt with the publication of the government Green Paper *Every Child Matters* in 2003 (HM Treasury 2003). This announced the government's intention to draw up new legislation that would address the concern raised by Lord Laming that accountability and safe management practice were still not a priority for the agencies involved with safeguarding the needs of children: '*The principal failure to protect her [Victoria] was the result of widespread organisational malaise*' (Laming Report 2003: para. 1.21; emphasis added).

The Green Paper sets out five outcomes, which all services for children should work towards achieving. These are represented in the Table 1.1.

Table 1.1   The five outcomes of Every Child Matters

Outcome	What it means
Be healthy	Being physically, mentally, emotionally and sexually healthy and having a healthy lifestyle
	Parents, carers and families promote healthy choices
Stay safe	Safe from maltreatment, neglect, violence, sexual exploitation, accidental injury/death, bullying, discrimination, crime, anti-social behaviour. Have security, stability and are cared for
	Parents, carers and families provide safe homes and stability
Enjoy and achieve	Ready for, attend and enjoy school. Achieve stretching national educational standards. Achieve personal and social development and enjoy recreation
	Parents, carers and families support learning
Make a positive contribution	Engage in decision making, law-abiding, positive and enterprising behaviour. Develop positive relationships, self-confidence and successfully deal with significant life changes and challenges
	Parents, carers and families promote positive behaviour
Achieve economic well-being	Engage in further education, employment or training on leaving school. Live in decent homes and sustainable communities, have access to transport and material goods, live in households free from low income
	Parents, carers and families are supported to be economically active

Source: *Every Child Matters: Change for Children*, DfES 2004a: 9

In order to achieve these outcomes, in *Every Child Matters: Next Steps* (DfES 2004b) the government announced its intention to focus on four main areas:

Supporting parents and carers through information, advice and support provided by universal services and through targeted and specialist services for parents of children who need them.

Early intervention and effective protection to be achieved by establishing multi-agency teams and co-locating services, improving information sharing, implementing the Common Assessment Framework and the Lead Professional role.

Accountability and integration by bringing together the commissioning of key services through Children's Trusts and requiring local authorities to set up partnership arrangements with a specific focus on Local Safeguarding Boards. Also by locating new leaders in the Director of Children's Services and the Lead Elected Member and creating a new national role for a Children's Commissioner.

Workforce reform by developing a pay and workforce strategy that addresses recruitment and retention issues within the children's workforce as well as improving its skills and abilities.

By and large local authorities with social services responsibilities welcomed the Green Paper, though concerns were immediately expressed about whether resources were going to be made available to fulfil such an ambitious agenda. Andrew Cozens, on behalf of the Association of Directors of Social Services, pointed out:

> The vision in the Seebohm Report was a preventative one with universal access at the point of need but it became diluted with scarce resources, focussed increasingly tightly on the relatively few with very high levels of need. Access to services became defined by eligibility criteria, so derided by the Victoria Climbié Inquiry Report. (ADSS 2003: 6)

Arguing that the resource requirements needed to be fully understood and then met, Andrew Cozens asserted that:

> Broadening the constituent population that can have early access to preventative services has to be reflected in the resource base available to all key stakeholders in the childcare sector. A step change of this kind should follow a national audit of the numbers of children who would benefit from specific and comprehensive intervention at an early stage. ADSS has repeatedly highlighted the need for a Wanless type review of social care to ascertain the range and scale of what is required and would again urge that such a review be conducted. (ADSS 2003: 6)

The ADSS did not get its Wanless type review. The government did, however, press ahead to provide the legislative framework for its Every Child Matters change agenda (DfES 2004a) for children's services in England through the

Children Act 2004. Its provisions aimed to promote integrated working amongst professionals involved in supporting children through the establishment of Children's Services Authorities and Children's Trusts and statutory Local Safeguarding Children Boards. A more detailed description of some its key provisions can be found in the Legislation Glossary.

The Every Child Matters initiative also led to the *Care Matters* White Paper (DfES 2007) and the Children and Young Persons Act of 2008. This aimed to ensure that children and young people looked after within the public care system received high quality care and services, which are focused on and tailored to their needs. In particular the Act endeavoured to improve the stability of placements and the educational experience and attainment of young people in local authority care or those about to leave care.

What then has all this meant for social work practitioners? Within local authority social work, this by and large has depended on local interpretation of the legislation and the finance available to implement the reforms, especially in relation to the integration of services. Most social workers, however, have experienced the separation of adult and children's services. Those working with children and young people are now employed by Children's Services Authorities (CSAs) together with all those previously employed by the Local Education Authority (LEA).

With the introduction of the CAF, based as it is on the Assessment Framework, social workers have increasingly experienced a common language when talking to other professionals involved in supporting children. There has also been renewed enthusiasm for multi-agency working, with some local authorities introducing virtual teams and others co-locating social work teams with other groups of professionals. Above all, listening to the 'voice of the child' became a priority not just for practitioners but also for managers, planners and councillors alike. At least that is what many involved in the world of children and families' social work believed until that particular bubble burst with the death of 'Baby Peter'.

The death of Peter Connelly (2007)

On 3 August 2007 Peter Connelly, a 17-month-old toddler, later more widely known as Baby Peter, was pronounced dead on his arrival at hospital as a result of multiple injuries. On 11 November 2008 his mother's partner and his brother were found guilty of his murder. His mother pleaded guilty to the same offence. At the time of his death, Peter was on Haringey Council's child protection register in the categories of physical abuse and neglect and was the subject of a multi-agency child protection plan. Peter had suffered 50 injuries despite receiving 60 visits from social workers, doctors and police over the final eight months of his life. The second Serious Case Review found that the interventions put into place as part of the child protection plan were 'insufficiently challenging to the parent [and] … insufficiently focused on the children's welfare' (Haringey Local Safeguarding Children Board 2009: 29). The fact that this was the same London borough in which Victoria Climbié died served to symbolise the failure of local authority social services departments to learn from the deaths of children known to them.

Peter's death thus caused yet another crisis of confidence in social work and again the profession was put on the defensive. As part of its response the government established the Social Work Task Force, chaired by Moira Gibb CBE, Chief Executive of the London Borough of Camden, and a former social worker. The purpose of the task group was to conduct a 'nuts and bolts' review of the profession and to advise on the shape and content of a comprehensive reform programme for social work. The Task Force considered what social workers said to them about what they needed:

- more time to work directly with children and their families
- regular high quality supervision and time for critical reflection
- better education and training
- more opportunities for career development
- improved IT and support
- stronger professional leadership, standing and voice

Having considered this alongside other contributions, the Task Force went on to identify what the social work profession needed to be (see Box 1.1) and made a number of recommendations that became the basis of the social work reform programme.

Box 1.1 The Social Work Task Force said that the social work profession needed to be:

- confident about its values, purpose and identity;
- working in partnership with people who use its services, so that they can take control of their situation and improve the outcome;
- working cohesively with other professions and agencies in the best interests of people in need of support;
- demonstrating its impact and effectiveness and, therefore, its value to the public;
- committed to continuous improvement, with the training and resources it needs to be effective and a vigorous culture of professional development;

- understood and supported by employers, educators, government, other professionals and the wider public; and
- well led at every level: in frontline practice; in influencing the shape and priorities of local services; in setting and maintaining the highest possible standards within the profession; and in influencing policy developments and priorities at national and political level.

Facing Up to the Task: Interim Report of the Social Work Task Force (2009)

This review was undertaken alongside the government-funded Children's Workforce Development Council's (CWDC) three-year social work programme (see CWDC 2010). This intended to drive and support improvements in the way social workers are recruited, trained and supported to work with children and families in England. The programme included piloting a programme of enhanced support for newly qualified social workers (NQSW) and those in their early professional development (EPD) and developing roles such as the advanced social work professional (ASWP) that would encourage and enable experienced practitioners to remain in practice. What this will all lead to in the context of children and family's social work remains to be seen. However, the fact that the majority of local authorities are participating in the NQSW and EPD pilots and some have already established ASWP roles, is evidence that some things are already changing, at least for a number of qualified practitioners working on the front line.

Social work reform 2010 onwards

In May 2010 the Conservative/Liberal Democrat Coalition government came to power against a backdrop of a global economic crisis and recession. Massive public spending cuts have ensued and local authorities have been faced with reduced income from the government of about 26% between 2011 and 2015. It has also been predicted that approximately 500,000 jobs will be lost to the public sector – many of these from within local authorities. The impact of much of this has yet to be fully realised, particularly with regard to early intervention and preventative services and to social care services.

The Coalition government has, however, given its support to the Social Work Reform Board, also chaired by Moira Gibb, which is now charged with progressing the recommendations of the Social Work Task Force. As one of the Coalition government's first steps was to rename the Department for Children, Schools and Families (DCSF) as the Department for Education (DfE), this step served to alleviate apprehension amongst some social work professionals that the new government lacked commitment to progress the work of the Social Work Task Force.

The government has also commissioned reviews of a number of services affecting children and families which will also have implications for social care. These include:

- Munro Review of Child Protection
- Family Justice Review
- Allen Review into Early Intervention
- Frank Field Review of Tackling Poverty

In the social care sector organisations that support social work delivery are also changing. The Children's Workforce Development Council (CWDC) will cease to exist as a non-departmental public body, with its workforce development functions being absorbed by the Department for Education by 2012. The General Social Care Council will cease to exist by 2012 with the renamed Health Professions Council taking on registration of social workers and the regulation of social work degree courses. The College of Social Work, currently under development, is expected to become the voice for social work and to provide leadership for the profession.

The Social Work Reform Board progress report *Building a Safe and Confident Future: One Year On* (2010) considers five areas that have been identified as in need of reform:

- an overarching professional standards framework that includes a single nationally recognised career progression route and expectations at each stage of a social worker's career
- standards for employers and a supervision framework
- principles that should underpin a continuing professional framework
- requirements for social work education
- partnerships between employers and educators

During 2011 the Reform Board expects to test these five areas with both individuals and organisations, whilst at the same time developing other areas of work, such as the national social work supply and demand model and the proposed Assessed and Supported Year in Employment (ASYE). It is likely that the ASYE will replace, though be informed by, the Newly Qualified Social Worker programme.

Little reference here is made to pay, other than to say that the Reform Board is working with Local Government Employers and the Trade Unions to ensure that the 'right links are made to support the implementation of the National Career Structure' (Social Work Reform Board 2010: 15). Difference in pay is problematic as it means that social workers do not get the same remuneration for doing the same extremely complex job. This is unlike most other public sector professional groups. It also sets local authorities in competition with one another which impacts adversely upon both recruitment and retention.

This is not an easy issue to resolve because to reintroduce national pay scales would involve some social workers receiving less and others more. It

would also not be easy for those local authorities having to pay social workers more to find the additional funding required, especially in the current
economic climate. However, the inability of some local authorities to fill
vacancies and to retain staff can lead to turbulence in the workforce and to
over-reliance upon agency social workers. This results in too many children
receiving services characterised by delay, lack of continuity and drift. The
need to provide some kind of national framework for pay scales therefore
remains an important element in the jigsaw of reforms required.

There is also a seeming lack of commitment to ensure that all social workers
have access to the post-qualifying award and to ensure that only those social
workers who have achieved at least the Higher Specialist PQ (if not the
Masters) Award are eligible for the Advanced Social Work Professional (ASWP)
role. In the authors' view these are missed opportunities. The fact that take-up
of the PQ award by employers has been patchy is cited as the reason. However,
the lack of commitment of some, though by no means all employers, to providing funding for PQ is an issue that needs to be addressed as part of this process
of reform. Enabling experienced social workers the opportunity to refresh and
reflect on their practice, within an academic framework, is a vital developmental opportunity that needs to become an essential rather than a desirable aspect
of social work continuous professional development. It is difficult to see how
the ASWP role can deliver 'excellence' in practice without it.

In May 2010 the government commissioned Professor Eileen Munro, Reader
in Social Policy at the London School of Economics, to undertake a further
review of child protection work. Intended to build upon the work of the Social
Work Task Force, Professor Munro has been asked to look at how bureaucracy
can be reduced and how social workers can be helped to spend more time with
children and their families. The first part of the review, called the *Munro Review
of Child Protection – Part One: A Systems Analysis*, was published in 2010.

In this report Munro noted that reforms introduced by previous governments were well informed and well intentioned and yet had not led to the
expected improvements in front line practice. In fact, Munro concluded, past
reforms have had unforeseen consequences and this had led her to adopt a
systems approach to the review to enable the understanding of 'how reforms
interact and the effect these interactions have on practice' (Munro 2010: 5).
On a more positive note, she affirmed that knowledge about interventions
that work had substantially increased and that there was both good practice
and research findings to draw from and build upon.

The main problems identified by Munro in the report include:

- Social workers too focused on following procedures and consequently spending
  insufficient time assessing and supporting children
- A performance-driven culture in local authority social work that results in social
  workers being unable to exercise their professional judgement

- Too much emphasis on identifying families that need an assessment and not enough on putting children's needs first
- Inflexible ICS, locally procured IT systems, that fail to maintain a narrative about the child and are perceived as unhelpful by practitioners
- Serious Case Reviews focusing on what went wrong rather than learning from good practice and what could be done better
- Delays in the family courts adversely impacting upon the welfare of the child
- Demoralisation of social workers employed by organisations that fail to support them appropriately

Munro does seem to have identified some key issues for the profession, though interestingly she says virtually nothing about workloads, either in terms of volume or complexity. What is important here, however, is how the Munro Review dovetails with other developments. An historical problem has been the number of organisations involved in setting social work standards. This has resulted in a lack of coherence as there is no one organisation that can claim to be the voice of the profession. It is therefore essential that the transfer of the GSCC functions to the HPC, the establishment of the National College of Social Work, the Social Work Reform Programme and the outcome of the Munro Review all align and so together contribute to the strengthening of the social work professional base and its delivery of services to Children in Need.

Munro's final report, *The Munro Review of Child Protection: Final Report A Child Centred System* was published in May 2011. It sets out 15 recommendations which together aim to 'help to reform the child protection system from being over-bureaucratised and concerned with compliance to one that keeps a focus on children, checking whether they are being effectively helped and adapting when problems are identified' (Munro 2011: 5). Munro proposes that only a move from a compliance and blaming culture to a learning and adapting culture will improve the scope for practitioners to apply professional judgement when assessing and supporting children. The report identifies the following principles of an effective child protection system:

- The system should be child centred
- The family is usually the best place for bringing up children
- Helping children and families involves working with them
- Early help is better for children
- Children's needs an circumstances are varied so the system needs to offer equal variety in its response
- Good professional practice is informed by knowledge of the latest theory and research
- Uncertainty and risk are features of child protection work
- The measure of the success of child protection systems, both local and national, is whether children are receiving effective help

(*The Munro Review of Child Protection: Final Report A Child Centred System*: 23)

Munro suggests a more a more local approach to child protection that allows not only for innovation, flexibility and adaptability of response but is also freed up from the constraints of national performance indicators. Whilst acknowledging the importance of gathering data about performance she asserts that the data currently gathered is focussed on process rather than on outcomes, quality of service and service improvement. Critically, she argues, only a knowledgeable and skilled social work practitioner base, informed by research and other sources of evidence and capable of communicating with children and making relationships with families, can effectively help protect children. Munro goes on to recommend that the Social Work Reform Board's Professional Capabilities Framework be specific about the capabilities required of social workers to work effectively with children and their families. She also recommends that the Framework should inform the content of: social work qualification courses; ongoing post graduate professional development and the appraisal of social worker's performance.

Munro reminds her readers that social work is a profession intrinsically involved in the management of uncertainty and risk. Decisions about the likelihood of further harm are inevitably fallible as even where sound professional judgement concludes that the likelihood of further abuse is low that does not mean conclusively that it won't happen. 'The ideal would be if risk management could eradicate risk but this is not possible; it can only try to reduce probability of harm' (Munro 2011: 18).

Munro endorses the 10 underpinning principles of the *Framework for the Assessment of Children in Need and their Families* (DH et al. 2000) but expresses concern about how the Framework has become linked to performance indicators, process and recording forms. She recommends that guidance on undertaking assessments should continue to be statutory but proposes that the distinction between initial and core assessments as well as their associated timescales be removed. Munro acknowledges that *Working Together to Safeguard Children* (DCSF 2010) provides a necessary set of rules, so that all organisations are clear about their roles and responsibilities for protecting children. However, it also contains a vast amount of professional guidance in the midst of which those rules can get lost. Munro therefore recommends that these documents are revised to ensure that assessments are proportionate to need, families get help quickly, and professionals work together collaboratively.

Munro also questions the effectiveness of the Ofsted inspection regime in driving child centred practice and improving outcomes for children. She proposes that inspectors should examine the child's journey through the system and the quality and effectiveness of the help offered during that journey. In future, she suggests, inspections should be 'broad, covering the contribution of all children's services to the protection of children and be conducted on on unannounced basis in order to minimise the bureaucratic burden of inspection' (Munro 2011: 46). She also proposes that Ofsted's role of evaluating Serious Case Reviews (SCRs), undertaken by local safeguarding children boards (LSCBs), to learn from serious incidents of non accidental harm to or death of a child, should immediately end. Munro points out that though the current model of undertaking SCRs is generally successful at identifying what had happened to the child, it is less successful at identifying why. Skewed by the 'hindsight bias' SCR recommendations tend to focus on improving processes and procedures and there is usually little reference to the organisational and management issues that impact upon human behaviour. This results in a culture of human error being seen as the sole factor which then leads to individuals being blamed and to solutions that seek to eliminate the possibility of individuals making the same mistakes in the future. Munro proposes a very different approach that would involve the application of systems methodology to SCRs to enhance the learning from this process. She recommends the model developed by the Social Care Institute for Excellence (SCIE) as one that focuses on understanding professional practice in context with the result that any required changes can be 'grounded in practice realities' (Munro 2011: 61).

Other recommendations include:

- Amend statutory guidance to require LSCBs to produce annual reports for the chief executive and leader of the council
- Require local authorities to protect the roles and responsibilities of directors of children's services and lead members
- Initiate national research into the impact of the NHS reforms on safeguarding
- Place duty on local services to co-ordinate an 'early offer' of help to families below social care thresholds
- Require employers and higher education institutions to work together to prepare students for the challenges of child protection work
- Designate a principal child and family social worker in each local authority
- Establish a chief social worker at national level

The Coalition government welcomed the final report and has indicated that it will give the recommendations careful consideration, responding later in 2011. There is also much in this report for local authorities to digest and consider, as its content poses some significant challenges at a time of a changing political and economic environment. A move from the current command-and-control culture to a learning and adapting culture as proposed by Munro will not be an easy task for such bureaucratic and hierarchical organisations. Munro suggests that managers will need to be aware of how their organisation works as a system in order to achieve a redesigned structure that supports social workers spend time with the children and families and to ensure continuity in social work service delivery. The new system needs to both listen and learn.

> The review asks local authorities to take more responsibility for deciding the range of services they will offer, defining the knowledge and skills needed and helping the workers develop them. For example, a local authority wishing to implement a particular evidence-based way of working with children and families needs to consider what changes might be needed in the training, supervision, IT support and monitoring to enable this to be carried out effectively. To keep the focus on the quality of help being given to children and young people, they need to pay close attention to the views and experiences of those receiving services and the professionals who help them. (Munro 2011: 8)

Conclusion

This chapter has sought to assist the reader understand the historical and current social policy and legislative context of social work with children and young people. This context often makes social work a controversial profession as it executes the power invested by legislation to intervene in family life and because of the complexity of the interventions it undertakes. At times these controversies have sapped the confidence of the profession, which is now waiting to see how the social work reform programme proposed by the Social Work Reform Board and the outcome of the Munro Review will strengthen their professional base and renew professional confidence.

The next chapter will consider what all this means for social workers currently employed in a children's local authority setting.

Recommended further reading

Nigel Parton, *Safeguarding Childhood: Early Intervention and Surveillance in a Late Modern Society*, Palgrave Macmillan (2006)
In this book Parton critically assesses the latest developments in child protection thinking and practice, explaining how changes in philosophy and intervention have been informed by cultural, economic and political contexts.

Lorraine Fox Harding, *Perspectives in Child Care Policy*, Longman (1997)
This seminal text presents four different value perspectives on child care policy. Fox Harding discusses how these perspectives differ in their underlying values, concepts and assumptions concerning children, families, the rights and powers of parents and the role of the state.

Eileen Munro, *The Munro Review of Child Protection*, Department for Education (2011)
This publication sets out for discussion the characteristics of an effective child protection system and the reforms required that might help that system.

Chapter 2

Social Work in a Local Authority Setting

Defining social work

We have already discussed the public perception, strongly influenced by adverse media coverage, of social workers as well-intentioned do-gooders who frequently get things wrong either by not intervening soon enough or by being overzealous and authoritarian. Yet if members of the public were pushed to describe what social workers actually do and what influences their practice, their answers would probably be vague, disparate and not particularly accurate.

What then are the answers to these questions?

Learning points

- Social work ethics, values, roles and theories
- Working for a local authority
- Ingredients for effective practice

Defining social work is not a straightforward issue and has been the subject of much discussion amongst social work academics. Stevenson (2004), for example, describes social work as a reactive activity that exists in response to the tensions evident between the individual and family and the wider society or state. The professional identity of social workers has developed through its questioning of who the profession should be serving – the state or the individual and by seeking to answer such questions through adherence to a particular set of ethics and values. Stevenson stresses the important contribution social work makes to social justice as it challenges social exclusion by protecting the vulnerable.

Thompson (2005) proposes social work as a contested concept with different groups and interests, representing consensus and conflict models, competing for dominance. He proposes an existentialist perspective of social work that focuses both on social stability and social change, arguing that much of social work practice is concerned with helping deal with existential challenges. These constitute challenges that arise:

- naturally at different points of life
- for specific individuals in particular circumstances
- from the individual's position in society, e.g. poverty, racism, sexism

Thompson does not believe that it is possible for the profession to be value-free or neutral, as this will inevitably favour the dominant status quo. He therefore proposes that social work needs to be explicit about its values and base its practice on the principles of existentialism by being sensitive to the interactions between the personal and the social; responsive to existential challenges; systematic; reflective and emancipatory.

The International Federation of Social Workers and the International Association of Schools of Social Work have adopted the following definition of social work

> The social work profession promotes change, problem solving in human relationships and the empowerment and liberation of people to enhance well-being. Utilising theories of human behaviour and social systems, social work intervenes at the points where people interact with their environments. Principles of human rights and social justice are fundamental to social work. (cited in the BASW Code of Ethics for Social Work, 2011: 1)

The British Association of Social Workers (BASW) launched this definition at their Annual Study Conference in 2002 and added to it as follows

> Social workers attempt to relieve and prevent hardship and suffering. They have a responsibility to help individuals, families, groups and communities through the provision and operation of appropriate services and by contributing to social planning. They work with, on behalf of or in the interests of people to enable them to deal with personal and social difficulties and obtain essential resources and services. Their work may include, but is not limited to, interpersonal practice, group work, community work, social development, social action, policy development, research, social work education and supervisory and managerial functions in these fields. (BASW Code of Ethics for Social Work 2011: 1-2)

BASW also describes social work as being to five basic values

> Social work practice should both promote respect for **human dignity and worth** and pursue **social justice**, through service to **humanity, integrity and competence**. (BASW Code of Ethics for Social Work 2011: 2)

The current social care regulatory body is the General Social Care Council (GSCC), though its functions will transfer to a renamed Health Professions Council by 2012. In *Quality Assuring for Child Care Social Work* the GSCC defines the values of social work as follows:

> Social workers assist people to have control of and improve the quality of their lives and are committed to reducing and preventing hardship and disadvantage for children, adults, families and groups. Social workers practise in social settings characterised by enormous diversity. This diversity is reflected through religion, ethnicity, culture, language, social status, family structure and lifestyle. They work with individuals and families from backgrounds and cultures of which they may have had little direct experience and intervene in the lives of people whose life chances may have been adversely affected by poverty, ill health, discrimination and/or disability. In intervening in people's lives to achieve change, social workers must recognise the interrelationships of structural and individual factors in the social context in which the service operates and the need to address their impact on the lives of children and adults. (GSCC 2000)

All these definitions and interpretations locate social work as a profession that concerns both the individual and wider society. Social workers therefore have to manage the contradiction of being obliged by their ethical base to advocate on behalf of marginalised individuals whilst being employed by the very state that has contributed to their marginalisation.

The definitions and values espoused by BASW and the GSCC say little about the use of statutory powers to intervene in the lives of individuals without their consent. It therefore goes without saying that social workers need to be both knowledgeable and skilled to work effectively in such a complex and conflictual context. This is particularly relevant when considering the type of work social workers in a children's local authority setting are engaged with. Though there are times when social workers will be working with parents who want to work positively with social workers to effect positive change in their children's lives, there are also times when parents engage only with reluctance and sometimes with open hostility. To negotiate the world of children's social care and emerge professionally confident and competent two ingredients are essential – good organisational support and a professional evidenced-informed approach to practice.

Working for a local authority

There are 150 councils with social service responsibilities. Each of these, as a result of the Children Act 2004, will have a lead member for and a director of children's services. These services, at a minimum, will consist of local authority children's social care and education services. By local agreement they could also incorporate other services, e.g. leisure or health. Social care services for children and young people must undertake statutory responsibilities in relation to 'Children in Need' as defined by the Children Act 1989. They can also provide non-statutory services, such as preventative family support services, deemed appropriate and affordable in the context of local budgets.

Local authority social workers are usually organised in teams with each team managed by a first line manager, often called a team manager or team leader. With the changes wrought by the implementation of the Children Act 2004 social workers might now find themselves in a multidisciplinary team or co-located with other professionals, e.g. health visitors. Central government does not concern itself with agency structures, so there is a wide variation of structure across local authorities. However, a common feature is an increasing number of specialisms, so that some social workers may deal with responding to referrals and undertaking assessments, whilst others are involved in intervention and care proceedings or supporting looked after children living in adoptive, permanent fostering or residential placements.

Line managing the team managers/leaders will be a more senior manager who will usually either take responsibility for a specialist area or a geographical area. The hierarchy will continue upwards to a Head of Service who will usually be directly accountable to the Director. The Head of Service can also be responsible for provider services such as fostering, adoption and residential and for the local Youth Offending Service (YOS). The work of social workers will be supported by a number of other non-operational service areas such as administration, finance, planning, policy and procedures, contracting and human resources.

Organisational support for effective practice

The nature of local authority children's social work means that it is extremely difficult to become an effective social worker in a local authority without good organisational support. It is therefore worth spending a little time considering what organisational support should look like.

Recruitment and induction

Newly qualified social workers are no different from other employees, in that they should be recruited to posts, against job descriptions that clarify the main purpose, scope and roles and responsibilities of the job. The job description will be underpinned by a person specification that details the qualifications, experience, knowledge and skills required to undertake the work successfully (ACAS 2010). Usually newly qualified social workers start at level 1 and within a given timescale, and as they evidence competence and the ability to work independently of their manager, they will progress to level 2 and in some authorities again to level 3 or senior practitioner roles. As social workers progress this brings increasing financial rewards. Being a level 1 social worker should afford some degree of protection from the more complex casework. As one of the recommendations of the Social Work Reform Board is the introduction of a nationally recognised career progression route, these local variations may in the near future cease to exist.

In many local authorities newly qualified social workers are also participating in the Children's Workforce Development Council's (CWDC) Newly Qualified Social Workers (NQSW) pilot programme. This is designed to support the development of practitioners in their first year of practice through access to high quality supervision and training, the completion of a portfolio in which they evidence the achievement of 11 learning outcomes and a protected caseload. This programme is now available to NQSWs in most local authorities and those that participated in the first pilot will move into the CWDC's Early Professional Development (EPD) pilot, which is designed to support social workers through their second and third years of practice (CWDC 2011). The NQSW pilot programme is informing the development of the Assessed and Supported Year in Employment (ASYE) as proposed by the Social Work Reform Board.

Newly appointed social workers, whether experienced or not, should always experience an induction or programme of events, through which they are introduced to their colleagues and working environment. The CWDC has also established *Induction Standards for Use in Children's Social Care* (2006: 3). This sets out 'what new workers should know, understand and be able to do within six months of starting work' under the following headings:

- understand the principles and values essential for working with children and young people
- understand your role as a worker
- understand health and safety requirements
- know how to communicate effectively

- understand the development of children and young people
- safeguard children
- develop yourself

A good induction can make a big difference to a practitioner's confidence and performance. The world of children and families social care is both complex and stressful and for young inexperienced practitioners the local authority context can be a daunting one. Good induction is therefore also crucial to retention, as failing to put the right support in at this early stage can demoralise and lead quickly to practitioners feeling demoralised and 'burned out'.

Supervision and appraisal

Social workers should routinely and regularly meet with their team manager for supervision. Social work has a long and strong tradition of professional supervision and when done well it provides a critical source of developmental support to practitioners involved in a multifaceted and often extremely stressful area of work. Good quality supervision will encompass a number of issues and should always incorporate discussion of staff development, staff care and mediation into the process (Morrison 2000). Simply focusing supervision on individual performance management is likely to create an atmosphere of mistrust and devaluing (Thompson 2005) and therefore this approach should be avoided if supervision is to achieve its objectives.

Kadushin (1976) viewed supervision as having three main roles:

- a supportive or debriefing role that restores the practitioner to the point where they can continue to practise effectively
- an educative or reflective role that should bring theory and research findings onto the agenda to assist in working out what went well and what could have been done differently
- a management role that ensures the practitioner is working consistently within agency policies and procedures

The role of supervision in promoting and delivering good quality services to children and young people cannot be underestimated. Where both parties prepare for and use each session well, then safe and effective practice is both promoted and sustained. Clearly within the context of supervision the first line manager plays a critical role in assuring and maintaining best practice standards (Cunningham 2004).

Most local authorities have an annual appraisal process, which identifies strengths in performance and areas for further development. Developmental targets will be set and training needs identified as part of the appraisal. These should be subject to review during the year.

Working as part of a team

Social workers are commonly based in teams and are expected to attend team meetings. Bens (1998) says that effective teams use team meetings to do the following:

- Build relationships
- Learn team skills
- Set goals and objectives
- Plan work
- Coordinate work
- Discuss ways to expand empowerment
- Find and solve problems to continuously improve
- Work on innovations
- Give each other feedback
- Evaluate the team and the meetings in order to improve them
- Evaluate results achieved

Team meetings are, therefore, an important forum for information sharing and promotion of good practice. Team meetings should take place regularly and the team manager should promote good attendance. Some local authorities also promote team development days as the means by which team members can look together at areas of practice in more depth.

Social workers will also come together with other workers to form duty teams, which offer an immediate response to new referrals or to existing service users whose usual worker is unavailable. They will work as members of the 'team around the child' working with parents/carers and other professionals to accurately assess the needs of children and deliver appropriate services. Whatever the nature of the team social workers find themselves operating in, it is important that they accurately identify who are the team members. Developing trust between these members is a critical factor in enabling open communication and inclusive decision making (Statham 2004).

Continuous professional development

All social workers registered with GSCC have to undertake 15 days or 90 hours of post-registration training and learning (PRTL) over three years in order to maintain their registration. PRTL requirements are flexible and may include reading, attending training events, teaching or studying for a qualification. This is a minimum requirement and needs to be considered alongside the professional development responsibilities that are placed on both employers and employees in the GSCC Codes of Practice. As the responsibility for the registration of social workers transfers to the renamed Health Professions Council this process may also be subject to change.

Most local authority children's social care services commission an annual training programme to support the continuous professional development (CPD) needs of their social care practitioners. Many will also support social workers to undertake the Post Qualifying Child Care Award, which can be undertaken to a Masters level. It is not unusual to find that progression from being a level 1 social worker to a level 2 social worker is linked to the consolidation module of the Specialist Award.

More proactive social care services, however, are also seeking to raise the quality of service delivery through strategies that seek to promote evidence-informed practice. This is an approach that views continuous professional development opportunities, not just as accessing staff to training events and post-qualifying courses but as activity that can engage staff on a day-to-day basis on their own worksites, with the aim of improving the quality of their decision making and interventions.

Organisational support for evidence-informed practice

So what exactly is evidence-informed practice (EIP). Originally called evidence-based practice (EBP), this approach promoted the idea that good practice is delivered by research-informed evidence (Webb 2001). Reference to EBP begins to appear in the mid-1980s to early 1990s in publications such as the Department of Health's *The Pink Book: Social Work Decisions in Child Care* (1985) and *Patterns and Outcomes in Child Placement* (1991a).

In 1996 the Department of Health supported the establishment of the Centre of Evidence-based Social Services at the University of Exeter, in collaboration with 15 social services departments. This was led by Brian Sheldon who, with Geraldine Macdonald, was concerned with what they believed to be the ineffective and subjective nature of social work decision making. They belonged to the 'what works' movement and advocated an experimental approach to EBP based on stringent evaluation of different interventions, using research techniques widely used in health research such as randomised control trials (Newman and Roberts 1997). Trinder (2000) advocated a more pragmatic approach to EBP that draws on a range of different types of research methodologies, including the results of service user surveys. This latter approach has been heavily influenced by the Dartington Research Unit, led by Michael Little.

Whilst the debate has continued about what constitutes credible and robust research in social care, the idea that decision making should be informed by the best available research evidence has become an increasingly orthodox position. The *Framework for the Assessment of Children in Need and their Families* (DH et al. 2000: 10) outlines a key principle of assessment to 'be grounded in evidence based knowledge'. In 2000 the Department of Health, in its *Quality Strategy for Social Care*, urged councils to:

> ensure … that knowledge based practice informed by research evidence is supported and applied in everyday practice … that there are clear mechanisms for keeping staff up-to-date with practice developments, research findings and action participation in research and learning networks … [and] that there is a shift to a culture of continuous improvement. (DH 2000)

Part of this quality strategy led the government to establish the Social Care Institute for Excellence (SCIE) with a specific remit for promoting evidence-informed practice. This was modelled on the National Institute for Clinical Excellence, the organisation responsible for national guidance on health promotion and the prevention and treatment of ill health. Working closely with government regulatory bodies such as the GSCC and the National Care Standards Commission, SCIE seeks to create an expert knowledge base using evidence based methodology to produce practice guidance for social care. Marsh and Fisher (2005) differentiates between evidence and knowledge by defining knowledge as a synthesis of evidence, practice wisdom and user experience.

A useful source of current thinking relating to EIP is a handbook called *Firm Foundations* written by Mo Barrett and Rhiannon Hodgson and produced by Research in Practice (RIP) in 2006. RIP is a collaboration involving the Dartington Hall Trust, the Association of Directors of Social Services and Sheffield University and has more than 100 participating agencies, including many local authorities. *Firm Foundations* seeks to provide practical guidance to 'organisational support for the use of research evidence'. Barratt and Hodgson summarise the debate about what constitutes evidence and describes EIP as a thoughtful reflective process during which practitioners consider research evidence, together with the knowledge gained from their own professional experience and the views of users to inform their decision making. They cite Brechin and Sidell (2000), who view social work practitioners as drawing on different sources of knowledge:

- Using research evidence (empirical knowing)
- Using different methods or approaches (theoretical knowing)
- Using knowledge based on experience (experiential knowing)

SCIE argues for 'a better understanding of the relationship between social care research and the work of social care practitioners, including what organisational structures are needed to realise the aim of using research to improve practice' (Walter et al. 2004). Barrett and Hodgson (2006: 19) further develop this argument by describing the key ingredients of organisational support for EIP as:

- Senior leadership that personally sells the benefit of EIP
- A clear strategy and champions of that strategy throughout the organisation
- Explicit expectations about research knowledge and its application
- Procedures that embed the use of research into practice
- A positive culture that provides incentives to work in an evidence-informed way
- Opportunities for reading and reflection
- Training to develop critical thinking skills
- Easy access to research overviews
- Information and research support staff
- Time to consider the practice implications of research findings with colleagues
- A local programme of research studies, routine service evaluation and consultation with service users

The impact of organisational support on the practitioner

What then should all of this look like to a practitioner working for a local authority social services department? This will obviously vary from one local authority to another and some will offer more organisational support than others. Ideally, however, on recruitment, practitioners should be able to see from job descriptions and person specifications, interview and induction processes what is expected of them in terms of roles, responsibilities and competence and that this should include expectations of research awareness and use. Practitioners should have managed and manageable caseloads and dedicated time allocated for learning and reflection. Every practitioner needs access to the Internet and a local library and ideally should receive support from specialist colleagues and training on how to access relevant research and other sources of evidence that enables and promotes good practice. Discussion about the evidence informing decision making and proposed interventions and the opportunity to test out hypotheses should feature in supervision. Opportunities for shared learning should be built into team meetings and team development days.

Practitioners should have access to professional development opportunities through formal training programmes and post-qualifying awards. Additionally, access to locally commissioned practice seminars, including multi-agency practice seminars and research seminars will help keep them up to date, well informed and appropriately connected with partner agencies. They should be working for an employer who has good links with local universities, is a member of RIP and is engaged in national and local research projects. Practitioners will be encouraged to participate in these projects and will receive training on how to be research active and to think critically. They will be fully aware of how service users are being consulted and the impact this has had on service design.

All this activity will support and enable professional competence and enhance the credibility of the practitioner with the service user. This brings us to the second ingredient of effective practice and that is the individual approach the practitioner takes to their practice.

A professional approach

'Professionalism is the degree to which an individual possesses and uses the knowledge, skills and qualification of a profession and adheres to its values and ethics when serving the client' (Barker 2003: 342). Watson and West (2006) propose a new professionalism underpinned both by ethical practice incorporating:

- a strong, empowering value base which incorporates an awareness of the worker's approach to practice and how this impacts on service delivery
- anti-discriminatory and anti-oppressive principles
- accountability – both personal and professional

and by effective practice involving:

- a theoretical understanding of both the worker's and the service user's actions within a particular socio-economic context
- an understanding of the relevant current research evidence
- a clear process of evaluation which incorporates the service user perspective

Davies (1994) rightly asserts that inherent in the social work role is both power and responsibility:

> Empowered by legislation, she can affect for better or worse, the fortunes of all those who come into contact with her. The difference between good practice and bad practice can often be identified by the extent to which the social worker improves or damages the lives of the clients for whom she is responsible. (Davies 1994: 95)

It is critical, therefore, that social workers deploy this power and responsibility in their interactions with service users in a manner that is characterised by competence, confidence, sensitivity and the appropriate use of authority.

Analysis, critical thinking and reflective practice

Much has been written on these aspects of social work practice and for a more in-depth exploration readers will need to refer to authors such as Cottrell (2005), Fook and Gardner (2007) and Munro (2008). What follows is only intended to provide an introduction and to briefly summarise the issues that interplay between those aspects:

> Child protection work makes heavy demands on reasoning skills. With an issue as important as children's welfare it is vital to have the best standards of thinking that is humanly possible. Mistakes are costly to the child and the family. (Munro 2008: 153)

Taking a professional approach to assessment and care planning is vital in the complex and challenging world of social work with children and their families. Let's therefore look at what is involved in assessing and planning for children, and the role good quality analysis plays.

Assessing children involves gathering information, both past and present, about a child from those involved in caring for her/him, those involved in supporting her/him and from the child her/himself. That information should then be evaluated and judgements made about what is required to safeguard and promote the welfare of the child. Analysis involves reviewing the information gathered, which is often contradictory, confusing and incomplete, systematically and rigorously, in order to identify what is relevant and to determine what weight to give each element. It is this process that promotes the understanding of the world inhabited by the child and what is militating against her/his needs being partly or entirely met.

Analysis needs to be applied alongside critical thinking, which takes a questioning approach to the situation and information being evaluated. Critical thinking also involves self-questioning and maintaining an open mind to the information being evaluated. It is a process that challenges assumptions and thinking about different ways of understanding the information being considered. This is a demanding process as people are more likely to be drawn to information that confirms rather than challenges the ideas they already have about a person or a situation.

Critical thinking clearly links to reflective practice, which allows practitioners to look back on different aspects of their casework with children and their families and consider what went well and what didn't and what then could have been done differently and how. Reflection is a highly personal process that involves practitioners looking back on their experiences and how assumptions, beliefs and values have impacted upon their practice. This can be seen as putting all the responsibility for improvement on the practitioner and does not take account of the broader context in which the practitioner operates. To balance this a concept called reflexivity has been developed, which 'refers more to a stance of being able to locate oneself in the picture … [and] understanding the myriad ways in which one's own presence and perspective influence the knowledge and actions which are created' (Fook 2002).

It is helpful to consider the three concepts of analytical, critical and reflective thinking as different but linked modes of thinking that play a crucial role in delivering good quality assessments and care planning. These modes of thinking are all rooted in a solid knowledge base and draw on a range of skills. Research in Practice in their literature review *Analysis and Critical Thinking in Assessment* (Turney 2009: 7) lists the following skills and attributes necessary to support analytical, critical and reflective thinking:

- curiosity
- open-mindedness
- self awareness
- creativity
- sense making
- ability to manage uncertainty and not knowing
- ability to question one's own as well as others' assumptions
- ability to hypothesise
- ability to synthesise and evaluate information from a range of sources
- ability to present one thoughts clearly, both verbally and in writing
- observation skills
- problem solving skills

Being willing to repeat hypothesising in order to test out initial assumptions and conclusions and to take account of the child's changing needs and circumstances means practitioners must allow themselves to be wrong and for agencies to allow for this. It also allows practitioners to avoid the danger of over-sympathising with hard-pressed and stressed parents/carers and to guard against the rule of optimism when seemingly cooperative parents/carers are effecting no or minimal change in how they are parenting.

Social work theory

In the midst of values, knowledge, skills and modes of thinking, what role then does theory play in social work practice? First let's be clear about what a theory is. A theory is a statement of ideas organised in such a way that it helps provide explanation and understanding in and to practice (Fook 2002). Payne (2005) asserts that in social work the term covers three possibilities:

- *Models* that describe in a structured form certain principles and patterns of activity that provide for consistency in practice, e.g. task-centred practice
- *Perspectives* that express values or views of the world in an organised way that helps develop an understanding of the situation from different points of view, e.g. feminist or systems theories
- *Explanatory theory* that focuses on cause and effect and describes what works, e.g. cognitive-behavioural theory

Payne cites Sibeon's (1990) three-fold categorisation of theories: (i) theories as to what social work is; (ii) theories as to how to do social work; (iii) theories about the service user world. Sibeon suggests that the second category incorporates what he calls practice theories. These are the theories that inform social workers about what is important to assess, what the appropriate intervention is, how it should be delivered and how and when the intervention can be deemed to have produced a positive outcome for the service user.

Payne lists the following as practice theories:

- psychodynamic (including attachment) theories
- crisis intervention and task-centred models
- cognitive-behavioural theories
- systems and ecological perspectives
- social psychology and social construction theories
- humanism, existentialism and spirituality
- social and community development
- radical and critical perspectives
- feminist perspectives
- anti-discrimination and cultural and ethnic sensitivity
- empowerment and advocacy

It is not essential for social workers to have a grasp of all theoretical perspectives (Thompson 2005). They may not be convinced by some or be interested in others. However a key component of well-informed practice will be the application of theoretical knowledge. So that using a systems approach, for example, would lead the social worker, in the course of the assessment, to unravel the different systems impacting upon the child, e.g. family, kinship and community, in order to determine how the patterns of systems can be altered to improve the child's circumstances. Or, when applying attachment theory the practitioner is assessing the quality of the child's attachment to their primary carer and where an insecure attachment is identified the practitioner then assists the child and primary carer to forge a more secure attachment

The application of theory within social work practice will be explored further in the chapters that discuss assessment and care planning and in the three case studies designed to assist practitioners' understanding of the child's journey through Assessment, Planning, Intervention and Review (APIR). This will focus upon the application of three particular theories, specifically:

* attachment theory
* systems and ecological theory
* solution focused theory

Managing self in complex organisations

The ability to develop care pathways from the foundation of an iterative assessment process requires knowledge, confidence and skill in staff, underpinned by regular training and professional supervision. Resources which help structure practitioners' thinking about the complex lives of families, that assist them to record systematically and consistently and then assist their analysis and formulation of appropriate plans can make a significant contribution to effective practice. (Sheffield ACPC *Serious Case Review* 2005:115)

Social workers will find themselves working in diverse organisations all of which will give a different priority to being a learning organisation that promotes the development of it staff. Resource limitations, staff shortages, frequent restructurings all impact upon effective practice. A number of social work writers and the authors of Inquiry and Inspection Reports and Serious Case Reviews have noted that, though social workers are good at gathering information, they struggle to evaluate it effectively and to then draw appropriate conclusions. Analytical and critical thinking and reflective practice are processes that take time and time is not always easily available to social workers with busy caseloads working in an ever-changing environment.

Many recent research studies into the roles and tasks of social workers have also identified that increasingly more of their working time is taken up with administrative tasks (Lewis and Glennerster 1996; Postle 2002). In children's social care this was exacerbated by the introduction of the Integrated Children's System (ICS) in 2007. ICS was described as providing 'a conceptual framework, a method of practice and a business process to support practitioners and managers in undertaking the key tasks of assessment, planning, intervention and review' (DCSF 2008b: 1). Thus all casework activity is now framed by ICS as well as by child protection procedures and legal processes. ICS is designed to be supported by an electronic case record system and a key feature of this is a suite of exemplars for recording information, assessments, plans and reviews of plans that concern children. The Electronic Social Care Record (ESCR) incorporates both the recording of social work activity and any communication about the child, sent or received.

The introduction of ICS as an electronic system of recording social work activity has been enmeshed in controversy. Many social workers dislike the tick box approach taken in some of the assessment records and they complain that the electronic records take too long to complete, so distracting them from direct work with children and their families. The Interim Report of the Social Work Task Force said: 'We have heard concerns in many areas that compliance with the Integrated Children's System makes record keeping a burdensome process and drives a model of practice which can be at odds with professional judgement' (2009: 59). The Labour government responded by promising a 'usability review' and relaxing some of what was required of local authorities as they continued to roll out implementation and development of ICS. The review of child protection work, commissioned by the Conservative and Liberal Democrat coalition government, currently being undertaken by Professor Munro, has also been asked to look again at how the demands of case file recording can be reduced.

Nevertheless, a professional approach needs be taken to record keeping as this needs to be understood as part of the service provided to the child/young person. In 45 public inquiries into child deaths held in the UK between 1973 and 1994, record keeping was an area severely criticised, with the main criticism centring on the lack of information in the child's record, making it difficult to understand what had happened and why in relation to case management. Good record keeping 'enhances the quality of service delivery in relation to effectiveness, accountability and confidentiality. ... it provides an opportunity for critical reflection and evaluation, particularly in relation to decision making' (Trevithick 2005: 249). Records need to be written in the knowledge that the child/young person may wish to access and read them and should be encouraged to do so.

The competing demands of ensuring that children and their families are seen sufficiently to undertake assessments, implementing and coordinating the necessary interventions, talking regularly with other professionals in and outside of meetings, as well as the need to maintain up-to-date and accurate records often means that there is a need for ongoing reprioritisation of work and diary management. Sufficient time needs to be allocated to service user contact, travelling, attendance at meetings, talking to other professionals, supervision, training events, recording and report writing and it is not always easy to fit everything in. Social workers are usually responsible for their own diary management and they need to do this regularly and efficiently. What has been planned for the coming week will sometimes need to be reprioritised and rearranged, as working with vulnerable children and their families means that an immediate social work response is required, when the situations for children become acute. Professional behaviour, such as keeping appointments punctually and returning phone calls promptly, also contributes to helping the practitioner earn the respect of both service users and other professionals involved in the assessment and care planning process.

Maintaining professional boundaries ensures economic use of time and resources, as well as assisting with keeping to the task and roles agreed and formalising practical arrangements (Trevithick 2005). Clarity about professional boundaries helps children/young people and their parents/carers understand what to expect from the practitioner and to know what the practitioner expects from them. Key to this is how social workers explain the assessment and care planning process and then consult with children and young people and the adults that are important in their life. The views of those who feature in the assessment should always be secured and when they cannot be acted upon the reason for this must be explained. Children and young people need to actively participate in the decision making that affects their lives because this is empowering and it helps them make sense of what is happening to them.

Confidentiality remains a fundamental principle of social work and so it is important that service users understand that no information about them will be disclosed to other parties without their consent. The only exception to this is where the act of seeking consent would put a child in immediate risk of significant harm and where that is the case then only relevant information will be shared.

Finally, whilst it is right to expect the employing organisation to provide a continuous professional development framework for practitioners to access, it remains incumbent on individual social workers also to take responsibility for their own learning and development. They are accountable for the quality of their work and therefore need to take responsibility for maintaining and improving their knowledge and skills.

Conclusion

As a profession, social work clearly has a strong ethical and theoretical base. During the past 30 years, however, this has been put to the test by successive governments (Lymbery and Butler 2004). During the 1980s this stemmed from the Conservatives' dislike of public service and during the following two decades from New Labour's emphasis on regulation and performance.

Local authority social work has been being subject to managerial regimes that at times have been more accountable to central government and to public outcries than to local communities. Such pressures can lead to 'defensive social work' (Harris 1987) with social work managers being pushed into making decisions on the basis of what they can defend rather than on what would have been in the service users' best interests.

Nevertheless, with the establishment of a National College of Social Work as part of the reform programme recommended by the Social Work Task Force, there is the opportunity for promoting a greater understanding of the distinctive contribution social work can make and to put into place the resources to make that contribution effective. As an increasingly graduate profession, social work understands how to demonstrate competence and with a rich theoretical framework to draw on it can confidently assert its credibility as a profession that seeks to enable, empower and protect the vulnerable and to advocate on their behalf in an often unsympathetic world. Hopefully, from the point of view of the authors, the Social Work Reform Programme and the outcome of the Munro Review of Child Protection will turn this aspiration into reality.

Recommended further reading

Tony Morrison, *Supervision in Social Care*, Pavilion (2000)
This covers the fundamentals of good supervision, group supervision and the emotional impact of social work. It demonstrates the critical links between supervision, the quality of front line practice and service user outcomes. Morrison places emphasis on the role of emotional intelligence as crucial to both the quality of supervision and the quality of practice.

Eileen Munro, *Effective Child Protection*, Sage (2008)
Eileen Munro examines the context, purposes and operational requirements of effective child protection. The book is set in a social and historical context and incorporates evidence-based and practical guidance to good professional practice.

Malcolm Payne, *Modern Social Work Theory*, Palgrave Macmillan (2005)
This book offers a comprehensive survey of major theories relevant to social work practice and a clear assessment of the role and value of each approach based on the current critical literature.

Chapter 3

Working with Children and Their Families

This chapter will look at how to form positive working relationships with families. It will provide an overview of the assessment processes that underpin social work relationships with service users and address the issues of consent and confidentiality. The chapter will also look at challenging relationships, how you work with hostility and lack of cooperation.

Learning points

- The process of local authority social work
- How to approach a family with respect
- What to consider before making contact
- Consent and confidentiality
- Working with uncooperative families

Introducing the case studies

During the next three chapters case studies of three families will be used to promote an understanding of the social work task. The case studies will also be used to ask key questions about the areas of social work activity these chapters discuss and to help develop a fuller understanding about how these ideas work in practice.

The detail of each of the three case studies can be found towards the end of the book. They are called:

- Case Study 1 – Elizabeth and Peter
- Case Study 2 – Maya and Ajay
- Case Study 3 – Charlie

In these case studies the children/young people's experience of the process of assessment and care planning, as well as the outcomes for all involved are fully described.

The case studies are inventions of the authors and are not based on real children. Any resemblance to real children is entirely coincidental. The following sets the scene for each of the case studies:

Elizabeth and Peter

Jenny has two children: Elizabeth, who is 13 years old and attends the local secondary school, and Peter, who is seven years old and attends a special school. Peter has moderate learning difficulties and is on the autistic spectrum. Peter receives regular short breaks, staying overnight with foster carers every 6 weeks, arranged by the local social services department.

Elizabeth's father is Mark, who lives locally with his second wife and two children. Peter's father, whom Jenny lived with for about a year, has not been in touch with the family for more than five years. Jenny has a white Christian British background and the family live in a private rented house in a small market town.

Jenny displayed behavioural problems as a child and a teenager, and this at times led to a strained relationship with her parents. When Jenny was 24 years old she was diagnosed with bipolar disorder. Her mental illness is managed through medication and support from the local community mental health team.

Jenny's fluctuating mental health and her need for support in relation to Peter's disability means that both she and her children have regularly needed social work intervention.

Jenny's mental health worker has recently developed concerns about Elizabeth's behaviour and the impact this is having on Jenny's mental health. Elizabeth has been staying out late without Jenny's permission and refusing to go to school. This is leading to arguments and a tense atmosphere within the home. Jenny has rejected her parent's advice about how to manage the situation and is not currently in contact with them. The mental health worker decides to undertake a common assessment.

Maya and Ajay

Roshni and Kripa are married with two children, four-year-old Maya and one-year-old Ajay. Maya attends a local Sure Start nursery. The family are British/Asian of Indian/Hindu origin. Both Roshni and Kripa and their children were born in the UK and live in privately owned accommodation in a large city.

(Continued)

(Continued)

Roshni's sister, Asha, who is also a neighbour, has called the police three times in the last six months after hearing Roshni and Kripa arguing. This often involves Roshni crying out and subsiding into tears. Each time when the police have arrived Kripa has already left the home. Roshni then reports that, though they have argued, she is fine and that the arguments have been about money and the children.

The latest incident left the police concerned that the children were awake and distressed after witnessing the events, although again Kripa was not home when they arrived. They advised Roshni that they would have to refer the matter to social services. Maya was late for nursery the next day and seemed withdrawn to nursery staff. She said that daddy had hurt mummy and that daddy had also broken a window. Maya showed her nursery teacher a cut on her hand she said she had got from the broken glass. The nursery decided to talk to Roshni about the need to contact social services about the family's situation.

Charlie

Charlie is a dual heritage White/British and Black/African Caribbean six-year-old boy. He is being looked after in the care of the local authority since his parents were arrested for a number of offences, including using and dealing in drugs. Charlie is the subject of an Interim Care Order granted by the local Family Proceedings Court and is cared for by white foster carers. His mother, Lisa, who has always cared for him, is likely to be given a prison sentence. Michael, Charlie's father, who was arrested at the same time as Lisa, acknowledges Charlie as his son but has never actively parented him. He is also likely to get a prison sentence. Social work assessments and court decisions need to focus on where Charlie should now live and how to safeguard him from risk when his parents are released from prison.

Working with children and their families

Eligibility for service

The statutory entitlement to a social work assessment derives from the Children Act 1989 and its provision for a child to be assessed with a view to providing services, if the child is likely to be a Child in Need. Calder and Hackett (2003) point out that the government guidance issued, when the Children Act 1989 was implemented in 1991, recognised that budgets and resources are finite and that to a certain extent local authorities had to be allowed to define which children in their area were 'in need'. As local authorities adopted their own interpretation this inevitably operated as a threshold for children needing to access a service. Research evidences that thresholds vary between local authorities and that locally determined criteria of need influence who receives services (Cleaver and Walker 2004). Where the threshold is high children are unlikely to receive a service unless deemed at risk of significant harm and potentially in need of protection. Where set lower, a child will receive a social care family support service. This variation does lead to tensions between social services departments and other agencies with a remit for supporting children as such thresholds are rarely considered to be low enough by such agencies struggling to manage their concerns about vulnerable children.

Most children and young people will have their needs met by a combination of their family, community and universal services but some children will have additional or specialist needs that mean they need support from targeted and/or specialist services. A very small number will not be able to have their needs met adequately or safely by their birth families and these children will need to be cared for by kinship carers, adopters, foster carers or within a residential setting. It is important to understand that when children with additional needs are identified early, the combined support that can be offered by universal services, e.g. school/health visitor and targeted support, e.g. a parenting programme/family support worker, can often sufficiently improve the child's situation and avoid the need for the more specialist support offered by social workers or mental health workers.

The Common Assessment Framework (CAF) was introduced by the government, as part of the Every Child Matters agenda, in 2005. This was to help practitioners outside of social services involved in supporting children identify and respond to concerns they have about a child. It provided a standardised approach to assessing children with additional needs. The CAF is intended to promote the earlier identification of need, particularly from within universal services, e.g. by health visitors or teachers. It aims to assist these professionals assess the needs of children, the strengths in their situation as well as the impact of how they are parented and any environmental factors on their development and overall well-being. This assessment should then equip the professional to agree with children and their families what support they need and may lead to the establishment of a multidisciplinary plan coordinated by a Lead Professional. This should ensure that the right support is made available to the child and without such support the child's situation could deteriorate to the point where referral to social services becomes necessary. Often the capacity of social work access and assessment teams is eaten up by assessments of children that should have been supported by universal and targeted services, through the application of the CAF. This can have dangerous consequences for those children who do have more complex needs as it dilutes the service that should be made available to them.

Accessing a social care service

The majority of referrals of children to social service departments are made by parents, relatives, neighbours, other adults but mostly by other professionals. Children rarely refer themselves; when they do, it is usually because they are a teenager at risk of family breakdown with no money and nowhere to go. If a professional makes the referral, they will usually be expected to do so in writing, unless the child is thought to be at immediate risk of significant harm.

As there is now a growing expectation that a common assessment will have been undertaken prior to referral and a multidisciplinary plan have been put in place, the most recent common assessment and multi-agency plan should accompany the written referral. This should evidence that the family has been involved in the decision to refer to social services and that the adult with parental responsibility has given consent to contacting and sharing information with other agencies involved in supporting the child. This can only be waived if securing consent would place the child at immediate risk of harm. The social worker who assumes responsibility for assessing the child should build on the information contained in the CAF and the plan. This will prevent the child and family from having to provide the same information again.

> **Case Study Exercise**
>
> Consider which other professionals could have assisted each of the children in our case studies and whether this assistances could have prevented referral to Social Services.

Introducing Assessment, Planning, Intervention and Review (APIR)

The Framework for Assessing Children in Need and their Families (2000) (Assessment Framework) provides a clear map of the social work process as well as tools for undertaking and recording assessments. The Looked After Child materials provides a similar map in relation to children in public care. The then-Department for Education and Science (DfES) integrated both frameworks in 2007 and the result, the Integrated Children's System (ICS), has been implemented across all children's social services departments. Some of the more controversial aspects of ICS have already been described in Chapter 2.

The intent behind developing this framework was to ensure consistency in the nature and quality of the information social workers collect and record about children. This should lead to well-informed up-to-date assessments and effective care plans, the mechanisms by which services are identified and provided to children in need.

The Assessment Framework (DH et al. 2000: 10) sets out the following underpinning principles:

Assessments

- are child centred
- are rooted in child development
- are ecological in their approach
- ensure equality of opportunity
- involve working with children and families
- build on strengths as well as identify difficulties
- are inter-agency in their approach to assessment and provision of services
- are a continuing process, not a single event
- are carried out in parallel with other action and providing services
- are grounded in evidence based knowledge

APIR, as framed by the Integrated Children's System, constitutes the following elements:

Contact and Referral – contacts are usually made over the phone or in writing. Where a contact includes a request for service then that constitutes a referral. A decision should be made within 24 hours of the referral as to whether a child is potentially in need and therefore requires an assessment. It is important that contacts and referrals are responded to by experienced social workers. As they make the necessary checks and undertake discussions with relevant professionals they will make judgements about whether the child needs a social work assessment or whether they could be more appropriately assisted by another agency.

Initial Assessment – an initial assessment should be completed within 10 days of the referral. This will include gathering information from relevant agencies, interviews with the parents/carers and child/young person and possibly with other significant adults. The child/young person, when of sufficient age and understanding should always be seen alone and their views secured. This information will be considered and analysed by the assessing social worker who will discuss with and make recommendations to their team manager about what needs to happen next to support the child. Where the needs of the child are complex, one of the recommendations may be that a core or a more in depth assessment is required.

Strategy Discussion – where there is a likelihood of or actual significant harm then a strategy discussion will take place during the course of the initial assessment. This discussion will always involve the police and social services but often will also include the referring agency and other involved agencies. This discussion will agree if s47 enquires are required and then plan how the enquiry will be undertaken.

Core Assessment – Where a strategy discussion has established the need for s47 enquiries a core assessment will automatically commence and the enquiries will form part of that assessment. A core assessment will also be undertaken if the child has complex needs, e.g. arising out of neglect or from enduring health needs or significant disabilities. A core assessment should be completed within 35 working days of commencement.

Multi-agency Meeting – this can be a CIN meeting, a Child Protection Conference/Review Conference or a LAC Review meeting. These meetings bring together those involved in supporting a child, at the conclusion of an initial assessment or in the early stages of the core assessment process, to agree an initial multi-agency plan designed to support the child. Within child protection processes, if a child is made the subject of a Child Protection Plan, a Core Group will be identified who will meet sufficiently regularly to ensure that the plan is being implemented.

Care Plan/Intervention – where the initial or core assessment has concluded that the child is in need, a Child in Need plan should be established that will describe how the child's needs should be met and by whom. Where a Child Protection Conference has decided that a child is at risk of harm then a Child Protection Plan will usually be established. The plan will be multi-disciplinary and will clearly describe the nature and objectives of any social care intervention. As well as a Care Plan, Looked after Children will need additional plans developed to meet their needs, such as a personal educational plan, health plan and contact plan.

Review – All plans must be subject to review to see if they are being achieved within the agreed timescale. Children subject to a Child Protection Plan and Looked after Children will always be reviewed formally and within a timescale laid down by regulation. These meetings will always be chaired by someone who is independent of the child's case management. Where the child is looked after this will always be by an Independent Reviewing Officer. Social workers are required to up date the assessment of the child's situation, prior to these review meetings taking place. Local authorities have varied patterns for reviewing children in need. However, good practice would suggest that a child's situation needs to be reviewed every 8 weeks.

Some elements of this process, particularly those relating to timescale, maybe subject to change consequent to the *Munro Review of Child Protection*.

Taking a referral

Establishing basic information about a family and securing a description of the child's current situation from the referrer and all agencies involved with the family is necessary so that an informed decision can be made about whether an assessment is required. The prior application of the Common Assessment Framework (CAF) should have ensured that professionals already involved with the family have gathered the relevant information about the child's situation to enable them to try to solve the difficulties or challenges to the family without involving social services. However where these interventions have not been successful, the information recorded on the Common Assessment and in the multidisciplinary plan can be provided to social care services and will be used to inform the referral. The information needed to make this decision is as follows:

- Names and any known-by names of the child; the child's parents/carers; siblings and relevant adults
- Dates of birth and current addresses of all children of the parents/carers and of all relevant adults
- Ethnicity of the children and parents/carers
- Any known disability or mental health issues
- First languages and/or communication methods of parents and child
- Description of current situation and history
- Previous involvement with agencies
- Names and contact details of all agencies currently involved and reason and nature of agency involvement
- Referrer's concerns and the basis of the concerns
- The nature of any support offered to date
- Any known risks in relation to contact with the adults

What could be the consequences for Maya and Ajay if the referral information was either incomplete or incorrectly recorded?

Case Study Exercise

Getting the assessment started

This information will enable the receiving social worker or manager to determine whether it is likely that a child is in need and that an initial assessment of need should be undertaken. It needs to be understood that incomplete or inaccurately recorded information could lead to flawed management decision making about eligibility for service. Children in Need are assessed under s17 of the Children Act 1989. However, where it has been established there is evidence of actual or risk of harm, the child will be assessed under s47 of the Act and social services will follow government guidance as outlined in *Working Together to Safeguard Children* (DCSF 2010). Consent of the person with parental responsibility to refer to or to share relevant information with other agencies must be secured unless this would put the child/young person at risk of harm.

Where concerns exist about significant harm a strategy discussion will have taken place during the initial assessment to establish whether s47 enquiries are necessary and to plan how these enquiries will take place. These discussions will have considered whether there is an immediate need to secure the child's safety and if so how this will be achieved. Should the outcome of the enquiries determine a need for a multi-agency child protection conference then this meeting should take place within 15 days of the strategy discussion that agreed the need for a s47 enquiry. The core assessment will need to be completed within 42 working days of referral.

An initial visit and all interviews with service users should have a beginning, middle and end. First impressions count and in social work the relationships often have to be built quickly and in difficult circumstances. It is obviously important to consider the skills and knowledge required to achieve good working relationships before knocking on the door for the first time. Where it is known that English is not the first language of the family the services of an interpreter should be secured to assist with the interview. Similarly where a member of the family has a hearing impairment the services of a BSL interpreter may be needed.

Thought needs to be given prior to the visit about what information needs to be gathered and what issues need to be discussed. It can be very helpful to write out an interview schedule for the visit, one for the adult and one for child. This will be based on the following good practice principles:

Beginning – this involves arriving on time and stating name, job title and employing agency. Identification should be shown before entering the home. In unannounced visits it will be necessary to briefly explain the purpose of the visit and to secure agreement for entering the home. On entry it is important to secure the names of the individuals present and the whereabouts of all children known to live in the home and then to further clarify the reason for the visit. Establish the family's view of the reasons given for the visit and what they would like to get out of it. Explain roles and responsibilities and what is involved in the assessment process. Give them written information, which they can refer to once the visit is over, and allow plenty of opportunity for questions. From the adult and child's perspective they will want the social worker to be respectful, obviously knowledgeable and competent, an active listener (Lishman 1994) and a person with whom they can engage and learn to trust. Any lack of cooperation when visiting to evaluate child protection concerns will need a firm though unfailingly polite response.

Middle – the interview starts. Questions will be asked about each child who is the subject of the assessment in relation to their development concerning health, education, relationships, emotional well-being and behaviour. The nature of the child's attachment to his/her primary carer will be observed and parental response to the needs and wants of the child will be evaluated. Information about the wider family and environmental aspects and family history will be gathered. Each child being assessed will be seen on their own. Verbal children will be asked about their view of what has happened and of their situation and what they would like to change. Their sleeping arrangements should always be seen.

End – this will involve summarising what the visit was for, what has happened in the course of the visit and what is likely to happen next. This should include when the family should expect to hear from or see the social worker again. Contact details should always be left.

Communicating with children/young people

Fundamental to establishing whether a child is in need and how those needs should be best met is that the approach must be child centred. This means that the child is seen and kept in focus throughout the assessment and that account is always taken of the child's perspective. (DH et al. 2000: 10)

Preparing to talk to children/young people is essential if the social worker is to successfully assist the child tell their story (Howes 2010). Holland (2010) discusses how children/young people

are looking for reliability, honesty, flexibility and action. Additionally, they want to gain a sense that the practitioner is not always siding with adults' perspectives, but listening to and empathising with the child or young person's experience. (2010: 114)

Howes talks of the need for social workers to be knowledgeable, skilful and tenacious as they seek to find out what the child has experienced and what they want to change in their situation. Within this process they need to be sensitive to the child's age, disability and ethnicity. When talking to children she suggests that social workers should (2010: 132):

- use simple language
- keep sentences short
- use familiar words
- avoid unnecessary words
- use action words
- use their usual way of talking
- use terms the child can picture
- remember the child's experience
- speak to express not impress

Ethnicity and culture

Respectful relationships include consideration of ethnic differences and cultural backgrounds. An awareness of cultural difference and an understanding of the implications of different backgrounds are vital in order to establish relationships based upon mutual respect. Acknowledging the difference and checking out the cultural norms are important for building an understanding of how the families functions. Social conventions are the commonly expected behaviour that mediates relationships between family members and between adults, such as the use of first names, taking shoes off when you enter a home, whether children are allowed to eat food in front of the television. The impact of social convention and how these vary between different cultural groups and minority ethnic communities will need to be considered when working to develop respectful relationships. Starting relationships at the highest level of social convention, i.e. clarifying how to address an individual, asking whether it is OK to sit down and then moving into shared familiarity, is likely to ensure you do not offend and maintain a suitable level of professional boundaries.

The aspects attributed to respectful relationships do not mean that the participant always 'gets their own way' or will be happy about the outcome of relationship but that, with reflection, they can see that they have not been silenced or left out of the process.

Disability and mental health

The Disability and Equality Act 2010 defines a disabled person as someone 'who has a physical or mental impairment that has a substantial and long-term adverse effect on his or her ability to carry out normal day-to-day activities'. In effect this means people who are substantially and permanently affected by physical and/or sensory impairments, long-term medical conditions, learning disabilities or mental health problems. This definition is inclusive of those who have chronic substance misuse issues.

When assessing disabled parents, it is important to recognise that if an adult's parenting needs are responded to within the adults' social care and health framework then children are less likely to become in need. In order to provide disabled parents with an accurate and fair assessment consideration therefore needs to be given to undertaking a joint assessment with adult social care and/or health services. Disabled parents have the right to an assessment of their needs for support in their daily lives and such assessments should include any assistance required with parenting roles and tasks. If a parent's difficulty in effecting a parental role arises solely from their disability then Adult Services have to consider funding a service that compensates for lack in parenting capacity.

SCIE (Morris and Wates 2007) identifies four key features of good practice in assessment and planning:

- preventing avoidable difficulties by identifying need early
- ensuring clarity of responsibilities between adult and children's services
- having mechanisms in place for coordinating assessment planning and review
- making links with a range of support services

Learning-disabled parents often need to overcome preconceived ideas among other people about their ability to parent. For example, there may be a willingness to attribute potential difficulties they may have in parenting to their impairment rather than to disabling barriers or to other factors that affect the parenting of all parents. This has been described as the 'presumption of incompetence'.

> The absence of explicit standards and the uncertain nature of the links between parental competence and child outcomes render parents with learning difficulties vulnerable to discrimination. (Booth and Booth 1996)

This group of parents are more likely to require financial, practical and social support if they are to perform their parenting role as effectively as they want (Booth and Booth 1998). When children's and/or adult services carry out assessments, write plans and provide services to learning disabled parents, information should always be provided in accessible formats. Communication should happen in ways that are accessible and take account of the nature of the disability.

Key messages from disabled parents

Social workers who are good at communication:

- Are respectful
- Turn up on time
- Speak directly to parents
- Don't use jargon
- Think before they talk to you
- Listen and 'hear' you
- Explain what is happening
- Do what they say they will do
- Be honest if they cannot help you
- Are patient
- Make enough time to communicate with you.

CHANGE (2010: 18-22)

Design a first interview schedule for your first visit to Jenny and Peter.

Case Study Exercise

Respectful relationships

It is evident that children's social workers will work with families through intensely stressful periods in the family's lives (DH 1995). During the course of a social work intervention with the family the grounds for intervention may change and the relationship with the adults vary due to the child's fluctuating circumstances and ongoing assessment by social workers of the child's situation. Maintaining respectful relationships or 'helping relationships' which model good human interaction, despite the changing situation and stress experienced by the adults and children/young people, will increase the likelihood of accurate assessments, participants' engagement and opportunity for change. The potential for aggressive behaviour is a constant possibility within child protection and child welfare work. However, respectful relationships can reduce its occurrence (Cleaver and Walker 2004; Clifford and Burke 2004; Littlechild 2005).

Respectful relationships should be maintained between social workers and parents or carers and their children. As children/young people are often powerless in the relationship with adults, the importance of reflecting on your personal interaction with children and young people in order to maintain respectful relationships will be vital. Making positive relationships involves:

- being reliable
- carrying out commitments
- completing assessments within timescales
- acknowledging and building on the positives in the situation whilst identifying the problem areas
- ensuring everyone involved feels listened to and has had their views taken into account.

Poor relationships will ensue from:

- repeatedly being late or cancelling appointments
- being difficult to contact and not responding promptly to messages
- not listening and taking the views of others into account
- not explaining your actions
- not taking responsibility for the outcome of your assessment by asserting the manager takes all the decisions
- focusing on the parent/carer and not the child/young person
- focusing on and acceding to the more powerful adults in the family
- making judgemental comments that make the recipient feel inadequate.

It is easier to slip into the behaviours that lead to poor relationships when the child/young person lacks the opportunity to be heard, to influence or to complain. Young people who have been looked after report their experience of social workers include all of the behaviour described above (Morgan 2006). Morgan quotes a young person who summed up that from his point of view the ideal social worker would be someone who understands more from a child's perspective about any situation as not all children have the ability or maturity to understand fully what the social worker is saying or see from an adult's perspective. (Morgan 2006: 27)

Respectful relationships can be described as being based on honesty, openness and fairness. The casework heritage of social work provides the framework for respectful relationships. This can be seen in the casework model called person-centred practice developed by Rogers (1980) and Egan (1994). The principles of partnership working with parents in recognition of parental rights and responsibilities were also enshrined in the Children Act 1989.

Case Study Exercise

What would you need to do to commence a respectful relationship with Elizabeth, Peter and their mother, Jenny?

Honesty and openness

Honesty and openness has been noted in various studies as fundamental to successful relationships (Searing 2003; White and Featherstone 2005), and will be achieved by the application of listening and communication skills. The literature relating to the skills required by social workers in relation to listening and communicating is extensive. Honesty will require the ability to listen to others' opinions and views even if you don't agree with or believe them and to then share the reasons for disagreement or lack of belief. Skills are also required to communicate difficult information to parents and children, especially about what might happen unless the change required does not happen. Openness means that all known information is shared and accompanied by an explanation of what the information means, together with an acknowledgement of disagreements or differences of opinion.

Providing information clearly will ensure adults and young people understand the reasons and basis for the decisions that will affect their lives. How information is used often comes as a surprise to families who have not received an adequate explanation of the implication of that information within a social work assessment. It is also important to remember that children/young people have the right to understand how information will be shared and the limits to confidentiality.

Understanding the limits of confidentiality in the social work relationship at the start of the relationship will prepare individuals involved for what happens with information they provide and how information about them will be shared. Making the link between what professionals and family members have said/been observed doing and how this impacts on the assessment of the child's situation must be effectively communicated, even if those receiving the information do not agree with the conclusions reached. This is fundamental to an honest relationship where the parties understand how the other has reached their judgement.

Openness and honesty is a two-way process. When a commitment is made but doesn't happen, it can be viewed as a lie or untrustworthiness on the part of the social worker and undermines their credibility. Making any promises in social work should be avoided given the consistently changing environment in which social workers operate. Even the most stable family situation can unexpectedly change. However, following through on tasks committed to, is evidence of professional competence. Where an agreed action has not had a successful outcome then it is important to explain why and to do so at the earliest opportunity.

How would you ensure that Charlie understood what was happening to him and why at the point he was received into care, and at the same time minimise his distress?

Fairness

Fairness is based upon an understanding of how decisions have been made, an opportunity to have your opinion listened to and an opportunity to challenge others. Fairness is also a perceived even-handedness. This includes consistent responses and observing others being treated in the same way as you. It is recognised that parents may not agree with social work decisions but their views must be acknowledged and the reasons for not acting upon them explained. Power differences between the social worker and the parents will impact upon the perception and reality of fairness. Gender, class background, race and employment status will impact upon the social worker's relationship with a parent or child. The ability to reflect on the relationship and to empathise with the service user will be vital in maintaining respectful relationships. Steps will need to be taken to acknowledge and militate against the systematic unfairness and oppression within society in relation to minority groups. This may mean the involvement of high quality interpreting services or voluntary agencies that work on behalf of minority groups.

Consent and sharing information

The concept of consent is often focused upon during the referral stage. How you approach a family should be influenced by your knowledge of whether or not consent to contact social care services has been obtained by the professional or member of the public contacting you. Whether or not consent has been obtained will influence the parents' view as to the openness and honesty of professionals involved in their family. Where consent is not given initially the professional should persist if the concerns do not reduce.

> Consent is agreement freely given to an action based on knowledge and understanding of what is involved and its likely consequences …

> Informed consent is where a person giving the consent understands why particular information needs to be shared, what information might be shared, who will use it and how, and what might happen as a result of sharing or not sharing the information. (DCSF 2008a: 32)

Social workers involved with working with other professional groups will need to be clear about issues of information sharing and consent to take action. The DCSF (2008a: 32) established seven golden rules for information. Those involved in sharing information need to:

- remember that the Data Protection Act 1998 provides a framework for ensuring that information about living people is shared appropriately
- be open and honest from the outset about why, what, how and with whom information will be shared with individual's consent, unless inappropriate or unsafe to do so
- seek advice if unsure or if in doubt what constitutes inappropriate or unsafe
- share information with consent where appropriate
- base information sharing decisions on considerations of safety and well-being
- ensure that information shared is accurate and up to date and is necessary for the purpose for which it is being shared, is shared only with those who need to have it, and is shared securely
- keep a record of their decision and reasons for it

Section 47 of the Children Act provides the local authority with the authority to make enquiries necessary in order to establish whether a child is at risk of significant harm. When initiating a S47 enquiry the local authority does not need consent to share and seek information if this would put the child at further risk of significant harm. However, even during s47 enquiries, parents should be informed of all actions and encouraged to give their consent where it would not impact upon the safety of the child and the effectiveness of the enquiry.

The Children Act 1989 formally introduced the concept of partnership working and this emphasised the need to work with parents. Consent can be one of the building blocks of this partnership, demonstrating respect toward the family. Parents do not often object to multi-agency liaison and often expect it, assuming this will improve the service they will get. However, their understanding of how the information gathered influences the assessment is not often understood (Spratt and Callan 2004).

Outside of s47 enquiries consent from parents will always be needed unless an Emergency Protection Order, Interim Care Order, Care Order or Placement Order is in place in relation to that child. Where any of these orders is in place, the local authority shares parental responsibility. In these circumstances even though the local authority does not require consent it is good practice to seek it.

> In Jenny's case she initially refuses to give consent to her mental health worker to contact social care services – what are his options?
>
> Lisa refuses to meet with the social worker to discuss her opinion on her son being brought up by her sister. Does the social worker need consent to progress with the assessment of her sister? Does Charlie have any right to say he does not want his aunt assessed?

Working with uncooperative or hostile families

Apprehension about social work intervention is almost certainly likely to exist regardless of the pathway into social care services. However, as the research undertaken by Spratt and Callan (2004) indicates, apprehension does reduce the likelihood of successful working relationships. Understanding parental anxieties and a degree of anger from parents, where the normal emotional reaction is likely to be anger, will be a feature of social work with children and families. However some relationships remain hostile and when situations change within the family situation, previously successful relationships can become problematic and difficult.

'Developing Violent Scenarios' is a term used by Littlechild (2005) to describe common social work situations where violence has not as yet been expressed but where the social workers is working in an atmosphere of intimidation and threats. Physical violence is not the only challenge to successful social work. Parental behaviour may include passive resistance, active resistance, threats and violence all of which will impact on the ability of the social worker to engage and build an accurate picture of the situation.

Understanding the reason for the behaviour, where possible, will assist in establishing the significance of the behaviour to the assessment of the situation. Parents may not be able to explain why they are behaving with hostility or see their behaviour as problematic. How this type of parental behaviour impacts upon the child and what this says about the parental potential for working in partnership in order to meet the child's needs will need to be factored into the assessment.

Social work agencies should have a clear protocol and policy on violence and threats at work, and social workers need to be familiar with this policy. The impact of hostility on the assessment should be explored in supervision and how the assessment and work with the family should be undertaken should then be agreed. Strategies need to be developed to minimise the impact of the hostile behaviour such as joint visits, visiting parents separately, office interviews aimed at developing individual relationships, involving other agencies that have positive relationships in order to mediate and promote an accurate assessment of the situation. However, a clear message is required that this behaviour is not helping the situation, and the boundaries beyond which the local authority or agency will not tolerate hostile behaviour need to be provided. This can be sometimes be more powerfully provided with the manager involved with the case, if necessary.

At the referral and first visit stage of social work, the most likely difficult parental behaviours are a refusal to let the social worker into the home, the parent(s) not being present, or aggressive behaviour during the interview. These three responses need to be understood against existing information on the child's situation in order to assess how to progress. If there is evidence from the limited information or contact to date that the child is at risk of significant harm then a continued effort must be made to see the child and engage the parents. This may include a joint visit with another agency, telephone calls to the parents to explain the process or intercepting the family when they are known to be visiting another agency such as school. However if this continues to fail or the risk is considered immediate and significant then the use of court orders and the assistance of the police may be required.

If there is no evidence of risk of significant harm and the lack of engagement does not in itself lead to the potential for significant harm, i.e. the child is experiencing some form of neglect and needs a service to promote their well-being, alternative appointments should be offered and then a clear time frame given within which the family need to respond. Should this still fail to elicit a response then again a discussion should take place with the referrer or with a professional who has a working relationship with the parents about how to secure engagement. As part of these conversations it is worth checking the accuracy of the family's address and that the family can read any letters sent, with the original referrer. A multi-agency plan must continue to be in place to support the child, until the engagement of the family with social care or appropriate family support services has been secured. This plan should be reviewed as part of these discussions to ensure it is adequately addressing any unmet need.

Authoritative social work

The move towards family support and partnership working during the late 1990s and the increased awareness of power within the social work relationship have led social workers being required to mediate increasingly complex relationships with adults. Social workers have the role of providing support and promoting change whilst assessing and judging parental ability.

The social work task requires the sharing of difficult information and managing sometimes challenging behaviours, whilst maintaining working relationships in order to meet the child's needs. This can result in avoidance behaviour by the social worker, which can be demonstrated by

- allowing adults to dominate discussion
- attempting to minimise the implications of the information being shared
- not fully sharing information
- ignoring hostile behaviour
- ignoring provocative language

These behaviours can be minimised by using supervision to reflect on the factors enabling or inhibiting the assessment process and to put strategies in place to address the inhibitors. The multi-agency network of professionals can also assist in providing a collective response and an unambiguous message to the adults involved. Being clear with parents about relationships at the start of the process and informing adults of likely outcomes of social work interventions can only benefit both the quality of the relationships and the assessment process.

Case Study Exercise

How would you prepare for an interview with Kripa in which you intend to convey your view of the impact of his violence upon his wife and children and the consequences if his behaviour does not change?

Conclusion

The first stages of social work interventions must involve, from the outset, an honest, helpful and respectful relationship with service users. As suggested in this chapter this stage of the social work task can be highly stressful and difficult for both the service user and the social worker. Being prepared, reflecting on practice standards and seeking appropriate support and guidance will help the social worker feel authoritative and behave authoritatively, in order to ensure the best outcome for the child. The next chapter will look at the detailed assessment process needed to establish the situation for the child and to determine the interventions required to meet their needs.

Recommended further reading

Department of Health, Department for Education and Employment, Home Office, *Framework for the Assessment of Children in Need and their Families*, Stationery Office (2000)
Drawn from a range of research studies, policy and practice experience, this framework provides a systematic way of analysing, understanding and recording what is happening to children and young people within their families and communities. Accompanied by practice guidance, assessment tools and exemplar records.

Department for Children, Schools and Families, *Working Together to Safeguard Children: A guide to inter-agency working to safeguard and promote the welfare of children*, DCSF Publications (2010)
This government guidance sets out how organisations and individuals should work together to safeguard and promote the welfare of children and young people in accordance with the Children Act 1989 and the Children Act 2004.

Jan Horwath (ed.), *The Child's World: The Comprehensive Guide to Assessing Children in Need*, Jessica Kingsley Publishers (2010)
This book seeks to integrate practice, policy and theory to provide a comprehensive guide to all aspects of assessment. It both describes the Assessment Framework and gives information about how to apply it effectively.

Chapter 4

Good Assessments: Preparation and Information Gathering

This chapter focuses on why assessments are undertaken, how to prepare for and plan an assessment, and the skills and tools required by social workers to undertake this complex task. The reader will be asked to consider the issues discussed in the context of the case studies and is invited to complete exercises to help them explore what is involved in the assessment of children and families in more depth.

Learning points

- The referral of children to children's social care
- Planning assessments
- The main types of assessment
- Information gathering

The *Framework for the Assessment of Children in Need and their Families* (DH et al. 2000) was implemented in 2001. Now incorporated, together with the Looked After Child (LAC) materials, into the Integrated Children's System, the model of assessment introduced by the Assessment Framework underpins the way in which local authorities approach their assessment of a Child in Need (CIN).

Research subsequent to the introduction of the Assessment Framework found that the Framework helped social workers to consider what information should be gathered and evaluated in the course of an assessment and that although they generally completed the information gathering element well, their ability to analyse that information was weak (Cleaver and Walker 2004). Chapter 5 will therefore explore the process and skills required for analysis of the information that has been gathered, for making judgements and decision making as part of the assessment.

Initial and core assessments

The Assessment Framework outlines the domains that should be explored as part of an assessment of a child's needs by the local authority after the acceptance of a referral from another agency or the family. The three domains are as follows:

- Child's Developmental Needs
- Parenting Capacity
- Family and Environmental Factors

Each domain is broken down into dimensions for exploration, as detailed in the framework guidance. By covering these three domains and the dimensions within them, a holistic picture of the child will be established. Where social workers choose not to cover elements of the framework this must be explained in the assessment, as should any variation in the time scales for assessments. The framework requires that an initial assessment should be completed within 10 working days of receiving a referral. This will determine whether a more in-depth or core assessment is required. If so, this will need to be completed within 45 days of the referral, i.e. 35 working days from the core assessment start date.

The Integrated Children's System (ICS), of which the Assessment Framework is now part, is underpinned by the concept that assessment is ongoing and not a single event fixed in time. New information should always be evaluated and, if significant, a further core assessment may be required. All the reports that a social worker should complete prior to a review are, within ICS, assessment reports. The Assessment and Progress records, which should be completed in respect of children looked after by the local authority, provide a tool for analysing the needs and progress of children and young people across the seven dimensions of a child's development used in the Assessment Framework.

In each case study list the areas of the children's and adults' lives that you would focus upon when undertaking the required assessments.

Case Study Exercise

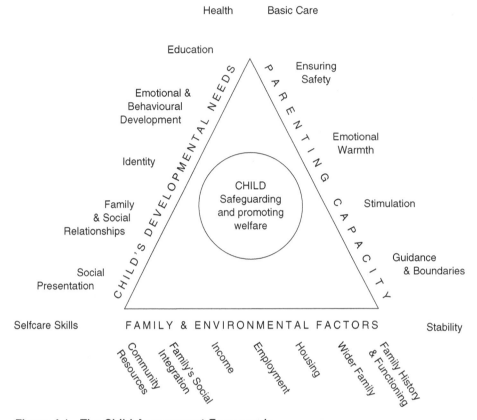

Figure 4.1 The Child Assessment Framework

Department of Health (2000) *Framework for the Assessment of Children in Need and their Families*. London: The Stationery Office, p. 17.

Planning an assessment

Several authors have recognised the usefulness of breaking down the assessment of children into different stages, stressing that these are suggestions and not prescriptive steps. Milner and O'Byrne (2009) look at the stages of preparation, data collection, applying professional knowledge, making judgements and lastly deciding or recommending what is to be done. Raynes (2003) uses a stepwise model to assist effective assessments and care planning. This includes planning, hypothesising, gathering information, testing information, analysing information and deciding on a care plan. Breaking down the process can help with organising information, making it available for discussion and review (Munro 2008).

Planning and preparing for an assessment is an important, necessary task which will help to ensure that a thorough piece of work is undertaken and will also save time during the assessment process. As social services have to make a decision about eligibility for initial assessment within 24 hours of receiving the referral and then complete the assessment within 10 working days, the assessment plan is usually formulated as part of a discussion with the team manager. The time available for planning and preparation will vary greatly. There may be only a matter of half an hour before undertaking an initial assessment allocated on duty, or there may be the opportunity for a full discussion of a complex court assessment in supervision. The preparation process requires the social worker to:

- be clear about the reason and purpose of the assessment
- be clear about what areas need to be focused on
- identify who needs to be involved
- be clear about the timescale for the assessment
- develop possible explanations and hypotheses about what is happening
- consider which social work theory or method is going to be applied
- establish what tools or techniques will assist the assessment process
- consider their value base

Purpose of the assessment

The reason and purpose for social work intervention should always be clearly understood by the child, parent and social worker. Most assessments will be to establish the needs of the child, and the parent's ability to meet these needs. As a social worker your initial information will generally be in the form of a referral taken by a screening social worker and it is important that the content is read carefully, even when there is little time. Any gaps, inconsistencies or lack of clarity should be remedied. Although not always possible, it is helpful to speak to the referrer prior to a social work visit so that a fuller understanding of the reason for the referral is obtained. The referral record should clearly detail the referrer's concerns and the basis of these concerns. It is important here to separate the referrer's opinions from their observations (Reder and Duncan 1999). The referral should also detail discussions the person taking the referral may have had with any other professional involved in supporting the child. If the child was previously known to the service, it will also be necessary to read any previous case records that relate to the child.

The findings of the assessment will have implications for the family, as the assessment may contribute to a child protection conference decision, court decision or the decision as to whether the carer can become a foster carer or adopter. This needs to be explained to and understood by the family from the start.

Often the first contact will be arranged by letter or telephone, and at this stage a brief and concise explanation of the reason and purpose of the visit will be necessary. The child's parents should be expecting this contact, as they will have given consent to the referral being made and also for the person making the referral to share information about their child. However, should the concern be such that to make the parents aware of the referral would place the child at risk of immediate significant harm, then consent may not have been secured. A home visit may be made without any prior notice and in these circumstances this will be the first the family know of a referral. Alternatively, contact with the family may need to be made through a school, clinic or another agency.

If we consider this issue in relation to Maya and Ajay, the police should have told their parents of their intention to refer the current and any other incident involving domestic violence to social services and why. Roshni, the children's mother, also gave her consent for the nursery to contact social services. Both parents should therefore be expecting contact, though social services will certainly have considered whether to see them separately in the first instance. In this example Roshni is seen at the nursery and Kripa, the father, is seen at home the following day, when Roshni and the children are safe at a relative's home.

In relation to Charlie, social services are contacted when he is taken into police protection and needs to be placed with foster carers. The main purpose of the assessment in this case will be to ascertain Charlie's needs and how they can be met. As care proceedings are to be initiated, the assessment will be presented to the court. There will be limited time to complete the initial report for the court prior to the Emergency Protection Order expiring but if an interim care order is granted, a further structured, more in-depth assessment can take place.

The completion of an assessment plan can be very helpful at this stage and this will outline the purpose of the assessment, the areas of focus, the people to be involved and the timescales (which will be decided by the court).

Knowing what to focus on

The Assessment Framework describes the key areas of a child's life and a parent's capacity to meet the child's needs. Once the reason for the assessment has been established, there may be specific areas requiring detailed assessment or focus.

The Assessment Framework notably does not include a defined 'risk assessment' section as it was designed as a framework by which need would be assessed and that this would incorporate an assessment of the child's needs in relation to living in abusive or neglectful circumstances. There has been debate about the benefit and challenges of this lack of a clear risk assessment (Calder 2003). Many local authorities and safeguarding children boards have developed additional guidance for workers to assist with risk assessments related to specific circumstances such as domestic abuse, substance misuse or situations of neglect.

The Assessment Framework distinguished between parental attributes and parental capacity. The attributes are factors such as poor mental health, substance misuse or learning disabilities that may negatively impact upon parental capacity or behaviour. There is a danger that during an assessment too much attention is given to the weaknesses in the child's situation and to the lack of parenting capacity. It is, however, also critical to examine areas of strength present in the family, in wider networks or in other professionals. Understanding the strengths will assist in assessing the impact they have on meeting the needs of the child. The strengths of the wider family may reduce the need for external professional support. For example, the input of a supportive grandparent or aunt may reduce the impact of neglectful parenting.

There are numerous supplements to the Framework designed to assist social workers assessing specific difficulties within family life, including issues of neglect, persons posing a risk, substance misuse, physical abuse and failure to thrive (Calder and Hackett 2003; see also local safeguarding children boards websites, such as Leicestershire and Rutland Safeguarding Board at www.lrlscb.org/). These supplements include additional topics to be added to the Framework and suggested questions, tools and techniques for assessing the impact of this area of difficulty on family life. The supplements add questions to each of the domains.

Who needs to be involved?

As well as the child/young person and their parents/carers, all professionals involved with the family and child should be asked to contribute to the assessment. At the planning and preparation stage consideration should be given to who the relevant professionals are, and how they will be involved in the assessment. Involving other professionals will ensure that both their knowledge of the child and their professional expertise will inform the assessment. They may have also known the family for longer or understand the cultural considerations of the family better. However, social workers should be willing to challenge their opinions and vice versa. It is appropriate to involve professionals working with the adults in the family as well as those involved with the children, for example, probation or mental health services.

Consideration of the role of family and friends in the assessment should also be undertaken by the social worker and, again, careful thought has to be given to who is to be involved, and how. The contributions of others should be clearly identified in the assessment record – unless the information has been provided by referees as part of an adoption or fostering assessment, as such references are given in confidence to help ensure complete honesty. Involving others will require the consent of the family unless the assessment is being undertaken as part of an s47 enquiry or court process.

Careful consideration has to be given to how to involve children in the process. This will need to take account of the child's age and stage of development and will involve imagination and good communication skills. The views of the child as well as their parents should always be taken into account and given appropriate weight during the analysis and inform recommendations.

In Maya and Ajay's case, the key professionals working with the family or with knowledge of them at the time of the referral are the police, nursery staff, the health visitor and GP. The key family members are the parents, the children and Roshni's sister and her husband.

In Charlie's case, the key professionals are the primary school staff, police, GP and drug services and possibly probation services. The key family members are the parents, Charlie, the maternal grandmother and maternal aunt and uncle, the paternal grandparents and paternal aunt.

Case Study Exercise

Who are the key professionals and family members for Elizabeth and Peter?

Timeliness and timescales

The Assessment Framework introduced timescales for assessments in order to ensure that where a child was potentially in need they received an assessment and a service in a timely way and without delay. Even if the Munro Review of child protection does away with fixed timescales, assessments will always need to be undertaken within a reasonable timescale.

Currently statutory timescales exist for most assessments:

- Initial assessments – 10 working days from date of referral
- Core assessments – 45 working days from date of referral, i.e. 35 working days from the end of the initial assessment
- Section 47 enquiries – child protection conference to be held within 15 working days of the strategy discussion that determined the need for the s47 enquiry
- Child Protection reviews – three months after the initial child protection conference and then every 6 months

- Looked After Children reviews – first review to be held within one month of accommodation, 3 months from the first review and then every 6 months
- Court assessment – timetable decided by the court

It is helpful to work backwards from the date the assessment record must be completed and establish what tasks must be completed by that point and when. Time needs to be allocated for writing the record and to follow up on any issues or information provided during the course of the assessment.

When planning a court assessment or core assessment, it is essential to complete an assessment plan clarifying who will be seen, where and when. Consideration should then be given to the areas you plan to cover in each of the interviews. Changing circumstances or additional information will mean that this has to be regularly reviewed but it does provide a useful framework for the worker and family.

Explanations and hypotheses

Having received initial information, as in a referral, and prior to any direct contact with a family, a social worker should begin to hypothesise about what is happening in a family and the reasons why. It is important that these hypotheses are transparent so that any bias or misunderstanding can be challenged (Raynes 2003). Holland (2011), who defines hypothesis as a testable proposition, emphasises the importance of workers recognising the range of sources from which a hypothesis can originate. The hypothesis or explanation of what is happening may come from the service user. Alternatively the hypothesis may be evidence-based or based on practice wisdom (Holland 2011).

When considering Maya and Ajay's circumstances, the social worker Milli Tucker could have a number of hypotheses based on the initial information that she has received and prior to undertaking the initial assessment. The aunt, Asha, has called the police to their house on several occasions, as she has heard fighting and things being thrown and is concerned that Kripa is drinking. Roshni says that she is fine. Subsequently Roshni has a black eye and Maya, a cut, from flying glass. Maya says that daddy hurt mummy. The hypotheses could include:

- Kripa may be violent towards his wife and feel that this is acceptable behaviour as he is head of the household.
- Kripa may only become violent following the use of drink or drugs.
- Kripa may be violent as a response to stress and feel worried about his behaviour.
- Kripa and Roshni may have a volatile relationship in which both are violent to each other.
- Maya may have cut her hand when Roshni was throwing items at Kripa. Roshni's injuries may have been caused by Kripa protecting himself.

This emphasises the importance of considering a range of alternatives and then, while gathering further information, analysing this information; throughout the assessment different hypotheses will be supported or discounted. This process continues and will be explored in further detail at different stages of the assessment process. It will contribute to an understanding of what is happening and why and what needs to happen to effect change. The social work interventions will be very different if the hypothesis that Kripa is violent only after imbibing alcohol is supported by evidence, in contrast to the response that may be made if Kripa's belief system incorporates a view that he is entitled to physically chastise his wife.

Specific social work method or theory

Howe (2009: 2) describes theories as 'particular ways of making sense' and different theories have specific approaches to undertaking the assessment process and interventions. Statutory assessments require certain areas to be covered but elements of theories can be applied and the principles behind approaches can and should be adopted by social workers undertaking assessments. There are many books on social work theory (Stepney and Ford 2000; Payne 2005; Howe 2009) but as outlined in Chapter 2, consideration will be given here to attachment theory, solution focused theory, and systems and ecological theory, which have very different ways of considering why something is happening and what might work in terms of intervention.

Attachment theory

Howe (2010: 184) describes attachment theory, which was developed by John Bowlby, as 'a theory of affect regulation and personality development in the context of close relationships'. It helps us to understand how children develop a sense of themselves (Fahlberg 1994) and the importance of them developing close relationships, particularly with their carer. An understanding of it can help practitioners to assess attachment, understand the impact of different attachment experiences and guide intervention.

Children, particularly babies, need to be protected and have their physical needs met. Attachment behaviours, for example crying or smiling (Howe 2010), are an attempt to get close to a carer who can offer this. If a carer responds to the need and is consistent in this respect, the child will learn to trust that their needs will be met and this is the basis of a secure attachment. Over time the child develops a sense of themselves and others and develops an 'internal working model' that can be carried through into adulthood.

Attachment experiences as a child can impact on adult relationships and how adults parent. This has implications when assessing foster carers or when undertaking kinship assessments.

Fahlberg (1994) discusses three processes that are important in the development of attachment and which can be used to assess attachment and inform intervention. First is the arousal-relaxation cycle, which begins when a baby has a need, for example, to be fed or changed. The baby expresses the need by crying, and to successfully complete the cycle the need is satisfied by the baby being fed or changed and the baby can then relax. Second is the positive interaction cycle, where the parent interacts with the child and the child responds. The child can also be the initiator of the interaction. The third element is 'claiming', and claiming behaviour includes, for example, recognising family resemblances.

These three activities can all assist with bonding and attachment and an absence of them can lead to difficulties. Children's needs may not be responded to for a range of reasons. A parent may not be aware of a child's needs or be able to respond to them if they are depressed or under the influence of substances. Children may also be living in an abusive or neglectful environment. The attachments may then be insecure.

When working with Maya and Ajay, an understanding of attachment theory and assessment of the children's attachment to both parents will contribute to our understanding of the family dynamics and emotional development of the children.

> How could you use the above information to assess Ajay's relationship with his mother and father?

Case Study Exercise

Systems and ecological theory

Systems theory helps social workers to move away from an emphasis on individual characteristics when undertaking an assessment and encourages them to look at relationships and how people are affected by family and other systems that they are involved with. The emphasis is not on the inner world as with attachment theory, but on understanding how systems impact on individuals and how the system can sometimes be changed or adapted if there are problems for individuals.

An important element of systems theory is the concept that the whole is more than the sum of the parts, for example an inter-agency core group working with a family may achieve more than professionals working independently of each other.

An individual's behaviour cannot be understood without an understanding of the systems that they belong to and therefore, if there are difficulties, the systems have to be explored and understood rather than the individual blamed.

Another important concept in Systems Theory is that the main goal of a system is to stay in existence and this may result in problems for individuals, for example scapegoating in a family.

Case Study Exercise

What systems affect your behaviour?

What systems have an impact on each member of Elizabeth and Peter's family?

The ecological approach recognises that individuals make an impact on their environment and vice versa. Brofenbrenner (1979) developed an ecological system of human development. Systems in which the child is directly involved, such as home or school, constitute the micro-systems and the meso-system is the interaction between the different elements, for example, the contact between home and nursery. The exo-system is a context where the child is not personally involved but which indirectly impacts on them, for example the parents' social network, and the macro-system is the wider context (Brofenbrenner 1979; Jack and Jack 2000).

The ecological approach looks at how individuals interact with the environment and as well as encouraging recognition of negative factors affecting the family, including poverty or discrimination, it also enables positive support networks to be explored. Also important is the concept of social capital 'which includes the relationships and exchanges between all members of a neighbourhood or society' (Jack and Jack 2000: 96). The Assessment Framework [DH et al. 2000] encourages an ecological approach with the domain of family and environmental factors, stressing the need to look at such areas as community resources and social integration.

Solution focused theory

Solution focused brief therapy (de Shazer 1985; Howe 2009) is much less concerned with why a difficulty has arisen. It works on the basis that the service user holds the solution to their problem and the worker needs to learn to see the service user's world. The service user sets out goals and ways to achieve them in a way that is realistic to their lives. The goals need to be realistic, specific, concrete and behavioural, as well as stated in the positive, i.e. something the service user will do rather than not do. For example, a mother will take the child to nursery on time every day and spend 10 minutes in class with the child for the next two weeks in order to settle the child in class.

The therapy uses what is called the 'miracle question' to assist the service user in moving forward towards the new behaviours or change required. The social worker needs to ask the service user 'If a miracle occurred over night and the problem which you think is the most serious for your family was solved over night, what would be different in the morning? How would you know that the problem had been solved?' The service user's answers will give you the information about what the service user will be doing differently and what behaviours will have changed. It allows the service user to see the future and start to unpick what they might be able to achieve.

A goal for the service user may be to no longer have social services involvement and if a miracle occurred there would no further social work visits. This can be a starting point for work by exploring with the family what they think would need to happen for this to take place. It can help explore which perceptions and concerns are shared.

Many service users present as though their problems have always existed and they are not in control of their situation. With some families there may be no hope of change, but in many cases families will have had periods when they functioned reasonably well and the problems did not exist or were managed. It may be possible to ascertain what action is needed to re-establish what happened in the past by asking the family 'Can you think of a time when this problem has not affected your family?' 'What was different about your family?' and 'What would need to happen for this to happen again?'

The Assessment Framework developed questionnaires and tools that include scales that can be used in solution focused work, for example Parenting Daily Hassles Scale. This could be used, for example, to explore on a scale of 1 to 10 how difficult the parent finds getting the children to school.

Solution focused work asks service users to consider how they cope. By exploring this, present strengths and solutions are identified and it may be possible to utilise these further. For example, if a service user finds support from a friend or particular service helpful, it may be possible to extend this and incorporate it into the plan.

It is important to acknowledge what can be achieved and establish that it is safe and good enough for the child. For this model to work, the service user's goals need to be consistent with the goals of the local authority in some way. It would not be effective if the adult wishes to continue with a violent relationship and does not recognise the risk to the child, or if there is a lack of genuine cooperation – as considered in the Serious Case Review following the death of Baby Peter (Haringey Local Safeguarding Children Board 2009).

If you are going to undertake a solution focused approach, then you might start with the positives in the child's life and where there is success, rather than focusing initially on the areas of concern. When looking at areas of concern, the social worker can compare these with the areas of strength in order to understand how the strengths may mitigate the areas of concern.

During the assessment process you will start the intervention process with the family, hence the need to consider what method or theory you are working with at the earliest possible stage.

Assessment tools and techniques

It is useful at the planning stage to identify what tools or techniques may be useful during the assessment. For example, once you have established the timescale you will be able to identify how many home visits, unannounced visits and activities with the child you would be able to realistically undertake. The reasons for the assessment and the areas requiring specific assessment will influence the techniques used. Different tools and techniques are described in Table 4.1.

Which techniques would not be suitable for each case study?

The social worker's value base

Reflection upon your values and background should be considered in order to understand how your own views or those of the organisation you are working for might influence how the assessment is approached. Assessment is not value-free. The British Association of Social Workers (BASW) *Code of Ethics for Social Work* (2002) states that social workers will acknowledge the significance of culture in their practice, will recognise the diversity within and among cultures and will recognise the impact of their own ethnic and cultural identity (4.1.6[a]).

To increase awareness and consideration of this, McCraken (1988), in relation to social research, suggests that a 'cultural review' should be undertaken and this can be a very helpful process prior to undertaking a social work assessment. The social worker can consider the range of suggested questions independently, discuss them with a colleague, or reflect on them in supervision. The process can show gaps in knowledge that may need to be filled before the assessment takes place, but more importantly it is an opportunity to consider what values and assumptions are being taken to the assessment.

Table 4.1   Assessment tools and techniques

Tool/technique	Advantages	Disadvantages
Structured interviews		
A planned series of questions designed to explore specific areas	Ensures all key areas are covered Development of skilled interview techniques	Interviewees may wish to talk about different issues – if the focus is solely on prepared questions opportunities may be missed to explore other relevant areas Over-reliance on verbal communication. Where service user does not perform well in the interview judgements about them and their parenting can be made without utilising other available sources of information (Holland 2011)
Scales		
These can be standardised scales, which involve the service user answering a series of questions. The answers are scored and the final score will inform the judgement to be made Alternatively service users can be posed a specific question and asked to rate their response between 1 and 10, e.g. Parenting Daily Hassles Scale. This can be a trigger for further discussion and used to track progress with issues	Standardised scales – enable you to suggest a national average Task-orientated activity, which can be helpful for people who find talking difficult Can be used to demonstrate the progress made by a parent/carer or child	Value-laden approach, as national averages do not consider cultural norms within families
Observation		
Periods of observing the child and the child–parent interaction. Specific activities can be arranged to assist with the observation such as a trip to the park or visiting at dinnertime	Evidence of actual parenting or child behaviour rather than self-reported Opportunity to observe attachment between child and carer Builds an understanding of the situation for the parents and child Observation of children with limited verbal communication or different methods of communication enables the development of a better understanding of their needs and how best communication can be achieved	Observer's presence may influence the dynamic between parent and child and this has to be taken in to account Not an interactive activity, unless feedback given to service user at the time. The service user does not have the opportunity to reflect upon or explain their behaviour

(Continued)

Table 4.1 *(Continued)*

Tool/technique	Advantages	Disadvantages
Imaginative questioning		
Asking 'what if' questions or ideal situation questions in order to provide an insight into a desired future	Understand what the child or parent may wish to achieve in the future or what is wanted from interventions	Only provides information of what is wanted or desired. Does not inform how they can be achieved
Life story work/genograms		
Gather information by questioning about family history. A family tree can start the process of discussing family members and their relationship to the child or parent	Identify patterns of parenting or childcare practice. Allow service users to reflect on the impact of their childhood experience on their current parenting Identify relatives that are supportive, and those that add to pressure or are a risk to children	
Specific risk assessments		
A number of risk assessment tools exist for social workers. These are often based upon a series of questions or processes for understanding information	Provides an indication about likelihood of future harm occurring	Only as good as the information fed into the assessment. Generally based upon a 'normal' situation and therefore may not consider specific or 'different' aspects that relate to the case, e.g. belonging to a specific religious group or family living with extended family
Reports from other professionals		
	Information from professionals, which can inform the specific area of the child or adult's life, which the professional is involved in supporting Professionals will have a different relationship to the family and therefore provide a different perspective	Professional may only focus upon their area of expertise in relation to the child or parent and not link this to an impact on the child or parenting Without specific instruction about what is wanted from the report the professional may not answer the questions the assessment needs to address

Table 4.1 *(Continued)*

Tool/technique	Advantages	Disadvantages
Interviews or written reports from family or friends		
Adoption and fostering assessments require written references	Invites direct comments from individuals who know the adult/child from a personal perspective If given with assured confidentiality may provide important information related to the potential carer Family members may be able to reflect on their situation and provide their own comment on the situation/needs. Some individuals may prefer to communicate in writing	Relies on a level of literacy Cannot immediately probe or question the information provided Individuals likely to provide favourable comments as chosen by the applicant in fostering/adoption applicants
Direct work with children		
Child's ecomap	Opens communication between child and social worker (Fahlberg 1994)	Direct work skills needed to respond to different age and developmental stage
Use of toys, i.e. telephone, puppets	Useful to ascertain information and give information	
Feeling faces	Helps children to express feelings	
'Listening' to behaviours		Social worker could misinterpret behaviour

The cultural review can be illustrated by application to Case Study 2. The referral relates to Maya, a four-year-old girl and Ajay, a one-year-old boy, whose parents are British/Asian Hindu. An initial consideration for the social worker prior to undertaking the assessment would be:

* What do I know about the needs of a four-year-old and one-year-old child?
* What is the range of development that I expect to see and where do these expectations come from?
* Are these expectations, or the measures I use, appropriate in this context?
* For example, what do I know about language development where children are bilingual? Are the Sheridan scales helpful in this family?

- What do I know about the British/Asian Hindu community and, again, where does my knowledge come from? Do I hold any positive or negative stereotypes?
- How might this family view me and how might the organisation that I represent and the assessment be perceived?
- What are my agency's values and expectations and do I share them?'

(Based on McCraken 1988; Holland 2011; Dalzell and Sawyer 2007)

The aim of the exercise is to increase self awareness, particularly of the impact that our beliefs and values can have on families and the assessment process, and this reflection can be repeated throughout the assessment.

Initial and core assessments frame how social workers approach assessments and will inform how other assessments will be undertaken. Let us look at what other assessments are in the remit of social workers working in a local authority children's services setting.

Specialist assessments

Assessments required by the Family Courts

During court processes under s8 of the Children Act 1989, in private court proceedings, or under s31 of the Children Act 1989 in public law proceedings initiated by the local authority, specialist assessments can be requested. These requests may identify specific areas of focus such as a parenting assessment or an updating of the core assessment in a particular area. The court may also request assessments to be undertaken by expert professionals who specialise in such areas as drug or alcohol misuse, mental health difficulties or learning disabilities and their impact upon parenting capacity. The court will provide a clear timeframe for the completion of such assessments, which may be provided to court as part of the court statement or as a separate document alongside the court statement.

Assessments of a Person Posing a Risk

The Sexual Offences Act 2003 introduced the requirement for the local authority to consider undertaking a 'Person Posing a Risk Assessment'. This is an assessment of a person who has had contact with the police, which leads the police to believe that they may present a risk to a child or young person. Where the person has specific contact with a child or young person, this child or young person's needs should also be assessed. These assessments may be provided to Child Protection Conferences or to the Multi Agency Public Protection Arrangements (MAPPA) meetings in order to inform them of decisions about the children's welfare or the offender's surveillance and support in the community. MAPPA are meetings that bring together the police, probation, health service and local authority to plan how those individuals who have committed serious offences against people are to be managed on their release into the community.

Assessments of foster carers, adopters, step-parent adopters, private foster carers and special guardians

There are separate assessments that are required of adults who are not the biological parent of the child but who are caring, or will care, for children in a parental role. These assessments have legally described elements to ensure the suitability of the adults to become carers (Children Act 1989, Adoption and Children Act 2002, Children Act 2004). The children involved in these arrangements also require matching assessment to ensure that the proposed carer can meet their individual needs.

Assessments of an Unaccompanied Asylum Seeking Child (UASC)

For the purpose of immigration, the Home Office definition of a UASC is as follows:

> An unaccompanied asylum seeking child is a person who, at the time of making the application is, or (if there is no proof) appears to be, under eighteen, is applying for asylum in their own right and has no adult relative or guardian to turn to in this country. (Home Office UK Border Agency 2010: para. 349)

The United Nations Commissioner for children defines unaccompanied children as:

> those who are separated from both parents and are not cared for by an adult who, by law or custom, has the responsibility to do so. (UN High Commissioner for Refugees 1994)

The Local Authority has the duty to assist all Children in Need in their area under s17 of the Children Act 1989 and if necessary provide accommodation either under s17 or s20. Case Law has had an important impact on how local authorities undertake their responsibilities to UASCs. These cases were prompted by the fact that some local authorities persisted in supporting UASCs, especially those age-assessed as 16 years or older under s17, as it was the cheaper option.

Until 2003, when the Department of Health issued Local Government Circular LAC (2003)13, most unaccompanied child asylum seekers were given support under s17 of the Children Act 1989. The 2003 Circular, however, stated that, as a matter of policy, unaccompanied children with no parent or guardian in the UK should be supported instead under s20 of the 1989 Act:

> where a child has no parent or guardian in this country, ... the presumption should be that he would fall within the scope of section 20 [of the Children Act 1989] and become looked after, unless the needs assessment reveals particular factors which would suggest that an alternative response would be more appropriate. While the needs assessment is being carried out, he should be cared for under section 20. (DH 2003)

The 2003 Circular adds that if an older child does not wish to be 'looked after' under s20, then the local authority concerned might decide, after taking into account the child's wishes, that that child is able, with the help of s17 support, to look after him/herself. The Circular was issued around the time of the Hillingdon judgement, *R (Berhe) v Hillingdon London Borough* (2003), which was thought to have brought further clarity to an area that had previously suffered from some confusion.

This clarity, however, was undermined by an Adoption and Children Act (2002) amendment to the Children Act 1989 that allowed local authorities to provide accommodation under s17 without the children becoming automatically 'looked after'. The result of this amendment was that local authorities had a legal basis to provide accommodation as part of their Children Act support to unaccompanied children under s17. The 2003 Circular nevertheless had advised local authorities that the amendment 'did not affect the duties and powers of local authorities to provide accommodation for lone children under section 20 of the Children Act 1989'. However, in January 2005, a report by the Refugee Council, surveying 19 local authorities, indicated a disparity of responses by these authorities to this guidance, thus suggesting a continued lack of consistency of approach towards unaccompanied asylum seeking children (Dennis 2005).

The 2003 Circular had recognised the need for the assessment to include taking account of the wishes and feelings of the child and further advised that this consideration may result in a decision that the child is competent to look after him or herself, thereby making s17 support more appropriate than making the child 'looked after' under s20. However, in 2007, a further judgement made during the case of *H & others v Wandsworth, Hackney and Islington* [2007] 2 FLR 822, ruled that the duty laid out in s20 (6) to ascertain and give due consideration to the child's wishes and feelings in an assessment of his needs did not override the duty in s20 (1) to look after children who meet one or other of the criteria. This supported the Hillingdon judgement in that if unaccompanied children require the provision of accommodation because they fulfil the criteria in s20 (1) of the Children Act 1989, they are 'looked after' children and afforded all the protection and rights associated with that duty.

In addition, the Administrative Court (the High Court exercising its judicial review function) has considered local authority age assessments of young asylum seekers in a number of cases since 2003. Local authorities are now obliged to follow the guidance agreed in these cases in order for their age assessments to be lawful. This practice guidance was approved by Stanley Burton J in *R & B v London Borough of Merton* [2003] 4 All ER 280 [2003] 2 FLR 888 and Jackson J in *R (T) v London Borough of Enfield* [2004] EWHC 2297 (Admin) (Unreported). Taken together, but Merton in particular, these two cases provided the basis for determining whether an age assessment undertaken by a local authority social services department can be said to be lawful and therefore 'Merton-compliant'. The aspects of the Merton judgement that are of particular note include the following:

- Physical appearance and behaviour cannot be isolated from the question of the veracity of the applicant: appearance, behaviour and the credibility of his account are all matters that reflect on each other (para. 28)
- The assessment of age in borderline cases is a difficult matter, but it is not complex and can be determined informally, provided that safeguards of minimum standards of inquiry and of fairness are adhered to (para. 36)
- The decision maker cannot determine age solely on the basis of the appearance of the applicant. The decision maker must seek to elicit the general background of the applicant, including family circumstances and history, educational background, and activities during the previous few years. Ethnic and cultural information will also be important. If there is a reason to doubt the applicant's statement as to his or her age, the decision maker will have to make an assessment of the applicant's credibility, and will have to ask questions designed to test credibility (para. 37)
- The local authority must make an assessment on the material available to and obtained by it. There should be no predisposition, divorced from the information and evidence available to the local authority, to assume that the applicant is an adult, or conversely that he or she is a child (para. 38)
- The children's services department of a local authority cannot simply adopt a decision made by the Home Office. It must decide itself whether an applicant is a child in need (para. 39)
- A local authority is obliged to give adequate reasons for its decision that an applicant claiming to be a child is not a child (para. 45)
- It is not necessary to obtain medical evidence (para. 51)
- Where an interpreter is required, he or she should ideally be present during the interview (para. 55)

- The decision maker must explain to an applicant the purpose of the interview (para. 55)
- Procedural fairness requires the assessing officers to put to the child matters which they are minded to hold against him or her, so that there is an opportunity to rectify any misunderstanding (para. 55)

Assessing age is indisputably a complex task that requires specialist knowledge and skills. The assessing social worker should actively try to obtain as much *relevant* information as they can to make an informed judgement. In circumstances where, following their enquiries, doubt remains as to whether the person is a child, they should be given the benefit of the doubt and treated as a child. It is not necessary to determine age in a single interview and it may not be possible to do so. Where the assessment is made over a period of time, the judgement may well benefit from the involvement of other professionals and services – for example foster carers, doctors, teachers and even other young people. Services should be provided while the assessment is being conducted or is ongoing – until a decision is taken that the person is not a child. They should then be referred to adult services for support.

When assessing an UASC, social workers will need to take account of both past trauma, an uncertain future and issues that may arise from the young person's ethnicity, culture and language. Social workers will find it helpful to draw from the knowledge and experience of groups that specialise in working with refugees and from local community voluntary groups that work with communities that reflect the young person's background. Early attention to any health needs they may have and access to education is particularly important for this group of young people, who may find that as adults they have to return to their country of origin. Health promotion and educational achievement in this country will help their chances of a more certain future on their return.

Consider what type of assessments will need to be undertaken in relation to each of the children in the case studies.

Case Study Exercise

First contact with parents or carers and children and young people

Parents and children will have different preconceptions of social work and social workers. These may be based on personal experience or the experiences of people they know and/or media accounts of social work (Spratt and

Callan 2004). It is important to note that Spratt and Callan's research found that all parents, including those that self refer, were apprehensive of social work intervention. This apprehension increased when parents were unaware of the referral, had not given consent to referral or where an unannounced social work visit took place.

Providing clarity about the social work role and task at the start of the relationship is repeatedly identified as pivotal to establishing a positive working relationship with the parent and child (Spratt and Callan 2004). Families report it is helpful if social workers focus on the aim of the assessment and emphasise that it intends to achieve what is best for their child. It is essential to help parents/carers understand that the focus of the visit is the welfare of the child.

First contact with family where there is no immediate child protection concerns will usually commence with a letter or telephone call. The advantage of a letter is the time it gives parents/carers and the young person to reflect on the purpose of the visit and to work out what they want from it. The letter should make clear what social services offer, the purpose of the visit and the proposed date and time for the visit to take place. The disadvantage is that letters assume a level of literacy either in English or the language the letter has been translated into. A telephone call can allow an adult or young person to ask any specific questions prior to your visit but may also be more of a shock. They may not be free to talk on the phone or accurately record the date and time of the appointment.

Where immediate child protection concerns exist or a strategy discussion has determined the need not to give the parents or carers prior warning, first contact with the family may come about through an unannounced home visit or at another venue, such as hospital A&E department. These initial unannounced contacts hold a higher level of difficulty and risk to workers, as parents/carers will be unprepared and therefore more likely to be upset or hostile. Such contacts need thorough preparation.

In order to make first contact a manageable event, it is evidently important to prepare as discussed above. Other important elements to consider immediately before the visit are:

- reviewing referral details
- clarifying what additional information needs to be secured
- discussing and agreeing with the manager what issues need to be explored
- making sure of directions to the venue and allowing sufficient time to get there
- having appropriate identification
- taking steps to ensure personal safety, for example leaving information about destination and expected time of return and agreeing with a manager whether a joint visit is required. If there are any concerns about the safety of making a home visit then

alternatives should be considered, for example interviewing in a secure office or asking for police accompaniment
* taking a mobile phone and ensuring that there is someone that you can contact if you need to discuss information or something unexpected occurs. This is particularly important if the visit is out of office hours

Information gathering

Working Together to Safeguard Children (DCSF 2010: 147) states that the initial assessment should involve:

> seeing and speaking to the child, including alone where appropriate; seeing and meeting with parents, family and wider family members as appropriate; involving and obtaining relevant information from professional and others in contact with the child and family; and drawing together and analysing available information (focusing on the strengths and positive factors as well as vulnerabilities and risk factors) from a range of sources (including existing agency records).

This clearly describes the key elements required from any assessment. It is a process that is only as good as the information gathered and the quality of the analysis of this information. Understanding the implications of the information gathered and applying meaning to this in relation to children's lives should be factored into the assessment planning process.

ICS prescribes the range and nature of the information that must be gathered in the course of an assessment. Social workers must be able to evidence that they have covered and considered all the dimensions of each of the three domains of the Framework for Assessment but this should be viewed as a minimum and is not exhaustive. It can in certain circumstances be helpful to take a copy of the Framework outline on a visit to act as a reminder of the domains and also to involve the family in the process but it is very important not to confine assessment to the elements of the Framework.

In looking again at Case Study 2 we can explore some of the key elements of information gathering. Horwath (2010) discusses how an assessment can be affected by the way in which a family are engaged. When working with Roshni, Kripa, Maya and Ajay, although we are informed that they are bilingual and that the children are being brought up bilingual in English and Urdu, it should be confirmed with them that they are happy to undertake the assessment in English or alternatives arranged if this is not the case. It is important to be honest, open and respectful with families and to recognise the anxiety they may be experiencing.

Genograms are a helpful way of starting work with a family. Completing a genogram or family tree can ensure that you have the correct spellings for names, that all dates of birth are accurate and that you have established who

Genogram symbols

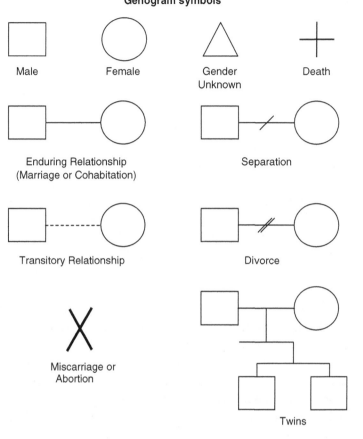

Family members who currently live in the same household are indicated by a dotted line drawn around them

Eldest children are placed furthest left and the youngest on the right

Figure 4.2   Symbols used in a genogram or family tree (based on Department of Health 1988)

lives in the family home. They can, however, be used more imaginatively with adults and children and initiate discussion and understanding of the relationships and support networks within the family, individuals' experiences of being parented or how loss and separations have been experienced. Children can be helped to complete genograms using photographs or drawings and they can be included as part of life story work. An example of a genogram can be found within each case study. Figure 4.2 gives the key to genogram symbols.

Ecomaps are also a useful assessment tool. The ecomap is a drawing that shows the child or family's links to other systems. The systems can include family members or more formal systems, for example social services or health services. The nature of the line from the child or family to the system is used to indicate the nature of the relationship, so that a solid line describes a strong relationship and a dotted line a weaker relationship. Again adults and children can help to construct ecomaps and the process can give a clear indication of which systems are supportive and which are stressful. It is an opportunity for family members to discuss what they find helpful and unhelpful and this can help workers and families to build on identified strengths in the network. An example of an ecomap can be found later in the book in Case Study 3.

Chronologies are helpful for gathering and organising information and should be completed for all cases regardless of the length of the intervention. They start with the earliest event and work to the most recent. They can begin to show patterns and themes in a family and there may be positive as well as negative indicators, illustrating, for example, how a family have previously coped with stress or overcome difficulties. It is important that chronologies are multi-agency rather than information merely being gathered from one's own organisation. Information from the police and health services in respect of Roshni and Kripa enables us to see where the concerns are, such as police call outs, but also the strengths, including the physical development of the children. A useful process is to discuss the chronology with the family and note should be made of any discrepancies or disagreements.

Observation is a very informative way of gathering information and can be used to assess a wide range of areas including child development and attachment relationships. There are many opportunities to observe, including visits to school or nursery or attendance at contact sessions. Half an hour watching a child at play can begin to teach you a great deal about their physical and emotional development and relationships. Observing a contact session, particularly seeing how parent and child meet and separate, how the child's cues are picked up by the carer and how reciprocal the relationship is, can form the basis of further discussion with family members and inform your assessment. Fawcett (2009) acknowledges that social work visits generally involve workers intervening but emphasises the value of observing and tuning in to children. Even when uninterrupted observation is not possible, taking note of what you see, and your interpretation of this, is a very important aspect of every visit. It is also helpful to observe children or members of the family in different settings and compare your findings.

Listening to the voice of the child or young person

It is essential that the child's understanding of their situation and what elements they would like to change are obtained. This may involve a discussion about options. It is particularly important to consider how to secure the views of

- pre-verbal children
- children without speech or with limited speech who use alternative methods of communication
- children whose first language is not English

There are imaginative and simple ways to undertake direct work with children of a range of ages (Fahlberg 1994). When working with Maya it may be helpful to work with her on drawing a child's ecomap with a picture of her house and school and her aunt and uncle's accommodation.

Drawing different rooms in a house sometimes gives children an opportunity to talk about what happens in them and likes and dislikes. Feeling faces are also appropriate for four-year-olds, and Maya can draw a face or pick a face from a sheet of drawings to help her express emotions in different circumstances.

With Charlie the social worker could use joint story telling (Fahlberg 1994). With this technique the social worker begins a story about the child's identified favourite animal and elements of the child's experiences are included in the story. The child is asked to continue the story and may be able to share feelings, thoughts and hopes.

An important element of any work with children is to ensure that it is undertaken in a setting where they are comfortable. Some children may be happy to be seen at school whilst others may feel having a social worker visit makes them stand out. Some children may wish to discuss things out of the family home or foster home whilst others only feel safe in this setting.

Even when an assessment is pressured and time is short it is extremely important that children are seen and talked to on their own when possible. Having a relationship with a child makes it much more likely that you will notice any changes in their behaviour or appearance and that they will be able to tell you if they have difficulties.

Conclusion

This chapter has explored the key elements of planning an assessment, emphasising that you should be as prepared as possible prior to making contact with a family and looking at the range of ways that you can do this. This includes being clear about the reasons and focus of the assessment, developing possible explanations about what is happening and why, and considering social work theory, tools and techniques. Information gathering is then discussed, recommending the use of a range of methods including genograms, chronologies and observation. The importance of working directly with children is emphasised and ways of doing this considered with reference to the case studies.

Having planned and prepared for the assessment and completed the element of the assessment involved in gathering the initial information, it is time to consider the next critical stages of assessment: analysis, decision making and care planning.

Recommended further reading

Jane Aldgate, David Jones, Wendy Rose and Carole Jeffery (eds), *The Developing World of the Child*, Jessica Kingsley Publishers (2010)
This book adopts an ecological perspective on understanding child development and emphasises the importance of direct work with children.

Peter Reder and Sylvia Duncan, *Lost Innocents: A Follow-up Study of Fatal Child Abuse*, Routledge (1999)
The follow-up to *Beyond Blame: Child Abuse Tragedies Revisited*, this book reviews knowledge about fatal abuse and looks at the recognition and assessment of risk, how to improve communication between agencies and improve preventative strategies.

Vera Fahlberg, *A Child's Journey Through Placement*, BAAF (1994)
A resource book for professionals working with looked after children. It contains chapters on child development, attachment and bonding, separation and loss, minimising trauma associated with placement moves and direct work with children.

Chapter 5

Good Assessments: Analysis and Decision Making

Having looked at the planning of assessments and the gathering of information we will now consider how this information is analysed and used as the basis of decision making and interventions. There will be a discussion of how to discard or accept explanations of what is happening and of the factors that can assist and hinder analysis and decision making. These will include other agencies' assessments, the impact of values, applying knowledge from research and experience and, perhaps most importantly, listening to the views of children and their families.

Learning points
- What analysis is
- Who and what should contribute to analysis
- How to reach decisions

Analysis

Definitions

Analyse – Examine methodically and in detail the constitution or structure. (*Concise Oxford Dictionary*)
Analyse – To examine in detail in order to discover meaning, essential features, etc. (*Collins Concise Dictionary*)

Social work practitioners are good at gathering information but often struggle to understand the implications of it and reach conclusions (Holland 2011). It is very important to move beyond data collection, as the purpose of assessment is to guide action (Reder et al. 1993: 83). Analysis takes the assessment beyond surface considerations and description, and attempts to explore what issues are present and why. It considers the relationship between what is happening and the impact of these events and circumstances on the child/young person and other family members. The assessment should help the practitioners and the family to identify what needs to change for the child and consider what interventions and services should be offered to bring about these changes. Analysis requires the social worker to consider the information gathered during the assessment in light of the child's needs, parental capacity and the family and environmental factors (*Assessment Framework*, DH et al. 2000). The Framework does, however, fail to encourage exploration of other important areas, and consideration should be given to the impact of socio-political factors impacting on the child and family, including oppression and government policies (Calder 2003).

Hypothesising

In Chapter 4 we looked at explanations and hypotheses. At the point of referral, practitioners should begin to hypothesise about what is happening in a family and the reasons why, but this process should continue throughout the assessment. Having started with a range of possible ideas, there should then be an evaluation and testing of the explanations using a variety of methods (Dalzell and Sawyer 2007). The understanding achieved will inform the decision making, intervention and action.

Prior to undertaking the initial assessment on Elizabeth in Case Study 1, Patsy, the social worker, will already have several hypotheses as to why Elizabeth is behaving as she is, based on the information in the CAF. This will include the impact on Elizabeth of her mother's mental illness, her struggling with her brother's disability, difficult peer group relationships and lack of privacy at home. Patsy may have other hypotheses which come from her knowledge of research and practice experience. She may be concerned that Elizabeth is being sexually exploited or misusing substances, as she is out late at night, missing school and her whereabouts are unknown. Whilst completing the initial assessment Patsy will test out the range of hypotheses. This is done by meeting with individual family members and speaking to professionals, using observation of the family, interviews, questionnaires and scales. Importantly, Elizabeth is seen on her own. Patsy then has further information which can discount or support some of the hypotheses. During this assessment further hypotheses are added which increase her understanding of the complexity of the situation, for example Elizabeth is involved in the care of her brother and struggles to establish an identity distinct from her mother. At this time Patsy may have discounted the hypotheses that Elizabeth is misusing substances after her enquiries or feel that she needs to explore this more fully before it can be dismissed.

> How would you test out the hypotheses relating to the violence in Maya and Ajay's home?

Case Study Exercise

It is important to be clear about the source and validity of your hypothesis. When looking at Patsy's hypotheses in relation to Elizabeth, they are from research findings regarding the impact of mental illness and substance misuse on parenting capacity (Cleaver et al. 1999), other professionals' assessments, information from the family and knowledge from experience.

During the analysis social workers should consider all the areas below as a source of hypotheses with regards to what is happening and why, and also as an aid to what intervention may work with the family:

- the information gathered or provided
- other agencies' assessments and opinions
- values and their impact upon decision making
- applying knowledge from research and other knowledge bases
- applying knowledge from experience
- managers' opinions and views
- voice of the child and other family members

The information gathered or provided

Although the usefulness of breaking an assessment down into different stages has been recognised, these stages overlap and there is not a precise time when information gathering stops and analysis begins. When completing an initial assessment, core assessment or assessment for court, there will be deadlines to be worked to, and your analysis will have to be presented at these times. If there are gaps in the information, these should be highlighted, with an indication of how, or if, this can be remedied. If, for example, you have been unable to contact a parent or professional, dates could be given of attempts to do this, or dates in the future when they will be available.

The fact that a person has not made him or herself available or cooperated with the assessment will be part of the analysis and you may have a hypothesis as to why this is and what the implications are. If you think that the person is not cooperating because they are anxious about social work involvement, they may want to consider having a family member or familiar professional involved. Sometimes the reasons for hostility, avoidance, or lack of cooperation are unclear. It is important to consider ways of increasing cooperation. Lefevre (2008: 80) discusses the relationship between professionals and service users and the importance of treating people with dignity and respect, being reliable, accountable and transparent. Also stressed is the importance of empathy, approachability and humour. Many families' contact with social workers has not been made voluntarily and ways of engaging them have to be creative and recognise that practitioners and service users are often coming from very different positions (Calder 2008).

Models of change can be very useful in establishing where service users are in terms of motivation and readiness to change and engage. They may be in a very different starting position to the social worker.

Model of change

Prochaska and Di Clemente (1982: 282) look at stages that are passed through during the 'course of change' though they recognise that the process is often not linear. Although used more frequently in the area of addiction, Morrison (2010: 313) recognises the range of areas where this framework can be utilised, including working with parents on a voluntary basis, statutory basis or in conditional voluntary situations where statutory involvement may be necessary if there is not engagement. The stages are:

1 **Pre contemplation** – the individual may or may not be aware of the problem but there is no thought of changing behaviour and there may be denial or defensiveness.
2 **Contemplation** – the individual has some awareness of the problem and is deciding to make some changes.
3 **Determination** – the individual is showing serious commitment to changing.
4 **Action** – the individual actively modifies behaviour.
5 **Maintenance** – the individual sustains the new behaviour.
6 **Relapse and lapse** – relapse is when the individual resumes the problematic behaviour. This is contrasted with lapse where the individual may be in a situation where the problematic behaviour is at high risk of returning but an appropriate response is made.

This model provides social workers with one way of understanding the stage that an individual is at and why they may be unwilling to cooperate. They may disagree with the person that has referred them that there is a problem, or be unable to contemplate change for other reasons, for example depression. It is important to consider the realistic time frame for change against the social work timetable for change, which will be dictated by the needs of the specific child. This can be an area of contention between adult and children's services. Twelve months may seem a realistic timescale for a person with a long history of substance misuse to become stable. For a newborn baby 12 months without the security of a permanent placement could impact on attachment relationships and development.

It is important that you do not stop gathering information as this may later lead you to an alternative explanation and understanding of a situation. Case Study 1 involves an assessment of Geoff, who is a person posing a risk. Geoff has a criminal record that includes two unrelated offences of unlawful sexual intercourse with a 12-year-old, the offences being separated by 10 years. The social worker, Adela, has to analyse the information which she has gathered and ascertain if Geoff is a risk to 13-year-old Elizabeth. Adela concludes that the risk to Elizabeth is medium to low and this is based on the information that Geoff lives with his mother in a small flat and she is aware of his offences and what happens in her home, which is an inhibiting factor. Geoff is anxious not to return to prison and having cooperated with the assessment, is not currently having contact with Elizabeth. If new information is received, for example that Elizabeth is again meeting Geoff at a mutual friend's home or that Geoff is no longer living with his mother, then the assessment would clearly have to be revisited.

Munro (2008: 138) explores a number of ways that practitioners have of not recognising information that challenges their assessments and these include: avoidance, forgetting, rejecting and reinterpreting. Workers are often reluctant to revise assessments and this can have serious consequences. In the case of Victoria Climbié (Laming Report 2003), Victoria was classified as a 'child in need' and the social worker concentrated on supporting the carers with housing issues. When Victoria sustained injuries the aunt's account wasn't doubted, Munro (2005) suggesting that the social worker wasn't seeing the situation as an investigation in spite of indications that there should be a decision to initiate a s47 enquiry.

Ways to try to avoid some of these pitfalls with regards to information are:

- keeping an open mind with regards to the analysis and being willing to revise it if new, conflicting information comes to light
- not seeking only evidence that supports your hypothesis
- not discounting information from sources until you are clear it is safe to do so; for example, information from neighbours or children is sometimes under-valued.

Holland (2011) suggests other methods to assist the analysis are:

* seeking out evidence to challenge your explanation
* using different methods to gather information, for example direct observation or questionnaires, as well as interviewing
* managing the information so that it is readily available and sources are clear

Other agencies' assessments and opinions

The multi-agency process should not cease at the information gathering stage. It is equally important to secure from the professionals involved in supporting the child and family their understanding of what is happening, why and how the child's needs can best be met. This may result in conflict as different professionals may express different views. Considering the evidence and reasons for the views being expressed will form part of your analysis. It will also be important for you to explain and evidence your analysis and the interventions planned as a consequence.

Occasionally professionals may decline to express an opinion, for example a worker who supports a carer with regards to their substance misuse may not want to comment on parenting capacity. They may be concerned that giving an opinion will impact on their relationship with the service user, or they may feel unqualified to comment. Professionals have the right to identify the limits of their knowledge and professional opinion and it is important that social work professionals are aware of the roles and responsibilities of other professionals so that they know what information they will be able to provide (Seden 2007).

Specialist information from them can assist your analysis. If the drugs support worker tells you that a parent continues to use illicit drugs and has been involved in criminal activity to finance the use, this may raise concerns for you and at the very least ensure that you explore with the parent where the child is at these times.

The importance of inter-agency working is stressed by the Children Act 2004 and *Working Together* (DCSF 2010). The complexities of it are discussed by Munro (2008) who, as well as acknowledging the value of pooling resources and expertise to achieve a more holistic picture of a situation, also warns of the dangers of 'group think'. This can include a group overestimating themselves, which could entail the members taking excessive risks. A second danger is of closed-mindedness, an illustration being given of professionals stereotyping each other and then not valuing each other's views as a consequence of the negative stereotypes. A third result of 'group think' can be pressures towards conformity and this could mean that minority views are ignored or discredited or that individuals do not feel confident to disagree with others. The dangers outlined may be more obvious in an actual group setting, for example a child protection conference or core group, but elements could apply in the less formal discussions with other professionals. It is important not to discount a person's analysis or understanding of a situation because it disagrees with your assessment or because you have had a difficult working relationship with the person in the past. Alternatively you should not just accept a person's analysis because you feel pressurised by their professional status. The evidence to support the analysis should be scrutinised and understood.

Calder (2003) highlights other obstacles to inter-agency working including agencies being guided by different legislation and guidance, variations in training, workers being socialised into their own professional role and differing professional and organisational priorities, structures and systems.

Reder and Duncan (1999: 10) stress that information is not the same thing as meaning and that 'communications simultaneously contain messages about the information itself and about the relationship between the participants'. Responsibility therefore has to be taken by the sender and receiver to ensure that they have expressed and understood what is meant. Confirming in writing your understanding from telephone calls or face-to-face meetings is a way of ensuring that all parties know what was agreed and have not just heard what they want to hear. If a duty phone call is received by a social worker at 4.30 pm on a Friday prior to their two weeks' leave, they may not want to hear that a situation is urgent and that it needs a response that day. If information indicating concerns is received regarding a family when the practitioner had been feeling positive about the progress and was recommending that involvement end, then this new information may be minimised or ignored.

Values

Supervision should be used to reflect on personally held values and their impact on the practitioner's response and analysis, ensuring that their conclusions are justified. Earlier we discussed the importance of undertaking a cultural review when preparing for an assessment. Account needs to be taken of personal characteristics throughout the assessment, as this can impact on our analysis and subsequent decision making. Our gender, age, sexuality, race or other characteristics may mean that we over-emphasise some issues and possibly neglect others. For example, strongly held negative views about the parenting capacity of parents who suffer with depression or have a learning disability may lead to a conclusion that does not take into account strengths and safety elements in an assessment.

Applying knowledge from research and other knowledge bases

There are very varied opinions as to how the most accurate assessments are completed, some supporting a scientific, objective, formal reasoning approach, whilst others value intuition and subjective knowledge. Munro (2008) highlights the move towards evidence-based practice, assessment tools and procedures as supporting the analytical approach but clearly sees the value of intuition and does not see the two as mutually exclusive.

There are a number of tools that can be used to evidence assessment and decision making (*Working Together*, DCSF 2010) including:

* The Strengths and Difficulties Questionnaires
* The Parenting Daily Hassles Scale
* The Recent Life Events Questionnaire
* Alcohol Scale
* Adolescent Wellbeing Scale

These can be used alongside other forms of practice and are not for using in isolation. Although they provide scales and questionnaires, their usefulness is often in the discussion that the tools can initiate.

Research evidence related to the area of need identified in your assessment should always be one consideration informing the analysis of the information gathered. However, the difficulties of utilising research should also be acknowledged and Calder (2003: 47) stresses that research is 'not simply a process revealing an objective truth'. Different people may reach very different conclusions when looking at the same piece of research. He also acknowledges that practitioners may not have the time to access research materials and that there can be anxiety around including research findings in reports, which may then be scrutinised and challenged, particularly if the work is in the court arena. The families and situations that are being assessed are complex and unique and care must be given when applying generalised research findings to a specific situation.

There is an increasing body of research that can provide guidance. To help with this there are a number of websites now available to social workers, where research that has been subject to a quality review and research overviews can be located. The Social Institute of Excellence (SCIE) is a government-funded organisation designed to ensure that social workers have access to the best available information. Research in Practice (RIP; www.rip. org.uk) is another organisation that seeks to promote the use of research within assessment and care planning processes.

As well as empirical research informing practice, knowledge of law, policy and procedures is important. Social workers also need a large repertoire of practical skills as previously discussed.

Applying knowledge from experience

Social work analysis and decision making will inevitably be influenced by experience. This experience needs to be considered in the context of the practitioner's value base and the outcomes of past work. Learning from what has worked and what has not worked in the past constitutes an essential element of the development of professional expertise. Care has to be taken, however, not to generalise and apply findings from previous experience inappropriately. Again it is important to stress that each child and family are unique.

There are long-standing debates on the role of intuition in making judgements and it is often compared unfavourably with an analytical approach. There is increasing recognition that it is helpful to see these on a continuum and that both have a usefulness (Munro 2008). Practitioners need to be able to move between the two or use a combination of both and consider which may be the most appropriate for different situations. Helm (2010: 154) gives detailed consideration of how to use intuition effectively. He looks at some of the characteristics of intuitive thinking, including that it is quick, reactive, unconscious and involves thinking widely about a large amount of information. This is compared with analytical thinking that is slow and deliberate and where there is a conscious thinking process and fewer issues considered.

Practitioners do sometimes speak about having a 'gut feeling' and Munro (2008) warns that this can lead to over-confidence and an unwillingness to consider the alternatives. Practitioners can often explain their feeling or hunch and this may be based on a combination of research knowledge, experience of similar situations and knowledge of behaviour from a work and personal perspective.

Managers' opinions and views

The sharing of case information with managers is an essential aspect of supervision. Supervision is a forum where a social worker's assumptions, hypotheses and understanding of a situation can be discussed and, if necessary, challenged. Managers may be able to identify gaps, or areas that require further assessment. It is the forum where practitioners can critically reflect on their practice and Baldwin and Walker (2005) recognise that there will be several cycles of reflection and practice during the assessment process. Interventions and the review of plans will also take place in this setting.

If the practitioner and manager hold different views, it is important to explore the basis of this difference. Disagreements should be recorded but managers hold casework responsibility. If a practitioner believes that a child or young person is at risk of harm as a result of the difference of view then it would be acceptable to ask the manager to review the case and seek a senior manager's opinion on the case.

Voice of the child and other family members

As previously emphasised, the relationship established with the service user will be a very important factor in the quality of the assessment and subsequent intervention. The current timescales for undertaking initial and core assessments can make it difficult to develop a trusting, constructive working relationship with a family, Calder (2003: 35) commenting that 'engagement is a process, not a set period of time'. The benefits of having timescales, including avoiding drift and delay, are recognised but the potential limitations to the quality of the assessment also have to be considered. If it is felt at the completion of an initial assessment that an accurate assessment has not been possible, this may be a reason to recommend that a core assessment is undertaken to enable a more intense and detailed piece of work.

In spite of the time constraints it is important that the family's understanding of their unique situation is obtained and Milner and O'Byrne (2009: 70) emphasise the need to 'co-construct shared understandings' with service users and be aware of power imbalance. They discuss the possibility of a 'plurality of truths' and that the service user's understanding may be different to that of the practitioner. Disagreement does not mean that the service user's perspective should be discounted. There may also be diversity of opinion in a family and attempts should be made to listen to all members.

It may be that the family understanding or explanation is unacceptable. For example in Case Study 2, if Kripa were to feel that he has the right to be physically violent to his wife, this clearly cannot be supported by practitioners. Work would then need to be undertaken with Kripa to challenge his view that violence to women is acceptable and to explain the concern that his violence harms Roshni and also his children.

Scourfield (2001a: 77), in a study of the culture of a social work team in the United Kingdom, looks at the social workers' opinions of women and identifies three strands: women being seen as oppressed, as responsible for protecting children and as making choices. The social workers' opinions of men (Scourfield 2001b: 85) included them being seen 'as a threat, as no use, as irrelevant, as absent, as no different from women, and as better than women'.

Men, including fathers and stepfathers, are still sometimes omitted from assessments and efforts should be made to include them from the start rather than concentrate on working with women and children only. Consideration should be given to how men in the family, including absent fathers, can be engaged directly and included at all stages, including the analysis and intervention. As with other family members, strengths as well as risks need to be identified and your analysis and interpretation of a situation should be tested out with the individual involved.

In what ways could Charlie's father, Michael, be engaged in the assessment?

Case Study Exercise

Holland (2011) acknowledges that children can be insightful, and imaginative ways of ascertaining their understanding and wishes and feelings are important. Practitioners may feel that time constraints make direct work with children impossible but the consequences of not including them and engaging with them can be very serious. A small amount of time talking to, or playing with, a child will help to form a relationship but also teach you a great deal about their development and relationships, their understanding of what is wrong and what would help.

Some children find it very difficult to express their views verbally and alternatives have to be considered. A social worker needs to have a collection of tools that can be used flexibly. Children may find it easier to draw what they are thinking and feeling and there are a range of books available which give colourful and imaginative pictures for children to write on or draw in. This can include opportunities to express what their worries are and what makes them feel safe, what they want to happen and how they can be helped in achieving it. Children may find it easier to talk using a puppet or toy telephone, all things that the social worker can keep in a box in the back of the car or carry on visits.

What tools may be helpful to engage Peter?

Case Study Exercise

Judgements

We have explored the importance of hypothesising and confirming and discounting explanations in an attempt to reach an understanding of what is happening in a family, so that decisions can be made with regards to interventions. When outlined as above, the process may appear logical and straightforward but all social work practitioners are aware that this is not the case. Hollows (2003: 61) recognises that the 'truth' of information that is obtained is not guaranteed. She also highlights the impact on workers of bombardment, interference and stress. Social workers have complex case loads and are working on numerous assessments at different stages in the process at the same time. Attention is drawn from one piece of work to another by a range of factors including telephone calls, reprioritising demands or crisis situations.

Hollows (2003) provides a useful framework for looking at judgements, which encourages the reconsideration of those that have been made.

Holding judgements: These are made when a quick decision is needed and there is little opportunity to hypothesise. An example of this would be an Out of Hours team being asked to visit a mother, previously unknown to Children's Services, who is caring for a baby and who appears to be intoxicated. When the visit is undertaken there is a neighbour present who offers to stay with the family overnight to ensure that they are safe. There may be few other alternatives for the worker to consider, other than removing the baby from the mother's care, and the worker agrees to the neighbour's suggestion. With little information or opportunity to hypothesise, intuitive decisions are often made at this stage, but there will be the need to revisit the judgement when more information is available. The danger occurs when holding judgements are allowed to continue without reconsideration.

Issue judgements: These judgements are made when there is more time for analysis and an opportunity to look at the wider circumstances. Following on from the above example, it may be that having had discussions with the health visitor and GP for the family the following day, and obtained their understanding of the situation, there are concerns that the mother is depressed following the birth of her baby and also a recent bereavement, and that she may be self-medicating. The main issues may therefore be the impact on the mother and baby of the mother's depression and experience of loss rather than a concentration on substance misuse. This clarification will clearly have an impact on the direction of the subsequent intervention.

Strategic judgements: These involve deciding what interventions will be appropriate when the issues have been clarified. They 'turn hypotheses into actions' (Helm 2010: 101).

Evaluative judgements: Evaluation of the issue and strategic judgements is important and reviewing of the progress of work necessary.

Decision making

At the end of the assessment work you will have progressed as far as you can with proving and discarding hypotheses, and taking into account all the above, reached some conclusion about what is happening and why. This can be illustrated with reference to Maya and Ajay in Case Study 2. By the time you have completed the core assessment on the two children, many of the initial hypotheses will have been confirmed or discounted. Following contact with the family and other professionals there is no evidence that Roshni is violent to Kripa and this has therefore been discarded. There is clear physical and verbal evidence from family and the police that Kripa is violent to Roshni and that the level of this is escalating and putting the children at risk. Evidence has been obtained through interviewing and observation.

The use of research findings has increased social worker Milli's knowledge of the complexity of the relationship between domestic abuse and substance misuse and that use of alcohol or drugs cannot be presumed to be the cause of domestic abuse. This is clarified by Humphreys, who says 'perpetrators of abuse may become drunk because they want to be violent' (Humphreys and Stanley 2006: 29). Milli has also discussed the family with her manager and gaps have been identified so that further work has to be undertaken into the impact of stress. This has established a clearer picture of what is happening and why and what interventions may work and which not, but there will still be a range of alternatives and a decision has to be made as to which route to follow.

Having worked through the different stages of the assessment a decision has to be made as to what the options are. Munro (2008: 106) provides a framework for looking at this with a decision tree that uses formal and intuitive knowledge. This involves considering:

- What decision has to be made?
- What options are there?
- What information is needed to help make the choice?
- What are the likely/possible consequences of each option?
- How probable is each consequence?
- What are the pros and cons of each consequence?
- The final decision.

Applying this to Maya and Ajay we can look at the options at the end of the core assessment and prior to the further violent incident, using the sequence above.

1 The decision that we want to make is how can Maya and Ajay be protected from the domestic abuse in their home.
2 The options could include:

A Child protection conference and rigorous child protection plan recommending Kripa leave the home
B Child protection conference with child protection plan and Kripa at home
C Continue to assess and monitor the family with Child in Need plan
D Initiate care proceedings

3   Further information needed to help determine which option may include checking with the legal department if the threshold would be met to initiate proceedings

4   Consequences need to be explored for all four alternatives but we will consider the second option B

  • A consequence of Kripa remaining at home may be that the family can be worked with as a whole, are still together and the domestic abuse will stop
  • Domestic abuse may continue and Roshni be harmed
  • Domestic abuse may continue and Roshni and/or the children be harmed

5   Consideration needs to be given to how probable each consequence is and Munro suggests that each probability is scored. If scoring out of 100% then the probability of the domestic abuse stopping might be scored at 40%, probability of risk to Roshni 40% and risk to the children 20%.

6   The next stage is to look at the pros and cons of each consequence, giving them an expected utility or desirability value. As Munro (2008) states, this involves value judgements and the opinion of different professionals may vary greatly. Yasmin, the support worker for example, may have very different views to the social worker. The utility value/desirability of the family remaining together and domestic abuse stopping is very high and with marks out of 10 could be given 9. Harm to Roshni and the children could both be scored at 1 as this is not wanted. The social worker would be concerned about adult or child being harmed and aware of the harm to children of witnessing domestic abuse. The probability scores are then multiplied by the desirability score and added together, and this gives you the total for the option. This process is repeated with the other three options and the option with the highest score will be the chosen option as it is combining what is realistic and desirable (Dalzell and Sawyer 2007)

Case Study Exercise

Repeat the process with option D and compare the score with outcome B.

Considering options and consequences in this way and then scoring them in relation to probability and pros and cons provides a logical and consistent process by which decision making with regard to risk management can be informed.

Conclusion

In this chapter we have looked at what is meant by analysis and the range of sources that can increase our understanding of what is happening in a family and why. No matter how rigorous an assessment is, there will never be perfect knowledge and information on which to base the analysis and decision making. However, by taking into account the areas discussed in this chapter, a comprehensive assessment and analysis can be undertaken which has meaning for both professionals and family and which leads to clear decision making, interventions and positive outcomes for the child/young person. The plans and interventions that should ensue from a good quality assessment are discussed in the next chapter.

Recommended further reading

Judith Milner and Patrick O'Byrne, *Assessment in Social Work*, Palgrave Macmillan (2009)
With a strong practice base, this book provides comprehensive guidance on undertaking assessments.

Duncan Helm, *Making Sense of Child and Family Assessment: How to Interpret Children's Needs*, Jessica Kingsley Publishers (2010)
This book provides practical guidance on undertaking assessments, with a particular emphasis on how to analyse information.

Eileen Munro, *Effective Child Protection*, Sage (2008)
This provides a detailed study of how judgements are reached and decisions made and explores how improvements can be made in these areas.

Chapter 6

Intervention and Planning

The term intervention is used to describe the action to effect change with the child, young person and parent/carer. As previously discussed, prior to the intervention consideration needs to be given to what services should be offered, the availability of resources and what is likely to bring the best outcome for the child. It will then be possible to establish a plan that outlines the actions required and who does them. *Working Together* also stresses the importance of working to 'timescales that are appropriate to the child' (DCSF 2010: 177).

Important elements of any intervention will be working with the child and family as well as other agencies involved in supporting the child. The plan will always be multidisciplinary and those involved will routinely meet to review it to make sure that it is still appropriate, is being implemented within the agreed timescales and that it is achieving its objectives. What actions and how they are to be implemented will depend upon the social work approach you are adopting and the desired outcomes you are seeking for the child.

Stages of assessment and planning are not sequential and planning should run concurrently with the assessment. So, if at the start of an initial or core assessment it is identified that action is needed to protect a child, or a service is required such as an urgent housing repair or mental health assessment, then this should be acted upon at the time, rather than waiting for the conclusion of the assessment. Assessment, planning and intervention should always be seen as ongoing events. Where the child's circumstances change or a new need is identified then this should be evaluated, as this may impact upon the social worker's analysis of the situation and lead to the need for a new or different intervention.

Learning points

- What intervention means
- Ensuring safety
- Effecting change

Interventions in local authority social work

Social work interventions

Understanding human behaviour will assist your ability to establish effective interventions with a family and it is important that social workers are knowledgeable about the range of models of change, including social learning theory and social skills training. They should be aware of the often conflicting variety of theories about what works and which are effective interventions. There is a range of books that explore these areas (Corby 2006; Howe 2009; Iwaniec 2006; Payne 2005; Stepney and Ford 2000).

Working Together (DCSF 2010: 177: 5.131) recognises that intervention may have a number of inter-related components:

- action to make a child safe from harm and prevent recurrence of harm
- action to help promote a child's health and development, i.e. welfare
- actions to help parent(s)/caregiver(s) in safeguarding a child and promoting his or her welfare
- therapy for an abused or neglected child
- support or therapy for a perpetrator of abuse or neglect in order to prevent future harm to the child and, where necessary, to other children

Local authority social workers are likely to be involved in all these areas, sometimes on the same piece of work, as they are not discrete categories.

Ensuring safety

The broad aim of any intervention is to ensure that the needs of the child are met, including their need for safety. Social workers should take immediate practical steps to ensure a child's safety, when this is deemed to be required. The safety of a child will need to be reviewed during the intervention as risks may go up as well as down during the course of social work activity. The following types of interventions may be used with each other to provide a package of safety to the child or young person.

Monitoring the implementation of plans

These are generally multi-agency agreements about who in the family will be seen and when. It should also include a plan of action should these contacts fail. An example of this would be where there are serious concerns about poor home conditions, school attendance and the child's physical development. Monitoring the plan may include weekly social work visits to the family to check home conditions and that family support is being utilised; the expectation of the child's daily attendance at school so that their educational needs are met and physical and emotional state observed; and monthly one-to-one sessions between the school nurse and the child so that both can discuss any health concerns. The contingency plan would be that the family social worker or duty officer will be notified and a social work visit undertaken if the child fails to attend school by 9.30am. Support provided by family and friends may be included in the plans, for example, a neighbour agrees to have the child one afternoon a week whilst the mother goes to counselling, or the child's grandparents offer some respite care one night a week.

Plans should always state whether there may be unannounced visits, i.e. visits made with no prior arrangement with the family. These visits can often be experienced by a family as a breach of privacy and are potentially invasive. They can also imply that there is a lack of trust between the social worker and family. To mitigate against the potentially adverse impact, when such visits are necessary the reasons for them should be clearly explained, for example to check that a person with a substance misuse history is not intoxicated when caring for their child or that a person posing a risk is not having contact with the family. It is important that practitioners and families are fully appraised about what is being monitored and why, as well as what practitioners are expecting of families and what families can expect from practitioners.

Written agreements

Written agreements do not in themselves secure a child's safety nor are they enforceable in law but they do establish clear ground rules and expectations for professionals, parents, carers and children, which, along with a monitoring plan, may assist the child's safety. These agreements may include working with the child or young person to reach an agreement about what they will or will not do, for example agreeing times that they are going to come home or they will ring to say where they are. It may include agreement with the child and carers as to who the child will have contact with and specify the nature of the contact. Alternatively it may specify individuals with whom there should be no contact and the reasons for this.

The consequences of a breach of the agreement should be specified and this may be that an initial child protection conference will be convened or Child in Need meeting held to determine a multi-agency response to the breach. Again, as with the monitoring plan, the agreement should specify what families can expect of the professionals involved. The family should be given clear information as to the frequency of visits or services that they can anticipate. They should also be given information as to how they can express disagreement or complaints.

Child protection conferences

These conferences (initial and review) are used to discuss and analyse the child's situation in a multi-agency forum and reach a decision as to whether the child has suffered, or is likely to suffer, significant harm. The conference will decide if action is needed to safeguard the child or promote their welfare and, if necessary, a clear outline child protection plan will be formulated. Parents/carers are usually invited to attend these meetings and there should be exceptional reasons for this not to be the case, for example risk of violence from them. Efforts should also always be made to involve the child/young person depending on their age and the content of the meeting. It may be inappropriate for the child/young person to attend the entire or any of the conference but they may wish to meet with the Chair of the meeting to express their wishes and feelings, or be present at the end to listen to recommendations.

The plan will specify how the situation will be monitored and progress evaluated and should clearly specify what interventions will take place and by whom. A Core Group will be identified that should meet within 10 days of the conference. This again should always include parents/carers and where appropriate the child/young person. The Core Group will consider the outcome of the core assessment and formulate the detailed child protection plan. Time and care should be taken when constructing the detailed plan and micro planning at this stage can help to avoid delay and drift in interventions and plans. Where possible the plan should include specific information as to what the professional or family member will undertake to do and dates should be given for this to be achieved. Rather than a vague recommendation that a parent will undertake anger management or accept support with a substance misuse difficulty, the name of the person who is going to provide this should be included, along with dates of the appointments. Contingencies should be built into the plan where possible. The Core Group must meet at a frequency sufficient to ensure that the plan is effectively monitored and implemented.

Consider who would be in the Core Group responsible for implementing Maya and
Ajay's child protection plan?

How would the Core Group ensure that the plan was being implemented and having the intended effect?

These fora demonstrate the overlap between assessment, decision making and
intervention, as it involves elements of all. Subsequent reviews, which take
place three months after the initial conference and then at least six-monthly,
will consider the progress and whether the need for the plan remains. It is
important to remember that although a decision may be reached that a child
protection plan is no longer necessary, the family may still need support and
services. It may therefore be appropriate to continue Child in Need meetings
and continue to review outcomes for the child in this forum.

Exclusion from the home

Abusers or a person presenting a risk may be asked to leave the home or have
no contact with the child. Legal orders such as a 'prohibited steps order' or a
'specific steps order' granted under s8 of the Children Act 1989 can sometimes be used to enforce this action.

Change of home

The non-abusing parent and child may be moved to alternative accommodation or have accommodation secured with safety equipment. This may be
effective in situations that involve domestic violence and where a safety plan
forms part of the overall plan for the child.

Residential assessment

The assessment of parents and child in specialist residential units can provide
intensive assessments in a safe and supportive environment. These may be
appropriate with parents and new babies, especially where this is the first
child and it has not been possible to previously assess parenting capacity. The
transition from the unit to the community should be carefully planned so that
there is not a sudden change in the level of support.

Family group conferences

Family group conferences were developed in New Zealand and are a 'kinship
led planning process' (Morris 2002: 131). A broad definition of 'family' is used,

which can include all people important to the child. The purpose of the conference is for the family to develop a safe and achievable plan for the child when the need for one has been identified. An independent person coordinates the conference and the child and its networks are given time in private to decide on a plan, on contingencies and on how the plan will be reviewed. The coordinator may be a social worker, CAFCASS family court advisor or other professional who has the skills and training to undertake this role.

Adult service assessment

Coordinating the social worker's assessment of the child with the assessment of a parent by mental health or disabilities social worker, employed in adult social care, may be necessary to inform the analysis of all the factors impacting on the child's situation and what is required to effect the necessary change. It may be necessary for the parents or carers to seek support and treatment from mental health or substance misuse agencies, attend probation service programmes, or for adult services to provide support to the parent to enable them to care for the child. The continuance of the child staying at home may be dependent upon the adult engaging with the treatment or service provision.

Where, for example, a parent has a mental health difficulty or disability, it is important to remember the role that adult social care services can play in providing the required intervention. The role played by Jenny's mental health worker in monitoring Jenny's mental health and ensuring that she continues to take lithium and maintains her mood chart is critical to ensuring that Jenny can parent appropriately. Alan Bailey also identifies an ongoing source of support for Jenny in the local MIND support group, a resource which a social worker based in children's social care may not have been aware of.

In the case of parents who have a disability, the Department of Health Circular 'Fair Access to Care Services' (DH 2010) gives guidance as to the support a person may be eligible for from adult social care. This will be dependent on how far the 'risks to independence and well being or other consequences' are seen as critical, substantial, moderate or low (DH 2010: 54) and the eligibility criteria of the local authority concerned. This may mean, for example, that where a wheelchair-using parent cannot take a six-year-old to school, that adult social care may fund transport. Alternatively, where a leaning disabled parent has difficulty establishing morning routines that makes sure a child is woken, has time to eat, dress, have breakfast and pack their bag and then leave the house in time to arrive at school by its starting time, adult social care may fund a family aide to support and guide the parent on school day mornings. Joint planning is very important in these circumstances. Though there may be different timescales and plans for individuals in the family, there does need to be coordination and understanding by the agencies involved of how these plans fit together.

An area of conflict between professionals working in adult social care and those in children's services can be lack of agreement regarding what is a reasonable timescale for an intervention and change. There can also be a danger of children's services concentrating on the child and child protection issues, and adult services looking at services for the adult without either service having an appreciation and understanding of the other's role.

As discussed in Chapter 3, when working with a learning disabled parent with parenting challenges for which the family need support, it will be important to work closely with other relevant agencies. Through all stages of the assessment, intervention and planning it is important to ensure that appropriate communication tools are used and the parent's understanding of information is checked out regularly. Information in writing should always be in *easy read* [CHANGE 2010]. If necessary, advice should be sought from adult social care, speech and language therapy or psychological services to assist understanding of how the individual understands, processes information and learns (Sheffield City Council Practice Guidance 2010).

When considering interventions, learning disabled parents may require more time to learn skills, and their ability and motivation to change and acquire the skills will have to be considered. There is a range of ways of teaching skills, including reducing tasks into smaller parts, providing feedback on work that goes well and modelling and role playing to illustrate what is expected or needs to be done, for example to illustrate how a baby is held or feeding bottle prepared. A positive attitude from both the worker and parent and an environment without distractions are thought to be conducive to learning (Sheffield City Council Practice Guidance 2010). Programmes based in the home appear preferable to those in an alternative setting (SCIE 2005). This may have implications if a residential assessment of parents is being considered.

A parent may not have involvement from adult services but consideration could be given to advocacy support for the family. Practice Guidance on working with parents with a learning disability provides excellent advice on this area of work, including supporting parents involved in the child protection system and child protection conferences (DH and DfES 2007).

It is important not to make 'presumptions of incompetence' when considering the parenting capacity of a learning disabled parent, and to ensure that a holistic assessment is undertaken that recognises their unique situation, rather than concluding without assessment that their disability will automatically result in difficulties. It is important, however, to recognise that their disability may mean that they experience difficulties, many of which are shared by other parents, which can make parenting challenging. This can include unemployment, isolation and exclusion and mean that they may need practical, social and financial support to undertake the parenting role (SCIE 2005).

When working with Elizabeth and Peter, how would you ensure that there was joint planning with adult services?

Case Study Exercise

Legal action and alternative care

Where it does not prove possible to achieve the cooperation of the family or the plan has failed to secure a sufficient level of safety for the child, it may be necessary to use legal powers in order to secure the child or young person's well-being whilst further assessments are being undertaken. This may lead to an application of an Emergency Protection Order (EPO) under s44 of the Children Act 1989 or an Interim Care Order (ICO) under s31. The child may then need to reside with alternative carers during the course of the intervention. This could be with kinship carers or, if no suitable kinship carers can be identified, within local authority care, i.e. foster care or a residential home

Effecting change

Alongside interventions related to the child or young person's immediate safety, interventions should be implemented to improve and enhance that child or young person's well-being.

We previously looked at how attachment theory, systems/ecological theory and solution focused therapy can help our understanding of what is happening and why. We will now discuss how they can inform our intervention. In some local authorities, specialist teams have been established to apply some of these specific methods of intervention with families and we will not only discuss how these are implemented but also what elements may be of value in achieving change for social workers who are not employed in these specialist teams.

Attachment theory

As well as providing an explanation of why something is happening, knowledge of attachment theory can be utilised when looking at interventions. It is possible to discuss with carers, whether parents or foster carers, what attachment is and what some of the key elements that assist attachment are, for example responding to the child's cues and interacting with the child.

Howe (2009: 182) recognises the importance of the work of neuroscientists in helping our understanding of brain development and the role played by relationships in development. We are born with a brain 'that works' (Gerhardt 2004: 37) but that needs social experience to develop certain capacities. Nerve cells are programmed from birth but there needs to be interaction with an adult who cares for parts of the brain to develop well. Although it is recognised that there are sensitive times for stimulation to take place, the brain can make some recovery if subsequently the individual who has had early difficulties experiences a good, warm, stimulating relationship. This is more difficult where there has been extensive neglect and trauma (Howe 2009). This does emphasise the importance of attachment relationships throughout the child's life.

In Case Study 3 Charlie has been assessed by the social worker as having an insecure attachment. Howe (2003) describes three patterns of insecure attachment:

- avoidant/defended
- ambivalent
- disorganised controlling

Charlie's attachment pattern could perhaps be most easily understood in relation to the second category of ambivalent. His mother is inconsistent in her response to him, depending on whether she is intoxicated. When misusing substances she is less likely to respond to his cues and signals and Charlie therefore experiences there being no link between what he does and the response he receives. This can result in children heightening their behaviour in an attempt to achieve a response and can help to explain Charlie being attention-seeking, angry and at other times clingy. As Howe (2003: 378) explains, the pattern is described as ambivalent because 'the child desires an increase in parental responsivity but also feels angry that parental care and protection cannot be taken for granted'. When Charlie's needs *are* responded to, he cannot be confident that this will last.

If Charlie was going to be rehabilitated to his parents' care, the intervention would need to include work with them on their understanding of their son's needs and their response to him. Occasionally workers are in a position to video-record a contact session and this can then be used as the basis of a discussion as to what the strengths are in the relationship and where there may be difficulties. Such opportunities are rare and it is much more likely that the work will be undertaken using the social worker's observations and parents' and child's perceptions. Parents or carers can be given examples of ways to bring changes to the relationship and it is useful to use Fahlberg's (1994) suggestions of responding to the arousal-relaxation cycle, initiating positive interaction and claiming behaviour.

In relation to the arousal-relaxation cycle, parents or carers can be helped to recognise cues and signals and to understand the importance of a consistent response. With Charlie's parents it may not be possible for them to respond consistently until they are drug-free but an important part of the assessment will be whether they recognise the impact of their behaviour. Positive interaction can be encouraged in many ways and include sharing an activity, teaching a new skill or supporting the child in some way. An important element of this is responding to the child when he/she initiates a positive interaction. Claiming behaviour can include identifying positive shared characteristics such as physical features or personality traits. All these can increase a child's sense of security and belonging.

> How could your knowledge about attachment theory be used in your work with Maya and Ajay's parents to effect change?

Case Study Exercise

An understanding of attachment theory and how children adapt their behaviour to cope when they do not feel secure can assist professionals working with children and also alternative carers, including foster and kinship carers. Children who are angry, attention-seeking and demanding can be exhausting to teach or care for and adults may be looking for the reason for this behaviour entirely in the school or home setting. Understanding why children may behave in this way can put the behaviour in context and offer suggestions for ways of working with the individual.

The above may make work with attachment difficulties sound very simplistic and easy to remedy and this is not the intention. Some children will have experienced trauma and neglect to such an extent that they will have great difficulties establishing trusting relationships and will have a series of broken placements. Some children will benefit from specialist counselling and therapeutic work, which may be long term and which is beyond the remit of this chapter.

Systems/ecological theory

The Multi Systemic Therapy (MST) approach looks at problems that have been identified in their broader systemic context. It views individuals as being surrounded by a network of interconnected systems that encompass individual, family and extra familial factors. Intervention may be necessary in any one or a combination of these systems.

The MST therapists have a small caseload of between four and six families and work with families over a 3–6 month period. The therapist will normally work with the family in the family home. They will observe behaviour and focus on achieving necessary changes. The treatment plan will be family-driven rather than therapist-driven. The model uses very measurable goals and will target specific, well-defined problems with clear action, which makes it easy to evaluate if change has occurred.

The therapist is the single point of contact for the family through whom all interventions and referrals for the family are routed. There is a strong emphasis on the positive and using the family or individual's strengths to bring about change. Therapists also have responsibility for holding other agencies to account and ensuring services are provided to meet the needs of the family. They are required to have specialist clinical supervision once a week and to have undertaken specialist training.

The intensive nature of intervention is beyond the resource capability of local authority social workers. Nevertheless it is important to understand that this therapeutic model draws on the social work systems theory and that the Assessment Framework requires social workers to consider the full ecological picture and the systems around the child. Elements of this model can therefore be successfully applied by social workers to effect change in the way a family functions.

When looking at Case Study 1 in relation to Elizabeth and Peter, the initial and core assessments are undertaken using the Assessment Framework and the interplay of the different systems in each child's life becomes very clear. What is also clear is the uniqueness of each child. A useful exercise in relation to Elizabeth and Peter is to look at the risk factors and protective factors in their lives. This could be completed under the domains of the Assessment Framework or looked at in the context of the individual, family, peer relationships, school and neighbourhood and community. The exercise can either be completed with family members or the social worker's analysis shared with the family. This can help to identify the systems that are supportive or increase resilience and those systems that are stressful or problematic. Work can then be undertaken to build on the strengths, for example building up contact with supportive extended family, or to attempt to address difficulties, such as the bullying experienced by Elizabeth at school.

Some advantages of this theory are that it encourages a holistic approach and exploration of social factors. Criticisms, however, include that it doesn't explain why things happen and connections exist or what we have to do to have an impact on the systems. It is also difficult to decide which areas are important and, when exploring wider issues, other more personal areas could be ignored (Payne 2005: 158).

Which systems in Peter's life are supportive and which are problematic?
What changes might take advantage of the strengths and reduce the difficulties?

Case Study
Exercise

Solution focused theory

As discussed earlier, for this model to work the adults involved need to have their own goals for change, which in some way need to be consistent with the goals of the local authority.

As part of the UK 'Option Two' there is a brief solution focused service which offers short intensive interventions to families whose children are on the brink of being brought into public care. The intervention is based in the community and uses motivational interviewing and solution focused counselling.

The model works on the basis that the service user holds the solution and the therapist needs to learn to see the service user's world. You cannot 'do brief therapy to someone', they need to see the benefit and be an active participant. Service users work out steps to achieve their goals in a way that is realistic to their lives. Child protection goals can often focus on the negative and are at times out of the control of the service user, for example, the alleged abuser not to visit the home. It is important to acknowledge what can be achieved and to establish if that is safe/good enough for the child. Establishing goals using these principles will also enable you to evaluate if the intervention is effective.

In the 'Option Two' model, families are provided with support from a worker on a daily basis and can access at least telephone support on a 24-hour basis. This intensive support lasts for 4–6 weeks but further support is offered after this to encourage the service user to work towards a positive future. Although a local authority social worker will not be able to offer this level of intensive support, the principles of shared positive goals with a clear vision for the future can be developed.

Social workers can therefore recognise any spontaneous improvement by asking at the start of each visit whether anything is better/changed since the previous meeting. Immediately recognising that there may be positives, and providing an expectation of improvement, avoids continually negative visits. Social workers need to know about positive changes in families in order to reinforce them and need to avoid discussions that simply focus on the negatives in the family situation. If you think one issue is very important and needs to be resolved but another issue is more important and difficult for a service user, consideration will need to be given to resolving both issues, either together or sequentially.

A solution focused approach could be considered when working with Jenny, Elizabeth and Peter in Case Study 1. Elizabeth is 13 years old and Peter is seven years old. They are both in the care of their mother and a starting point could be positive comments on this and how it has been achieved. Emphasis on exceptions to difficult and problematic times can assist individuals in understanding what their strengths and support systems are and these can then be built on.

The use of the miracle question can help social workers to understand what Jenny and the children want to change and how they think this can happen. Jenny may think that if the miracle occurred and her problems were solved, Elizabeth would be attending school and not staying out late. Elizabeth may have a very different perspective and feel that her problems would disappear if she had her own room and lived with her father. This gives family members an opportunity to say how the difficulties could be resolved for them and, if nothing else, can lead to more open discussion and pragmatic solutions. In the above example a downstairs room is changed into a bedroom for Elizabeth and Mark, her father, becomes a more active parent. Elizabeth agrees to be more communicative about where she is and come in at a reasonable time.

Scaling questions could be used with the family allowing them to rate how bad they feel a particular problem is. Peter could be asked scaling questions in relation to how worried he is about his mother, or how safe he feels at home. Any changes brought about by his increased understanding of his mother's illness or the positive impact of his increased contact with his grandparents could then be measured. When working with Peter, numbers could be replaced with smiling faces to indicate how positive or negative he feels.

There are many positive features to a solution focused approach, including its being strength-based and viewing the service user rather than the professional as the expert. There is transparency, with the emphasis being on gaining the service user's understanding of their situation and the assumption that they have the solutions to their difficulties, though they may require help to identify the goals. It is also much more likely that service users will engage with working towards outcomes that have meaning to them rather than goals identified by the practitioner. The approach does not see the service user as the problem and concentration on the future means that there is no blame and recrimination for past events. Myers (2008: 7) compares this with pathology-based approaches, in which he includes attachment theory, where there is a concentration on factors that have impacted on child development and where the intervention looks at how 'emotional hurt' can be mended. A further feature of this method is that it does consider that interventions do not have to be long term, even where there are entrenched difficulties, and that minimal intervention can be effective. This can be of benefit to service users who do not want lengthy involvement from practitioners and to service providers where there are resource concerns.

It is also necessary to consider the criticisms of the approach including that a concentration on the future means that important past information is not taken into account. Concerns have been expressed about 'start again syndrome' where there is emphasis on the present situation and valuable past information is not given enough weight. This can lead to important patterns or evidence of deterioration in a family's or child's situation not being recognised (Helm 2010). This may be particularly important in cases of neglect.

The Serious Case Review following the death of Peter Connolly ('Baby P') (Haringey Local Safeguarding Board 2009) considered the use of a solution focused approach which had been adopted by some members of the safeguarding team. Although the method was not directly linked to the outcome of the case, the report is clearly of the opinion that there is a lack of compatibility with this approach and the authoritative social work necessary at the time of protection enquiries, assessment and conference.

Direct work with children and young people

Practitioners need skills in building relationships and communicating with children/young people across a range of ages and abilities. There will, at times, be difficult and distressing information that has to be given to children or that they disclose to the practitioner. Work will need to be undertaken to help them with changes or painful loss in their lives. Aldgate and Seden (2006: 241) consider a range of principles which may be useful when undertaking direct work. These include skilful observation, sensitivity, careful listening, talking to children about things that interest them and being honest.

Elements of art therapy can be utilised and can help to increase self awareness and confidence (Ross 1997). This can include the young person drawing pictures of different elements of their personality, including how their angry self or scared self looks. This can lead to further discussion and exploration of the circumstances when this may arise and what helps and hinders.

Life story work can be undertaken with children of all ages and can utilise any interests or skills that they have. The work can, for example, be in the form of drawing, photographs or videos, or use toys or discussion. Rees (2009) makes the distinction between life story work and a life story book. She explains that children/young people should be routinely involved in life story work when this is undertaken and that it can help them understand their history and clarify things that they have been unsure about. This may include reasons for interventions and changes in their life or factual information about family relationships. A life story book is the end product which the child may or may not be involved in compiling. Life story work and books are frequently completed for children who are separated from their birth family and placed for adoption. Life story work can be helpful for a range of children, for example Charlie, where there is a move to a foster placement and then kinship placement.

Aldgate and Seden (2006) recognise that practitioners working directly with children and young people need appropriate training and supervision of their work. There may be areas of work in which the social worker feels less skilled, for example when therapeutic intervention is considered necessary for a child. It is then important to consider which professional is best able to undertake this work, recognising the importance of working closely with other agencies.

Interventions in local authority social work

Having looked at three specific models of intervention and direct work with children, it is important to review what the local authority social worker *is likely to be able to offer* to a child, young person and their family. The local authority social worker will need a pragmatic approach to intervention as she/he applies the Integrated Children's System. The child's plan is key to describing what aspects of the child's life need attention and what the intervention should be striving to achieve. The social worker will need to use the following types of interventions to implement plans for children effectively:

- Secure the child's immediate safety and welfare through the methods discussed earlier.
- Engage necessary services and resources through internal negotiation and collaboration with partner agencies to alleviate any practical presenting problems as identified in the assessment.
- Identify (or work with other agencies to develop) an approach to address any necessary parent or child behavioural changes. This may involve applying a specific theory or model or a referral to an agency that can offer a therapeutic intervention. The behavioural changes required should be described as clear, specific, goals which provide outcome-based descriptions in order for the family to be able to aspire to and demonstrate that they have achieved necessary changes.

- Establish parental strengths or alternative carer's strengths to identify whether they can take over aspects of the intervention in order that long-term independent change can occur. During the course of the intervention the aim should be to move the responsibility for the implementation of the plan from the social worker to the adult who is going to be responsible for the child.

A local authority social worker may use elements from Solution Focused Brief Therapy, MST, attachment theory, task-centred social work, cognitive behavioural therapy or other social work models to achieve the elements described above.

Regular reviews of the plan which describes both the intervention and desired outcomes will help to ensure both implementation and an evaluation of whether the intervention/s is/are securing the intended outcomes. They also offer all the agencies involved in supporting the child a chance to reflect on what has been achieved, address any new issues that may have arisen and plan for the coming period.

Desired or intended outcomes

Interventions should only be undertaken with the understanding of what the desired or intended outcome is. This should be discussed and understood and agreed by the family members, the child and other agencies involved. A desired or intended outcome may be a specific improvement in the child's life or an overarching change. These should be formulated from the assessment undertaken. The parent, carer or child should be asked and involved in establishing what their desired or intended outcome would look like.

If a local authority social work intervention is required the child will have been assessed as 'in need', i.e. in need of support or services to meet their health or development as described in earlier chapters. Three groups of children tend to receive services from the local authority social care service. Sometimes there will be children who fit with more than one group.

- Children at risk of significant harm
- Children at risk of family breakdown where accommodation by the LA has been requested
- Children with a substantial and enduring disability

Interventions put in place for Children in Need that arise from parental difficulties and/or risk of significant harm, will need to focus upon providing services to meet the needs of the child and establishing behavioural change on the part of the parent or carer to enable them to continue to care for the child without ongoing local authority intervention.

Here the desired outcome would be to both maximise the child's well-being and life chances and either to create sufficient change in parenting that the parent/carer can provide the long-term care for the child, or to establish that alternative long-term care is required for the child. The child may also need to be part of the change process for it to be successful.

Therefore social workers need to look not only at what services are going to be most effective for the child but also, often, how to achieve sustainable change.

Case Study Exercise

Make a list of the desired outcomes for Charlie at the point he has been placed in foster care.

Consider what interventions are needed to effect sustainable change.

Conclusion

Chapters 3 to 6 have charted the journey a local authority social worker undertakes as she/he gets started in their work with children and their families. As they assess and analyse information gathered through discussion and observation, they put into place interventions to effect the desired and often necessary changes required that will enable the child to continue living within their family and community in a way that promotes their well-being.

Towards the end of this book the case studies are considered in detail in order to help assist the reader consider the reality of what assessment and care planning processes constitute, both in terms of effective professional social work practice and also in terms of what the child and family actually experience. The dynamic of inter-agency relationships, across adult and children's services and inclusive of the voluntary sector, provides the context for effectively supporting children with additional and specialist needs and this is visibly demonstrated as the case studies unfold.

Further recommended reading

Dorota Iwaniec, *The Emotionally Abused and Neglected Child: Identification, Assessment and Intervention*, John Wiley and Sons (2006)
Ways of identifying and assessing emotional abuse and neglect are explained in this book, which also looks at interventions and includes examples of direct work with children.

David Howe, *A Brief introduction to Social Work Theory*, Palgrave Macmillan (2009)
This easy-to-read book provides a clear, brief discussion of a wide range of social work theories.

Sue Gerhardt, *Why Love Matters: How Affection Shapes a Baby's Brain*, Routledge (2004)
This very readable book looks at how early relationships shape the nervous system and the consequences of these interactions.

Chapter 7

Looking to the Future

This book has had at its heart local authority social work and a belief, rooted in a strong evidence base, in its capability to deliver good outcomes for Children in Need and their families. The values, ethics and theoretical base of the profession combined with the knowledge, skills and abilities of many local authority social workers, means that many children and their families receive a good quality service. This book has aimed to demonstrate this and to help, particularly newly qualified workers, understand what is expected of them and what they should expect of their employer to support them to deliver their professional role competently and confidently.

The authors, however, also recognise that one of the key issues for local authority social work is its' inability to deliver a consistently good quality of service and that some children have been failed in this process. Undeniably there is a good deal of truth in Eileen Munro's analysis of the position social work now finds itself in. That notwithstanding, the book is predicated on the strengths of the Integrated Children's System not as a system and certainly not as something that feeds performance indicators but as a framework that enables and promotes good quality holistic assessments of Children in Need, including those in need of protection and of being looked after.

The authors have presented the Assessment Framework as one which understands assessment as timely, focusing on the right things, ongoing, as multi-agency in nature and a process during which the child's voice is heard and taken into account. The authors have also argued that from good assessments effective plans can be established and positive change in a child's life can be effected. Wrapped round the assessment and planning process should be quality supervision which promotes analysis and critical reflection and allows for the testing of hypotheses. Underpinning assessment and planning should be the knowledge of child development and indicators of risk and abuse and the application of social work theory and skills. When local authorities are learning organisations the authors believe that they will and do provide their practitioners with the time to be reflective and the tools to keep up to date with practice issues and relevant research.

This book, thus far, has taken account of the current context for local authority social work practice and provided a model for both how local authorities should support and enable practitioners to practice well and for how social workers should take responsibility for their continuous professional development. It has then looked at practice and shows how to get started with families and to then assess and plan for the child/ren in those families.

The remainder of the book constitutes the detailed case studies which demonstrate how assessment and planning looks like in practice and what change can look like for children and their parents/carers over time. They aim to assist the reader to understand the reality of social work in a local authority setting and to get to grips with the "nuts and bolts" of effecting good outcomes for children.

Finally this is pivotal time for the social work profession. The work of the Social Work Reform Board and the potential outcome of the Eileen Munro Review of Child Protection on the whole augers well for social work. What does not auger will is the massive reduction in public spending that will start to impact from April 2011. This may mean that the necessary finance is not made available to make the reforms happen or to work well. Reducing early intervention and preventative services immediately puts more pressure on children's social care which itself may shrink as a result of the reduction to local authority budgets. Recession and the impact of cuts in welfare benefits may make more children vulnerable to poverty and this would lead to a greater demand upon children's service at a time that they are shrinking.

Whatever happens in this next phase it is clear that local authority social workers will still be needed to respond to Children in Need and it is the hope of the authors that this book will assist them in this task.

Case Study 1

Elizabeth and Peter

Background

Jenny is 32 years old and comes from a white Christian background. As a child and young person she displayed behavioural problems, which put a strain on her relationship with her parents, Mary and Eddie. Jenny continues to fall out with them on a regular basis which impacts on the level of support she receives from them. When Jenny was 19 years old she was diagnosed with bipolar disorder, a mental illness that is characterised by episodes of mania and depression. She takes lithium to moderate her mood swings and maintains a mood chart to help manage her illness. Her GP and the local community mental health team keep Jenny's condition under review.

Jenny has two children from different relationships. Her daughter, Elizabeth, is 13 years of age and attends the local secondary school. Jenny lived with Elizabeth's father, Mark, for two years before they separated. Mark is now married with two other children and they live locally. Elizabeth sees her father regularly but on an ad hoc basis. Mark's new wife does not encourage contact and Jenny is hostile to Mark. Elizabeth finds the complex dynamics stressful and distressing and tends to blame her mother for the situation.

Jenny's son, Peter, is seven years old. Jenny had only a brief relationship with his father and has not seen him since Peter was a baby. Peter has moderate learning difficulties and is on the autism spectrum. He is the subject of a statement of special educational needs and attends a primary special school. Peter receives a regular short break stay with local authority foster carers every 6 weeks. This is arranged by a children and families social worker, Patsy Evans, a practitioner with two years' post qualification experience, who specialises in working with children with disabilities.

Mary and Eddie, Jenny's parents, both work on a full-time basis and when the relationship with Jenny is OK, they do help out both financially and by spending time with the children. Jenny does not work and she lives in a privately rented two-bedroom house, which means that she and Elizabeth share a bedroom.

Key issues in this case study

The mental illness of a parent or a carer

Impact of mental illness

A wide range of mental ill health can affect parents and their families. This includes depression and anxiety, and psychotic illnesses such as schizophrenia or bipolar disorder. Depression and anxiety are common. At any one time one in six adults in Great Britain may be affected. Psychotic disorders are much less common, with about one in 200 individuals being affected. Mental illness may also be associated with alcohol or drug use, personality disorder and significant physical illness. Approximately 30% of adults with mental ill health have dependent children, mothers being more at risk than fathers.

> Appropriate treatment and support usually means that mental illness can be managed effectively and as a result parents are able to care successfully for their children. Mental ill health in a parent or carer does not necessarily have an adverse impact on a child's development. Just as there is a range in severity of illness, so there is a range of potential impact on families. The consequent likelihood of harm being suffered by a child will range from a minimal effect to a significant one. It is essential to assess the implications of parental ill health for each child in the family. This would include assessment of the impact on the family members of the social, physical ill health or substance use difficulties that a parent with mental illness may also be experiencing. After assessment, appropriate additional support should be provided where needed. (*Working Together*, DCSF 2010: 265-266)

> The majority of parents with a history of mental ill health present no risk to their children. However, in rare cases, a child may sustain severe injury, profound neglect or even die. Very serious risks may arise if the parent's illness incorporates delusional beliefs about the child, and/or incorporates the child in a suicide plan. (*Working Together*, DCSF 2010: 267)

Disabled children

Assessing disabled children

> In the past, disabled children have often been excluded from or marginalised within mainstream services, and many standard assessment frameworks and approaches have been developed with only non-disabled children in mind. The process of assessment and the likelihood of multiple assessment arrangements may compound the difficulties facing disabled children and their families and result in conflicting messages about the needs and the most effective types of intervention/or support.

The basic needs of disabled children are no different to those of any other child. The domains and dimensions of the Assessment Framework are relevant for all children. 'Professionals working with children need not and should not start from a different position when the children are disabled' (Middleton 1999: 92). While disabled children's basic needs are the same as all children's needs, impairments may create additional needs. Disabled children are also likely to face additional disabling barriers, which inhibit or prevent their inclusion in society. The assessment of a disabled child must address the needs of the parent/carer. Recognising the needs of a parent/carer is a core component in agreeing services, which will promote the welfare of the disabled child. (DH et al. 2000: 74)

Young carers

Children becoming young carers

Young people may not only become responsible for shouldering the burden of practical tasks, but also assume the emotional responsibility for a parent or younger siblings. To do this young people may curtail their leisure time and restrict their friendships ... It is essential that the needs of young carers are assessed to ensure that they receive the support they need. (*Working Together to Safeguard Children*, DCSF 2010: 269)

A group of children whose needs are increasingly more clearly recognised are young carers, for example those who assume important caring responsibilities for parents and siblings. Some children care for parents who are disabled, physically or mentally ill, others for parents dependent on alcohol or involved in drug misuse. For further information and guidance refer to the Carers (Recognition and Services) Act 1995: Policy Guidance and Practice Guide (Department of Health, 1996a) and Young Carers: Making a Start (Department of Health, 1998a). (*Framework for Assessment of Children in Need and their Families*, DH et al. 2000: 47)

Persons posing risk of harm to children/young people

Issues in assessment

The Children Act 1989 recognised that the identification and investigation of child abuse, together with the protection and support of victims and their families, requires multi-agency collaboration. This is rightly focused on the child and the supporting parent/carer. As part of that protection, action has been taken, usually by the police and children's social care services, to prosecute known offenders and/or control their access to vulnerable children. This work, while successful in addressing the safety of particular victims, has not always acknowledged the ongoing risk of harm that an individual perpetrator may present to other children in the future. Nor does it acknowledge that a young person may also be a perpetrator and that the same young person may simultaneously be either suffering, or likely to suffer harm, and present a risk of harm to other children and young people. (*Working Together to Safeguard Children*, DCSF 2010: 322)

Chapter 12 of *Working Together* (p.322) provides practice guidance and information about a range of mechanisms that are available when managing people who have been identified as presenting a risk, or potential risk, of harm to children. Areas covered include:

- collaborative working between organisations and agencies to identify and manage people who present a risk of harm to children
- the Multi Agency Public Protection Arrangements (MAPPA), which enable agencies to work together when dealing with people who require a greater degree of resources to manage the risk of harm they present to the public;
- other processes and mechanisms for working with people who present a risk of harm to children.

Episode 1 – Thresholds for assessment and consent

During Jenny's last review meeting with her mental health social worker, Alan Bailey, she tells him that that she is both fed up with and worried by Elizabeth's behaviour. School have advised her that Elizabeth is regularly failing to attend, despite the fact that she sets off every morning as if she is going. Elizabeth also goes out at night and stays out late. She refuses to tell her mother what she is doing and whom she is with, and they argue frequently. It becomes evident that Peter's need for continuity and routine is being seriously disrupted by the coming and goings of his sister and the resulting arguments.

Jenny is both agitated and tearful during this discussion and Alan is concerned about the impact Elizabeth's behaviour and the subsequent arguments are having on Jenny's fragile mental health. The insomnia she experiences as a result of her condition is getting worse and she is looking exhausted. She has also stopped maintaining her mood chart. Currently Jenny is not seeing her parents as she has argued with them about how she is responding to Elizabeth's behaviour. They think she should stop arguing with Elizabeth and give her clear consequences when she breaks the rules.

Alan talks to Jenny about her need for additional support and where that support could come from. He explains that he could undertake an assessment that would help them both understand what needs to happen to improve her situation. Alan also explains that the assessment would need to involve the other professionals involved with her children and that Jenny would need to give her consent to information sharing between those professionals.

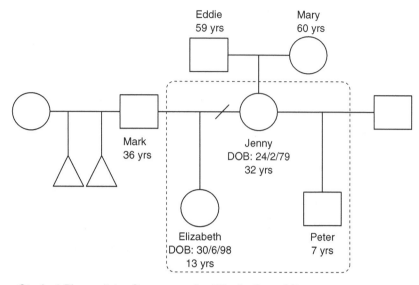

Case Study 1 Figure 1.1   Genogram for Elizabeth and Peter

Episode 2 – Assessment

The Common Assessment Framework for children and young people is a stan-dardised approach to undertaking an assessment of a child or young person's addi-tional needs … It has been designed to help practitioners assess needs at an early stage and work with children, young people and their families, alongside other practitioners and agencies, to meet those needs. (CWDC, 2009: 11)

> What could Alan do to help ensure that Jenny receives the right help both to improve her mental health and to manage Elizabeth's behaviour?

Common assessment – Elizabeth

Alan undertakes a common assessment in relation to Elizabeth and establishes the following:

Child's developmental needs

- Elizabeth is angry with her mother for being bipolar and because she is hostile to her father. (family relationships and emotional development)

- She does not have secure friendships in school and experiences bullying because she has a 'mad' mother and a 'retard' brother. (emotional development)
- She is a bright young person who is not attaining in line with her potential. (education)
- Recently Elizabeth has got in with an older group of children, some of whom have dropped out of school and others who have left. (social relationships)
- Although she loves her brother and does get on with him she struggles with his disability and the fact that life at home is organised around his and their mother's need for routine, and her brother's inability to cope with change or the unexpected. (family relationships)

Parenting capacity

- Though Jenny tries to set boundaries she is ineffective in this area and so cannot ensure her daughter's school attendance or her safety. (ensuring safety)
- Stress triggers Jenny's bipolar episodes and the frequency of extreme mood swings are currently concerning. (stability)

Family and environmental factors

- The fact that Jenny and Elizabeth share a bedroom is clearly problematic and denies Elizabeth any privacy or separate space in her home. (housing)
- Jenny's parents could be an ongoing and regular source of support but Jenny argumentative response to a problem she finds stressful means that this support is not always available. (wider family)

With Jenny's agreement Alan convenes a multidisciplinary meeting attended by Patsy Evans, Elizabeth's year tutor, Jenny, Mark and himself. Elizabeth was invited but refused to attend. Jenny had not yet repaired her relationship with her parents and so did not want them there. The meeting establishes the following multidisciplinary plan.

Multidisciplinary plan

- School will make learning mentor support available for Elizabeth to assist with attendance and bullying issues.
- Jenny agrees to attend a parenting support programme provided by a local children's centre. This is aimed at parents of teenagers and will assist Jenny to establish boundaries for her daughter that will keep her safe and ensure that she goes to school.
- Jenny agrees to see her GP to secure medication that will help her sleep and she also agrees to again maintain her mood swing chart.
- Patsy Evans will visit and ascertain whether Jenny and Peter need any additional support from social services. Jenny agrees to contact her parents and establish whether they would be prepared to talk to Patsy.
- As Alan's role is to provide Jenny with a service, it is agreed that Elizabeth's learning mentor will act as the lead professional in this case.

What does the lead professional do?

Where a child or young person with multiple additional needs requires support from more than one practitioner, the lead professional is someone who:

- acts as a single point of contact that the child or young person and their family can trust, and who is able to support them in making choices and in navigating their way through the system
- ensures that they get appropriate interventions when needed, which are well planned, regularly reviewed and effectively delivered
- reduces overlap and inconsistency from other practitioners

Evidence from practice suggests that the lead professional role is a key element of effective frontline delivery of integrated children's services. It ensures that professional involvement is rationalised, coordinated and communicated effectively. More importantly, it is intended to provide a better experience for children, young people and their families involved with a range of agencies.

> **Has the multidisciplinary plan addressed all the issues that are impacting upon Elizabeth's and Peter's development?**

The plan has not yet addressed Elizabeth's

- need for privacy in her home
- need for a stable relationship with her father that is not based on fantasy
- lack of engagement with the plan

Patsy visits and speaks to both Jenny and Peter. Although Elizabeth is present she refuses to engage. Jenny has started to maintain the mood chart again and the new drug regime is helping her to sleep. Some of the routines have now been re-established, particularly in relation to getting Peter off to school and at bedtime. However Peter is clearly worried about his mother's bipolar episodes and distressed by the ongoing arguments between Elizabeth and his mother.

> **What should Patsy do next to help her best understand what sort of help would most benefit Peter and Elizabeth?**

Patsy last updated the assessment concerning Peter 3 months ago as part of her preparation for the statutory review of his short break stays with his foster carers. However this did not take account of Jenny' deteriorating mental health nor Elizabeth's behaviour and the impact it was having on the family's functioning. In supervision with her team manager Patsy agrees to build on the common assessment completed by Alan Bailey and to undertake an initial assessment with regard to Elizabeth. It was also agreed that she would update the core assessment with regard to Peter. Patsy visits Jenny and both children and explains what this will involve and secures their consent to information sharing. Elizabeth is not particularly happy to involve herself in an assessment but eventually agrees to go along with it on the basis that it may well help her brother.

Consider what issues Patsy should explore with Peter and Elizabeth as she plans the assessments. What else will be involved in the preparation process?

Case Study Exercise

Initial assessment – Elizabeth

An initial assessment is defined as a brief assessment of each child referred to social services with a request for services to be provided. It should address the dimensions of the Assessment Framework, determining whether the child is in need, the nature of any services required, from where and within what timescales, and whether a further, more detailed core assessment should be undertaken. (*Framework for the Assessment of Children in Need and their Families*, DH et al. 2000: 31)

Planning the assessment

- Clarify the purpose and focus of the assessment.
- Who needs to be involved? – Jenny and Mark, Elizabeth and Peter, Jenny's parents (Mary and Eddie), school (learning mentor and year tutor), mental health social worker (Alan Bailey), children's centre (parenting support coordinator), GP.
- Schedule the meetings and discussions required within the 10 day timescale.
- Develop possible explanations and hypotheses about what is happening in this family and why.
- Decide what theoretical approach to adopt. Patsy decides to apply an ecological approach to help her understanding of the impact of the interplay between all the factors affecting the way in which this family is functioning. Patsy also decides to utilise the solution focused model to explore with Elizabeth and her mother what they would like to be different, what things they think need to change and how this could happen.
- Decide what tools to use. Patsy decides to:
  o use two of the Department of Health's Family Pack of Questionnaires and Scales developed by A. Cox and A. Bentovim in 2000 relating to Adult Wellbeing and Adolescent Wellbeing

- o   complete a genogram and a chronology
- o   observe how each family member relates/behaves to one another
- Access the research findings about the issues for young carers who live with poor mental health and disability.
- Consider own values and feelings in relation to mental illness and disability.

Gathering information

The Integrated Children's System describes the information that social workers need to gather to make a fully informed assessment of a child's needs. This is based on the domains and dimensions of the Assessment Framework. Chronologies, genograms and ecomaps are all useful tools that assist workers gather information about a child.

Patsy builds on the Common Assessment undertaken by Alan and discusses the situation with all the professionals currently involved in Elizabeth's life. Elizabeth talks to Patsy very reluctantly and will not talk at all about her school non-attendance and what she is getting involved with outside school and home. However, she says that she does like her learning mentor who is helping her deal with the bullying. She also says she hates her mother and what she sees as her mother's interference. Elizabeth clearly minds having to share a bedroom with her mother, as she has no private space of her own at home and she resents the fact that she cannot choose to live with her father. In this phase of the assessment Patsy learns:

Child's developmental needs

- Elizabeth is in good health physically. (health)
- She is struggling to establish an identity for herself that is distinct from her mother's mental health issues and her brother's disability. (identity)
- Caring for her brother when her mother is ill has led Elizabeth to develop good self-care skills. She also has had to develop independent living skills not usually required of a 13-year-old. (self care skills)
- Elizabeth physically presents as much older than her years and could easily be mistaken for a 16/17-year-old. (social presentation)
- Elizabeth believes that the only barrier to her living with her father is her mother's refusal to entertain the idea. (family and social relationships)

Parenting capacity

- Jenny usually provides Elizabeth with satisfactory basic care. However, when she experiences extreme mood swings, she struggles to prioritise her children and at these times Elizabeth has to take over some of the adult roles, e.g. shopping and clothes washing. (basic care)

- Jenny does understand Elizabeth's need for stability but does not see the important role her father could play in making Elizabeth feel secure, especially when her bipolar disorder is triggered. (stability)
- Jenny does have an emotionally close relationship with her daughter and even when in conflict keeps open the channels of communication. (emotional warmth)
- She understands the importance of school and wants Elizabeth to attend regularly and achieve. (stimulation)
- Mark is fond of his daughter but in no sense wants her to live with him and his new family. He does, however, acknowledge that he needs to offer more support and is prepared to discuss this with his wife. (stability)

Family and environmental factors

- The family depend on state benefits for income. The home is clean and furnished to a basic level only. (income)
- Mary and Eddie are delighted that Jenny is receiving additional support and are particularly pleased that she has agreed to attend a Parenting Programme. They are happy to offer both emotional and practical support. (wider family)
- The family are not well integrated into the local community. Jenny is socially isolated and she does not encourage Elizabeth and Peter to bring friends home. (social integration)
- The family do not normally take advantage of the community resources available locally. Accessing the Parenting Programme at the local children's centre was a major achievement for Jenny. (community resources)

Analysis

> Analysis of a child's needs is a complex activity drawing on knowledge from research and practice combined with an understanding of the child's needs within his or her family. (*Framework for the Assessment of Children in Need and their Families,* DH et al. 2000: 55)

Patsy now needs to consider whether Elizabeth is a Child in Need and if so what interventions could assist this young person. Her view will be informed by her analysis of how far Jenny and Elizabeth have insight into the underlying problems and difficulties and the degree to which they are motivated to change. A central element will be the family's explanation and understanding of what is happening and why, and what interventions they feel will help. Patsy will need to analyse the interplay between the different factors that are impacting upon the family's functioning and Elizabeth's individual needs. She should also consider how well they are likely to engage with any agency that provides them with a service.

Patsy herself had to work hard to recover her relationship with Jenny after twice being late for an appointment and on one occasion not turning up at all because she had to respond quickly to another service user. Elizabeth has not been particularly cooperative so far and has answered Patsy's questions monosyllabically.

Patsy concludes that Elizabeth does have unmet needs, particularly in relation to education, emotional and behavioural development, identity and family and social relationships. Jenny does, however, have real strengths as a parent. She is committed to managing her mental health issues and cooperates well with her GP and mental health worker to this end. When she is well, she meets her children's physical needs adequately. She has an affectionate relationship with Elizabeth and wants to support her to be successful at school. Patsy concludes that when she trusts the professional involved, Jenny engages well with the support being offered. Similarly there is evidence that when Elizabeth trusts the professional, e.g. her learning mentor, she does engage with the assistance being offered.

Patsy discusses the outcome of her assessment with her manager in supervision. She has concluded that Jenny and Elizabeth would be best assisted by a Family Support Worker joining the existing multi-disciplinary team and further developing the multi-disciplinary plan.

Case Study Exercise

Consider who should be invited to the meeting and what the objectives of the plan should be?

Core assessment – Peter

A core assessment is defined as an in-depth assessment, which addresses the central or most important aspects of the needs of a child and the capacity of his or her parents or caregivers to respond appropriately to these needs within the wider family and community context. (*Framework for the Assessment of Children in Need and their Families*, DH et al. 2000: 32)

Planning the assessment

- Clarify the purpose and focus of the assessment.
- Who needs to be involved? – Jenny, Elizabeth and Peter, Jenny's parents (Mary and Eddie), school (SENCO and class teacher), mental health social worker (Alan Bailey), GP, respite foster carers.
- Schedule the meetings and discussions required within the 35 day timescale.
- Develop possible explanations and hypotheses about what is happening in this family and why.

- Decide what theoretical approach to adopt. Patsy decides to apply an ecological approach to help promote her understanding of the impact of the interplay between all the factors affecting the way in which this family is functioning.
- Decide what tools to use. Patsy decides to use one of the Family Pack of Questionnaires and Scales developed by Cox and Bentovim for the Department of Health (2000) relating to Strengths and Difficulties.
- Direct work to be undertaken with Peter.
- Access the research findings about:
  - o the assessment and support of children with an ASD
  - o the issues for young people who live with poor mental health and disability.

Gathering information

Patsy builds on the last core assessment and the latest review report when undertaking this core assessment and focused on what has changed since the last review:

- Jenny's fluctuating mental health
- Elizabeth's behaviour and Jenny's response to it
- the lack of his grandparents in his life
- his deteriorating performance and behaviour at school which has just come to light

Child's developmental needs

During the core assessment Patsy ascertains the following about Peter:

- He does not feel safe at home. (emotional and social development)
- He is worried about his mother and does not understand why her behaviour becomes odd and her moods change. (family and social relationships)
- He is confused and upset by his sister's behaviour. (family and social relationships)
- He misses his grandparents. (family relationships)
- He is feeling increasingly anxious and this is having an adverse impact upon his behaviour. He is finding it particularly difficult to settle at night, his language is increasingly repetitive, as is his hand flapping. His responses to his mother and sister are often agitated. (behavioural development)
- He has stopped making any meaningful progress at school. (education)

Parenting capacity

- Jenny usually provides Peter with satisfactory basic care. However, when she experiences extreme mood swings, she struggles to prioritise her children and at these times Peter's sister, Elizabeth, has to take over some of the adult roles, e.g. shopping and clothes washing. (basic care)
- Jenny does understand Peter's need to feel safe and secure but does not see the important role her parents could play in this, especially when her bipolar disorder is triggered. (stability)

- Jenny does have an emotionally close relationship with her son but does not always respond appropriately when he becomes agitated as she then becomes agitated herself. (emotional warmth)
- She understands the importance of school and wants Peter to attend regularly and achieve. (stimulation)

Family and environmental factors

- The family depend on state benefits for income. The home is clean and furnished to a basic level only. (income)
- Mary and Eddie are delighted that Jenny is receiving additional support and are particularly pleased that she has agreed to attend a Parenting Programme. They are happy to offer both emotional and practical support. (wider family)
- The family are not well integrated into the local community. Jenny is socially isolated and she does not encourage Elizabeth and Peter to bring friends home. (social integration)
- The family do not normally take advantage of the community resources available locally. Accessing the Parenting Programme at the local children's centre was a major achievement for Jenny. (community resources)

Analysis

Analysis takes the assessment process beyond surface considerations and explores why particular strengths and difficulties are present, the relationship between these and the implications of them for the child and other family members, as well as considering what types of services would best help the child and family members. (*Framework for the Assessment of Children in Need and their Families*, Guidance Notes: Core Assessments, DH et al. 2000: 10)

Patsy has identified new needs in the course of this assessment and she concludes that the interplay between Jenny's mental health, Elizabeth's behaviour and his mother's response and the recent lack of contact with his grandparents to it, are all adversely impacting upon Peter's emotional wellbeing and educational achievement. Patsy suggests to his mother that Peter needs to be given more opportunity to be in environments that could deliver his need for routine and that this needs to involve his grandparents. She also helps Jenny to understand more fully the impact the current situation with Elizabeth is having on Peter, and Jenny agrees that she needs to adopt a different approach to Elizabeth's behaviour, as well as create more space for herself to act on the advice she is receiving from the parenting support programme. Patsy also points out that Peter needs help to better understand his mother's and sister's behaviour and to develop coping strategies both at home and at school.

Episode 3 – Planning

It is essential that the plan is constructed on the basis of the findings from the assessment and that this plan is reviewed and refined over time to ensure the agreed case objectives are achieved. Specific outcomes for the child, expressed in terms of their health and development can be measured. These provide objective evidence against which to evaluate whether the child and family have been provided with appropriate services and ultimately whether the child's wellbeing is optimal. (*Framework for the Assessment of Children in Need and their Families*, DH et al. 2000: 62)

Elizabeth

Patsy invites the following to the multidisciplinary meeting:

- Elizabeth (who refuses to attend)
- Parents – Jenny and Mark
- Peter
- Year tutor
- Learning mentor
- School nurse
- Parenting support coordinator at the local children centre
- Mental health social worker – Alan Bailey
- Team Manager of the Family Support Service
- Grandparents – Eddie and Mary

The meeting seeks to establish a plan that will address the following issues with regard to Elizabeth as a young person

- with a mentally ill parent who has to assume a caring role
- with a disabled sibling
- who needs a stable relationship with her father
- who needs to attend and achieve at school, to have a peer friendship group at school and not to be bullied
- who needs to stay safe, to have good sexual health and avoid drug/alcohol misuse
- who needs to have a mother who is a confident and effective parent
- who needs some private space within the home

The meeting agrees the plan laid out in Case Study 1 Table 1.1.

It was agreed that there was no further need for Patsy to remain involved and that Elizabeth could be supported through a multidisciplinary plan subject to a review in two months time. The family support worker agreed to take over from the learning mentor and act as the lead professional and coordinate the plan. Patsy's involvement and that of Social Services with Elizabeth ended at this point.

Case Study 1 Table 1.1   Multidisciplinary plan – Elizabeth

Intervention	Desired outcome/s	By whom	By when
Elizabeth will be offered a number of sessions with Alan regarding living with someone with bipolar and the strategies that can help with this	Enhance Elizabeth's understanding of her mother's behaviour and help her to develop coping strategies	Alan Bailey	Two months
Elizabeth will be offered a place in a support group run by MIND, for children of mentally ill parents. Elizabeth will also be invited to attend the support group for families with children on the autism spectrum with Peter and Jenny	Reduce feelings of isolation and difference Improve Elizabeth's self esteem Participate in a family activity and improve her support networks	Alan Bailey Patsy Evans	One week One week
Jenny will continue to attend the parenting support programme	Jenny more confident competent parent	Jenny/ SureStart Co-ordinator	Two months
Family Support will offer an intervention that will assist Jenny adopt and practise different and constructive strategies in dealing with Elizabeth's behaviour as outlined by the Parenting Programme	Jenny applying discipline in a realistic and measured way Elizabeth more willing to conform to Jenny's requests	Team Manager Family Support	Two months
Family support will help Jenny consider her housing options and whether a move to a 3-bedroom property is feasible. In the meantime Jenny will think about turning a downstairs room into a bedroom as an interim solution	Private bedroom space for Elizabeth, which will also make it possible to invite friends around	Team Manager Family Support	One month
Elizabeth will be offered a health promotion programme at school	Elizabeth well informed as to the risks to good health, including sexual health	Learning mentor	One month
The learning mentor will continue to see Elizabeth individually at school and will develop a circle of friends for Elizabeth and peer mentoring support	Elizabeth feeling supported in school Reduction in bullying Improved attendance and achieving	Learning mentor	One month
Mark will discuss with his wife an overnight stay at regular intervals and Jenny will cooperate with this	Improved quality in relationship between father and daughter	Mark	One month
Jenny will continue to make use of the medication and the advice of her GP and her mental health worker to keep her mental health as stable as possible	Improved stability in mental health	Jenny Alan Bailey GP	Ongoing

Consider each element of the plan in turn and the desired outcome/s. How would you measure success?

When measuring success consider:

- Is Elizabeth engaging with professional support?
- How far has the conflict between Jenny and Elizabeth reduced?
- Is Elizabeth responding to the boundaries being set by her mother?
- Has Elizabeth's attendance at school improved?
- Have the incidents of bullying decreased?
- Is Elizabeth developing any peer relationships at school?
- Does Jenny's mental health continue to be stable?
- Is Elizabeth seeing her father regularly and routinely?
- Do Elizabeth and Jenny think their life together has improved? If so what do they think has made the difference?

Peter

Patsy discusses Peter's situation with the professional responsible for reviewing his care plan – the Independent Reviewing Officer – who agrees to convene an early Looked After Child review meeting. The following are invited:

- Peter
- Parent – Jenny
- Elizabeth
- Mental health social worker – Alan Bailey
- Grandparents – Eddie and Mary
- Respite foster carers
- Class teacher

Changes and additions to his care plan, as laid out in Case Study 1 Table 1.2, are agreed.

Consider each element of the plan in turn and the desired outcome/s. How would you measure success?

When measuring success, consider:

- Is Peter visibly less anxious?
- Are his routines concerning school and seeing his grandparents and foster carers securely in place?

- Is Peter coping and achieving better at school?
- Does Jenny's mental health continue to be stable?
- Do Peter and Jenny think family life has improved? If so what do they think has made the difference?

Episode 4 – Intervention

Peter

Increasing respite with his foster carers and his grandparents proves to be hugely beneficial to Peter as this means he spends less time in the middle of Jenny and Elizabeth's conflictual relationship. Peter feels more secure now that his relationship with his grandparents has been restored. The plan for Elizabeth, even though it is proving to be only partially successful, has reduced the degree of conflict between mother and daughter, which also helps reduce Peter's anxiety level. Jenny's mental health is currently reasonably stable and Peter is learning to understand her condition better through his sessions with Patsy. School reports that Peter is able to concentrate again and though can still get distressed and anxious in class, his 'time out' is providing him with space he needs to calm down and to then re-engage with his class. Jenny and Peter have started to make relationships at the ASD support group. Elizabeth has yet to go with them.

Elizabeth

The family support worker, Helen Mitchell, has been designated as the lead professional with regard to the delivery of the plan for Elizabeth and as such she has responsibility for coordination and monitoring its delivery within the timescales agreed. She is also responsible for convening the review meeting in two months' time.

Helen works with Jenny to help her understand that arguing with her daughter is not making any difference to Elizabeth's behaviour and is simply making Elizabeth resentful and more determined to do her own thing. She also helps her understand how Elizabeth is struggling to cope with her mother's mental illness and her mother's attitude to her father. Jenny is learning a different style of parenting through the support programme she attends, which Helen is seeking to consolidate when she visits, but Jenny is not finding it easy to put the programme into practice.

Jenny strikes a deal with her daughter that if she goes to school and agrees to come in at night by the agreed time, then in return she will have her own room and be allowed an overnight stay with her father every week. This has

Case Study 1 Table 1.2   Looked after child (short breaks) care plan – Peter

Intervention	Desired outcome/s	By whom	By when
Provide more routine in Peter's life within safe environments • Short stay visits to increase to every four weeks • Contact with his grandparents to resume and will involve overnight stays	• Reduction in anxiety levels • Enhance feelings of safety and stability • Improved concentration at school	• Patsy Evans • Eddie and Mary	1 month
Patsy to undertake three sessions with Peter in order to assist his ability to live with a mother with bipolar and a teenage sister with emotional problems. She will use resources from the Parental Mental Health and Child Welfare Network to assist with this piece of work	Enhance Peter's understanding of his mother's and sister's behaviours and help him to develop coping strategies	Patsy Evans	2 months
Peter's individual education plan is amended to incorporating 'time out' from classroom learning when he becomes agitated and stressed at school	Provide Peter with a coping mechanism within his school environment	Class teacher	I week
Jenny will continue to make use of the medication and the advice of her GP and her mental health worker to keep her mental health as stable as possible	Improved parenting capacity through increased stability in mental health	Jenny Alan Bailey GP	Ongoing
Jenny and Peter will be invited to a support group for families with a child on the autism spectrum	Reduce Jenny's isolation and improve support networks for both Jenny and Peter	Patsy Evans	1 week

some success, particularly with regard to attending school, where, with the right support, life has begun to improve for Elizabeth. However, Jenny still has difficulty establishing where and with whom Elizabeth is spending her time outside of school. Her father has not yet persuaded his wife to agree to overnight stays but Mark is now seeing his daughter more regularly. Elizabeth has begun to realise that living with her father is not an option, not because of her mother's opposition, but because her father and his wife do not want this to happen. Elizabeth meets with Alan but declines the MIND support group. She is also unwilling to engage to any meaningful extent with Helen.

During a home visit Jenny tells Helen that she has been told by Elizabeth's school friend that Elizabeth has been seen entering and leaving the home of

Geoff, who has just been released from prison, where he was serving his sentence for unlawful sexual intercourse with a 12-year-old.

> Consider what Helen should do with this information and what her next steps will need to be.

Helen phones Patsy Evans who explains that Geoff is someone who should be considered as a Person Posing a Risk (PPR) to a child/young person and that an assessment of the risk he poses to Elizabeth and any other young person he is in contact with will be necessary. This assessment will need to be undertaken by a social worker experienced in undertaking s47 enquiries as part of a core assessment.

The matter is referred to an area assessment team. A strategy discussion with the police concludes that as there is no complaint nor evidence that a criminal offence has been committed and that social care should undertake a single agency investigation. The assessment is allocated to Adela Hussain, a practitioner with three years' post qualification experience. Adela plans to undertake a core assessment deemed appropriate within the Integrated Children's System for 11–15-year-old young people. She will also undertake a specialist assessment of the risk posed by Geoff to Elizabeth and any other children he may have contact with. In some local authorities probation officers undertake these assessments.

> What issues will the assessment of the PPR need to consider?

- The nature of Elizabeth and Geoff's relationship
- The nature of any other relationship Geoff may have with a young person under the age of 16 years or who may be vulnerable
- Elizabeth's attitude to having any further contact with Geoff and vice versa

Episode 5 – Assessment as an ongoing event – core and specialist assessments

PPR specialist assessment

Planning

- Who needs to be involved? - Geoff, Elizabeth and Jenny, Prison Service Probation, police, significant adults in Geoff's life, GP, other young people in contact with Geoff, if any, and their parents/carers.

- Schedule the meetings and discussions required within the agreed timescale for completing the assessment
- Establish whether Geoff has been assessed under the Multi-Agency Public Protection Arrangements (MAPPA) and the outcome of that assessment

Gathering information

Adela ascertains that Geoff has been released from prison on licence. He has been subject to Multi Agency Public Protection Arrangements (MAPPA) and assessed as medium risk. This means that he is viewed as unlikely to re-offend unless there is a change of circumstance, for example, loss of accommodation or drug or alcohol misuse. Geoff is willing to cooperate with the assessment and is anxious not to do anything that might jeopardise his licence. He agrees not to see Elizabeth again until the assessment is completed.

Adela establishes:

- Geoff is a 40-year-old white man, with some learning difficulties, who lives with his elderly mother. She suffers from poor health and does not often leave her bedroom. He is not in contact with any other family members.
- He is unemployed and has a criminal record relating to petty thieving, benefit fraud and two unrelated offences, separated by ten years, of USI, one with a 14-year-old girl and one with a12-year–old.
- There is no evidence that he is in contact with other PPRs.
- There is no evidence that he is having any routine/unsupervised contact with any other child/young person and he seems genuinely anxious about the consequences of breaching his licence.
- Geoff says that he met Elizabeth through an older teenager who lives nearby and who is a friend of Elizabeth's. He say that she has only ever visited in the company of this friend and they watched DVDs together.
- Geoff is evasive about the circumstances surrounding his offences against the two girls and though he did undertake a treatment programme in prison, his probation officer is not confident that it effected any real attitudinal change.
- He spends most of his time watching TV/DVDs and attending to his mother's needs – overall leading a stable lifestyle.
- The flat is small and his mother is in earshot of conversations in the other rooms.

Analysis

Adela concludes that the risk to Elizabeth is currently medium to low as long as Geoff's circumstances remain the same. His anxiety about returning to prison and his mother's presence in the flat are key inhibitors against re-offending behaviour. Geoff cooperated fully with assessment and there is no evidence that he is having any ongoing contact with Elizabeth.

Core assessment

Planning

- Clarify the purpose and focus of the assessment.
- Who needs to be involved – Elizabeth, Jenny, Peter, Mark, grandparents (Mary and Eddie), learning mentor, GP, family support worker (Helen Mitchell), school nurse and mental health social worker (Alan Bailey).
- Schedule the meetings and discussions required within the agreed timescale for completing the assessment.
- Develop possible explanations and hypotheses about Elizabeth's relationship with Geoff.
- What theoretical approach to adopt? Adela decides to use a cognitive/behavioural approach to her work with Elizabeth in order to help her understand how she is placing herself at risk.
- Access research findings about how to reduce risk factors when working with young people vulnerable to sexual exploitation.
- Adela needs to consider her own values and feelings about 'paedophilia' and 'paedophiles'.

Gathering information

Adela builds on the initial assessment and focuses on Elizabeth's behaviour that places her at risk. Like other professionals, Adela found it initially difficult to engage with Elizabeth and to begin with she was absent when she called to undertake an assessment interview. This led her to change tack and she arranged to see Elizabeth at school with her learning mentor, one of the few individuals trusted by Elizabeth. The learning mentor and Adela helped Elizabeth acknowledge that she did feel out of her depth and not always safe when with her older friends.

Jenny had panicked when she found that her daughter had been associated with a PPR and her initial response was to ground her indefinitely, only to find that her daughter would not comply, which led to more arguments. Adela and Helen worked together to help Jenny restore her relationship with Elizabeth and to apply boundaries more realistically. Jenny has not yet kept her promise to turn one of the downstairs rooms into a bedroom for Elizabeth and this has weakened her ability to successfully negotiate with her daughter. This becomes a focus of their discussions.

Child's developmental needs

- The lack of her own bedroom is key in motivating Elizabeth's desire to be out of the home during the evening and at weekends. She has no private space and nowhere she can take her friends. (identity) (family and social relationships)
- Elizabeth did not know of Geoff's criminal history but also did not appear worried about it when informed of it. She did, however, say that she has no interest in seeing Geoff again. (health) (emotional and behavioural development)

- Elizabeth did not always feel safe in the company of her older friends but her dependency on them was reducing as she was making some friends now of her own age at school. (identity) (family and social relationships)
- When with her older friends she admitted to being involved occasionally in drug experimentation with cannabis and ecstasy. (health) (family and social relationships)

Parenting capacity

- Jenny cannot prevent Elizabeth leaving the home and often does not know where she is when out. (ensuring safety) (guidance and boundaries)
- Jenny still does not fully understand Elizabeth's need to invite her friends into some private space at home and how this would help keep her safe. (ensuring safety)
- Jenny continues to offer her daughter basic care and emotional warmth.
- Mark does not attempt to influence Elizabeth's behaviour and finds it easier not to challenge her.

Family and environmental factors

- Jenny is on the waiting list for a 3-bedroom housing association property. Currently the waiting list is 18 months. (housing)
- Jenny's limited income also limits her housing choices. (income)
- The family's lack of social integration in the wider community increases the risks to Elizabeth when unsupervised out of the home. (social integration)

Analysis

Adela discusses with her manager the need to present the outcome of the core assessment and the PPR assessment to a child protection conference. They conclude that, as Geoff has been assessed as presenting medium to low risk to Elizabeth and that all parties are cooperating with the current plan the best outcomes for Elizabeth are more likely to be achieved by continuing to support this family through the existing planning process. They agree that Adela will convene a further planning meeting so that the current plan can be enhanced to take account of the outcome of her assessment. This will include all the interventions required to maintain her safety. Adela concludes that three changes are necessary to ensure Elizabeth's ongoing safety

- Building on parental strengths to make their guidance and boundary setting more effective.
- Ensuring that Elizabeth has her own bedroom and is encouraged to bring her friends home.
- Making Elizabeth more aware of the dangers of associating with known sex offenders.
- Making Elizabeth more aware of the dangers of taking illegal substances, especially when with those she cannot trust to look after her.

What does the plan need to address and how?

Planning and intervention

Adela invites the following to the planning meeting:

- Elizabeth (who for the first time attends)
- Parents – Jenny and Mark
- Peter
- Grandparents – Eddie and Mary
- Learning mentor
- SureStart parenting support programme coordinator
- Family support worker – Helen Mitchell
- Mental health social worker – Alan Bailey
- GP
- School Nurse

The meeting agree additions/amendments to the multidisciplinary plan already in place for Elizabeth, which was being coordinated by Helen Mitchell (see Case Study Table 1.3).

Case Study 1 Table 1.3   Updated multidisciplinary plan – Elizabeth

Intervention	Desired outcome/s	By whom	By when
The family support worker will continue to assist Jenny apply her learning from the parenting programme. This will have a new emphasis on how parents of teenagers can support them to keep safe	More competent, confident, effective parenting	Helen Mitchell	Over the next two months
Jenny agrees to turn one of the downstairs rooms into a bedroom for Elizabeth	Elizabeth has private space in her home to which she can invite her fiends. She is also at home more often	Jenny	Two weeks
In return Elizabeth agrees not to associate with Geoff. She also agrees that when she goes out she will tell her mother where she is going and will return at an agreed time. When out she will take her mobile phone with her and ensure it is on	Elizabeth is safe outside of the home	Elizabeth	Immediately
Mark agrees to attend the Parenting Support Group with Jenny and agrees to support Jenny to become a more effective parent	Elizabeth experiences a joint parenting approach to help her feel more secure	Mark	Immediately

Episode 6 – Review

It is good practice to review any plan at a minimum frequency of 8 weeks. The purpose of reviews is both to ensure that the plan is being implemented and achieving the desired outcomes. It is also an opportunity to consider whether all elements of the plan remain appropriate or require some amendment or addition. Plans need to be responsive to changing needs or circumstances.

Elizabeth

The combination of the support Jenny and Mark receive to become more effective parents, providing Elizabeth with her own bedroom, and building in trusted support at school, prove to be the key interventions in turning the situation around for Elizabeth. Her risky behaviour diminishes, she drops her older friends and the ongoing conflict between her and her mother begins to diminish. All the other elements of the plan provided a positive infrastructure within which these key elements took effect.

Peter

The key for Peter proved to be a combination of restoring his relationship with his grandparents, less exposure to the arguments at home, better understanding of his mother's mental health and improving the way in which school managed his distress.

In conclusion, Adela, Helen and Patsy all recognise that the success of the plans for both children was in large part due to the fact that Alan Bailey had recognised the problems early and had acted quickly to address them. Had the problems not been addressed by the right professionals doing the right things at the right time the problems could have become chronic and intractable. Fortunately for both children and their mother the timely interventions kept them living together as a sufficiently well functioning family.

Case Study 2

Maya and Ajay

Background

Roshni is a 27-year-old British Hindu woman of Asian descent. She is a trained hairdresser. She used to work full time but now just does hairdressing for weddings and for friends. Roshni has been married to Kripa, a 35-year-old British Hindu man of Asian descent, for five years. Kripa is a qualified computer engineer. He works full time, travelling long distances and often staying away from home on business. He started to drink alcohol to an excess about a year ago after being passed over for promotion and when an affair he was having with a colleague came to an end. Roshni is unaware of the affair. They own their own home in a multi-cultural neighbourhood in a city.

Kripa and Roshni have two children, Maya a four-year-old girl and Ajay a one-year-old boy. Maya attends nursery five mornings a week. Both children had an unremarkable birth and have achieved their developmental milestones. They are being brought up bilingual in English and Urdu.

Asha is Roshni's sister. She is 30 years old, married to Badri, with three children, and lives next door. Roshni and Asha's parents both died within two years of each other three years ago. Asha came to live near Roshni when they died. They have limited contact with their parents' siblings who live over 100 miles away.

Key issues in this case study

Domestic violence

Defining harm in relation to domestic violence

This clarifies the definition of harm in section 31 of the Children Act 1989 by making clear that the harm a child may be at risk of suffering includes 'any impairment of the child's health or development as a result of witnessing the ill-treatment of another person, such as domestic violence'. Ill-treatment is broader than physical violence and includes sexual abuse and forms of ill-treatment which are not physical, such as seeing a parent being harassed or intimidated by another person. (s120 Adoption and Children Act 2002)

Understanding domestic violence

Domestic violence against women by men is 'caused' by the *misuse of power* and control within a context of *male privilege*. Male privilege operates on an individual and societal level to maintain a situation of male dominance, where men have power over women and children. Perpetrators of domestic violence choose to behave abusively to get what they want and gain control. Their behaviour often originates from a sense of entitlement, which is often supported by sexist, racist, homophobic and other discriminatory attitudes. In this way, domestic violence by men against women can be seen as a *consequence of the inequalities* between men and women, rooted in *patriarchal traditions* that encourage men to believe they are entitled to power and control over their partners.

Research shows that violent men are most likely to perpetrate violence in response to their own *sexual jealousy* and possessiveness; their demands for domestic services; and in order to *demonstrate male authority*.

The vast majority of the victims of domestic violence are women and children, and women are also considerably more likely to experience repeated and severe forms of violence, and sexual abuse. Over two women per week are killed by current or ex-partners, and one in four women in the UK will experience domestic violence in their lifetime. (Extracts from the Women's Aid website, 2011; original emphasis)

Characteristics of domestic violence offenders

Research commissioned by Home Office in 2003 considered whether there were common characteristics amongst domestic violence offenders and identified two types of DV offenders:

- borderline/emotionally dependent offenders primarily characterised by high levels of interpersonal dependency, high levels of anger and low self-esteem
- antisocial/narcissistic offenders primarily characterised by hostile attitudes towards women and low empathy. These had the highest rate of alcohol dependence and previous convictions. (Gilchrist et al./Home Office 2003)

The use (or misuse) of substance is not however the underlying cause of domestic violence. If an abuser is alcohol/drug dependent, it is important that this is **treated in tandem** with addressing the violent behaviour. Addressing only one without the other is unlikely to prove successful. (Women's Aid website, 2011; original emphasis)

Impact of domestic violence

Domestic violence has an impact on children in a number of ways. Children are at increased risk of physical injury during an incident, either by accident or because they attempt to intervene. Even when not directly injured, children are greatly distressed by witnessing the physical and emotional suffering of a parent. Children's exposure to parental conflict, even when violence is not present, can lead to serious anxiety and distress which may express itself in anti-social or criminal behaviour. (*Working Together to Safeguard Children*, DCSF, 2010: 262)

Domestic abuse is also a child protection issue. If a woman is being abused by a current or former partner and there are children in the home, they are likely to have experienced abuse by the same perpetrator. A study of 111 NSPCC cases of child abuse (Hester and Pearson 1998) found that domestic violence was present in 62% of cases. The risks go further than physical injury. Even when a child is not directly abused (physically or sexually), there is a risk they will be harmed trying to help their mother. They will almost certainly suffer short- or long-term psychological trauma from having witnessed abuse. (*Responding to Domestic Abuse: A Handbook for Health Professionals*, DH 2005: 15-16)

Everyone working with women and children should be alert to the frequent inter-relationship between domestic violence and the abuse and neglect of children. (*National Service Framework for Children, Young People and Maternity Services*, DH and DfES, 2004: 166)

Episode 1 – Thresholds for assessment and consent

Asha has called the police three times in the past six months after hearing Roshni and Kripa fighting. She reports hearing items being thrown and the sounds of screaming and crying. Each time, by the time the police had arrived Kripa had left the family home. They have found Roshni and the children distressed. Evidence of assault was clear as Roshni was both bruised and bloodied. However she has insisted that she is OK and up to now Kripa has escaped arrest. Roshni has talked to Asha and reported she is fine and that the arguments are about money and the children's upbringing. Asha does not believe this is the whole story and thinks Kripa is drinking. Badri has reported to Asha that he has bumped into Kripa at the local shop and he has been buying vodka.

A further incident occurred and the police informed social services that Roshni had a black eye and the children were very distressed. Maya had a cut to her hand where flying glass had hit her. When Maya arrived at nursery she was still upset and when asked what was wrong told her nursery teacher that

Maya and Ajay

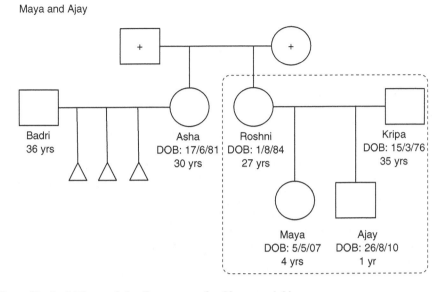

Case Study 2 Figure 2.1   Genogram for Maya and Ajay

daddy had hurt mummy. Nursery staff talked to Roshni about the incident and the need to seek the assistance of a social worker. Roshni gave consent to nursery contacting social services.

The Social Services Access and Assessment Team were already considering what action to take in response to the referral from the police. The fact that this was the fourth reported incident and both mother and one of her children had been injured as a result, had led the team manager to conclude that an initial assessment was required. This would determine whether Maya and Ajay were children in need and at risk of harm. The phone call from the nursery gave them the opportunity to arrange a meeting with Roshni at the nursery, without involving Kripa at this stage. This is an important consideration. Social services do not at this stage understand the factors that lead Kripa to be violent towards Roshni. A letter from social services arranging a home visit could have triggered a further violent episode. Contact via the nursery allowed the social worker to see Roshni without Kripa's involvement at this stage.

Episode 2 – Initial assessment

Milli Tucker, a British-born African Caribbean social worker with 12 months' experience, is asked to undertake an initial assessment.

Planning the assessment

- Clarify the purpose and focus of the assessment.
- Who needs to be involved? Roshni and Kripa, Maya and Ajay, Asha, nursery teacher, health visitor, G, police.
- Schedule the meetings and discussions required within the 10 day timescale.
- Develop hypotheses and explanations about what is happening in the family and why.
- Decide which theoretical approach to adopt. Milli decides to apply systems theory and an ecological approach to help promote her understanding of the impact of the interplay between all the factors affecting how this family is functioning. Her understanding of attachment theory will assist her understanding of the relationship between the children and their parents.
- Establish a genogram and commence a chronology.
- Consider how work with Maya be undertaken.
- Identify any gaps in information or knowledge, for example the impact of domestic abuse and alcohol misuse.

Gathering information

Milli meets with Roshni and her two children at the nursery. Roshni accepted that the violence was harming her and adversely affecting her children. Milli spent a little time with Maya in her nursery class and Maya told her that she missed daddy when he was away and wanted him to stop being naughty to mummy. Milli then contacted the health visitor who reports she last saw Roshni at home, 3 weeks after Ajay's birth. Roshni appeared to be coping well and she had no concerns. Roshni had been seen in the baby clinic on a monthly basis and had attended for all the children's immunisations and two developmental checks. Both children were deemed to be developing well and no concerns where noted.

Maya

Child's developmental needs

- Maya is in good physical health and the cut to her hand was minor, only requiring first aid. Her immunisations are up to date and she has met the usual developmental milestones. (health)
- She is showing signs of feeling insecure by waking in the night and being resistant to her mother leaving her at nursery. (emotional and behavioural development)
- Until recently nursery staff viewed her as a well-rounded child, learning and playing within the normal range. (education)
- Roshni reports that Maya's relationship with Kripa is distant because of the time he spends away from home and because of the arguments and violence when he is present. (family and social relationships)

Parenting capacity

- Roshni does generally provide Maya with good physical care and there is evidence of an emotionally warm relationship but the parent's relationship is impacting on Maya's sense of well-being. (basic care) (emotional warmth)
- Roshni and Kripa are not always keeping Maya safe and the conflict between her parents is undermining Maya's need for stability. (ensuring safety) (stability)
- Nursery view Roshni as a competent parent who ensures that her children are stimulated and respond to appropriate discipline. They have had no contact with Kripa. (stimulation) (guidance and boundaries)

Family and environmental factors

- Asha, Roshni's sister, is a good source of support. (wider family)
- Roshni has few friends. (social integration)
- The family are not well integrated into the local community, with exception of Maya's attendance at the nursery. (community resources)

Ajay

Child's developmental needs

- Ajay is in good physical health. His immunisations are up to date and he has met the usual developmental milestones. (health)
- He is showing signs of feeling insecure by his clinging behaviour, crying whenever Roshni leaves the room. He will not be comforted by Kripa. (emotional and behavioural development)
- Roshni reports that Ajay's relationship with Kripa is distant because of the time he spends away from home and because of the arguments and violence when he is present. (family and social relationships)

Parenting capacity

- Roshni does generally provide Ajay with good physical care and there is evidence of an emotionally warm relationship but his parents' relationship is impacting on his emotional well-being. (basic care) (emotional warmth)
- Roshni and Kripa are not always keeping Ajay safe and the conflict between his parents is undermining Ajay's need for stability. (ensuring safety) (stability)
- Nursery view Roshni as a competent parent who ensures that her children are stimulated and respond to appropriate discipline. (stimulation) (guidance and boundaries)

Family and environmental factors

- Asha, Roshni's sister, is a good source of support. (wider family)
- Roshni has few friends. (social integration)
- The family are not well integrated into the local community, with exception of Maya's attendance at the nursery. (community resources)

Asha was called to the nursery with Roshni's permission and agreed that Roshni and the children could stay with her for the next week. Asha expressed the view that Kripa has been drinking. At this point Roshni says she does not know if she wants to stay with or leave Kripa.

Milli visits Kripa the following day. He agrees to Roshni staying with her sister but wants to see his children. This is arranged with Asha taking the children to the house at teatime on Friday and Sunday. When he meets with Milli, Kripa denies that the violence is increasing in intensity and frequency and minimises the impact this is having upon Roshni. He refuses to accept that it is having any impact at all upon the children. He says that Roshni provokes the violence by berating him every night for being late and not helping with the children. Kripa says that he has one drink after work and that does not affect his behaviour. He does say that he has been depressed and fed up recently and at this point admits his affair. Kripa feels guilty about the affair but also upset that it has ended. He asks the social worker to not tell Roshni about it. He says any man would have an affair given Roshni's behaviour but refuses to expand on this statement.

Kripa thinks his relationship with his children is normal and he does not accept that he is emotionally distant from them. He expresses the view that mothers are the primary parent and are responsible for all the practical parenting tasks. As he is Roshni's husband and the children's father he naturally wants them home.

During this visit Milli observes the home conditions. The house has three bedrooms and is well furnished. Maya's bedroom was suitable for a four-year-old child and the bed had appropriate bedding on it, which looked clean. Ajay still slept in a cot in his parents' room. Again this contained adequate clean bedding. The house did, however, show some signs of neglect, with cluttered surfaces and floors and a lot of unwashed pots littering the downstairs rooms.

Kripa says that he would like to have counselling to help with his depression. Roshni says she needs space to think about what has been happening and going to her sister for a week would help. Yasmin Handa, an Asian/British Muslim family support worker, with 15 years' experience, is available to provide parenting and emotional support to parents with children who attend Maya's nursery. The nursery has some limited free places for children under three.

Milli convenes a Child in Need meeting and this is attended by Roshni, Asha (at Roshni's request), Kripa, the health visitor, nursery teacher and Yasmin. (Both children are also present but do not participate because of their age.) Roshni indicates that she had decided to return home.

At the end of the initial assessment the following plan was put in place:

* Kripa agrees to seek counselling from his GP to assist with his depression.
* Roshni agrees to have a weekly support session with Yasmin at nursery. This will focus on building self esteem and the choices available to Roshni.

- Roshni and Ajay agree to attend the carer and baby group at nursery to help Roshni feel less isolated and to allow Ajay play opportunities with other babies/toddlers.
- Roshni agrees to spend one morning a week with Maya in her class whilst Ajay attends nursery.
- A written contract is agreed between Roshni and Kripa to help them avoid arguments and decide on a course of action if they do argue.
- Kripa agrees to be involved in a swimming activity, twice a week, with Roshni and the two children to ensure they have quality time together as a family.
- Yasmin agrees to be the lead professional for the family.

Case Study Exercise

What was positive about this intervention?

This intervention allowed Roshni to be supported by a trusted family member and empowered Roshni by helping her feel more in control. Information provided by Asha allowed a fuller picture of the family to be revealed. Roshni was asked what she wanted to happen and although she does not know initially, the workers are clear that she realises that in the long term she can only stay with Kripa if the violence stops. Milli had obtained the views of all the key family members, including Maya.

The plan aims to encourage Roshni to spend more time with the children and to help build their relationship and reassure the children about their mother's availability. The time with Kripa is deliberately out of the home, in a less stressful environment, hopefully for them to spend some quality time together. The aim of counselling, along with the written contract, is to give Kripa the chance to reflect and seek support to develop alternative mechanisms for expressing his feelings and to consider his alcohol usage.

Nominating a lead professional means there is one individual whom the parents and children will know as the coordinator for their family's plan and locates responsibility with that individual to make sure all elements of the plan are progressed.

Case Study Exercise

What other agencies or services could have been asked to contribute to the assessment and plan? What other interventions could have been considered at this stage?

- The police could have further background information on the earlier incidents. They could also provide specific domestic violence advice to Roshni.
- The health visitor could have been asked to provide a more in-depth assessment of the children's health and development.

- Roshni could have been referred to specialist domestic violence services for advice and support.
- A safety plan could have been drawn up to agree a plan of action if Kripa does not keep to the agreement.
- Individual support could have been provided to Maya from the nursery to give her an opportunity to talk about life at home.

How should issues of ethnicity and religion be considered in this case?

- The parents should be asked about whether they are experiencing any direct or indirect racism from within their local community or in their lives.
- Cultural norms and religious beliefs in relation to domestic abuse need to be understood and discussed.
- Consideration should be made about how well the nursery reflects or promotes different cultures and religion in terms of meeting the family's needs.
- The social worker needs to consider her own beliefs and values and how this may impact on the family

Episode 3 – Core assessment

Yasmin sees Asha after school three weeks after the case has been closed by social services. Asha reports that the violence started again about a week after Roshni returned home. Asha has not called the police, as she has become frustrated with Roshni's ongoing acceptance of the violence. She wants Roshni to leave Kripa but Roshni continues to be reluctant to do this.

Yasmin sees Roshni the following day. She acknowledges that at least once a week since she returned home there has been an argument, which has ended in violence. However she does not want to involve social services again as she intends to sort it out herself. Yasmin notes Roshni appears to be holding her arm stiffly as if it was painful to move it and when she goes to pick up Ajay, she winces. Yasmin asks if her arm is OK. Roshni says it is nothing, a bit sore, but will get better. Yasmin talks to Roshni about the need to re-involve social services, as she is concerned that as Kripa continues to be violent the plan needs to be reviewed. Yasmin talks to the nursery teacher, who says that Maya has become more and more withdrawn and tired, falling asleep over her lunch yesterday. In the carer and baby group Ajay is becoming increasingly hysterical whenever Roshni tries to put him down. On hearing this Roshni reluctantly agrees to Yasmin contacting social services and Milli is allocated the case again.

She discusses the situation with her manager and together they consider the number and frequency of the incidents, combined with increasing evidence of the impact upon the children's emotional development, and conclude that a strategy discussion with the police is required. This confirmed the need for a s47 enquiry, as part of a core assessment. This assessment will consider the need for a multidisciplinary child protection conference. Milli plans the core assessment over four weeks, having sessions with the adults together and on their own, observing the children and working with Maya.

Gathering information

The strategy discussion had involved Milli in talking to the Domestic Violence Liaison Co-ordinator and obtaining full information about all reported incidents. They also discussed the need for a joint investigation. It was agreed that the police need to interview Roshni and Kripa with regard to the latest incident. They will also assist in developing a safety plan for Roshni and the children once the matter came to a child protection conference. Milli then talked to the health visitor who agrees to visit and provide an up to date assessment of the children's health and development. Milli contacts local voluntary sector agencies that provide support for women affected by domestic violence to ascertain what services are on offer to women in Roshni's position. She discovers one refuge that provides a counselling and advice service for Asian women.

Planning the assessment

- Hypothesise further as to what is happening and why. How can the different explanations be supported or discounted?
- Who needs to be involved? Roshni and Kripa, Maya and Ajay, Asha, the family support worker (Yasmin Handa), nursery teacher, health visitor, GP, police.
- Schedule the meetings and discussions required within the 35 day timescale.
- Decide what theoretical approach to adopt. Milli decides again to apply systems theory and an ecological approach to help her understanding of the impact of all the factors affecting the way in which this family is functioning. The further information with regards to the children's emotional health indicates that attachment in the parent–child relationships should be explored more fully.
- Decide what tools to use. Milli decides to use one of the Department of Health's Family Pack of Questionnaires and Scales developed by Cox and Bentovim in 2000, relating to Adult Wellbeing. She will also establish a genogram of the family.
- Observation of the family and how different members relate to one another.
- Direct work with Maya.
- Encouraged by her manager, Milli accesses the research findings about interventions that produce good outcomes for children witnessing domestic violence.

Maya

Child's developmental needs

- Maya was continuing to achieve developmentally within the normal range and her physical health was generally good. (health)
- Maya continued to enjoy her nursery sessions, which provided her with a source of safety and stability. (education)
- Her sleep continued to be interrupted by nightmares and she was often tired during the day. She was also presenting as withdrawn and recently has had some emotional outbursts, usually in response to another child's behaviour, which ends up with her weeping. (emotional and behavioural development)
- Maya often says that she wishes she could stay with her aunt Asha again and just visit her daddy. (family and social relationships)

Parenting capacity - Roshni

- Roshni is the main carer for the children. She has a close relationship with Maya, understands what she needs and appears to try hard to meet those needs. Yasmin however has formed a view that the marital situation is sapping Roshni's ability to think and act independently and is reducing the child focus she normally displays. (basic care, emotional warmth, stimulation, guidance and boundaries)
- Roshni can see that the situation between Kripa and herself is having a negative impact upon Maya but is unable to acknowledge the extent of the impact on her emotional well-being. There is also an ongoing risk that Maya could be physically harmed during the incidents of violence between her parents. (safety and stability)

Parenting capacity - Kripa

- Kripa only meets with Milli once during the assessment. He is offered another two appointments and fails to attend. Roshni questions why that matters, as he does not practically care for the children. Kripa states that he is feeling much better now the marital discord is all out in the open and that he understands that he and Roshni should not argue in front of the children. He reports it all started when they pushed and shoved at each other and it just seemed to escalate into a way of behaving, which he recognises is not helpful. He does not understand why his wife complains about him, as she doesn't even have to look after the children all the time now that Maya is in nursery school. He repeats that he is a moderate drinker but acknowledges he is not sleeping well and finding work stressful, which does make his mood bad at home. He minimises the impact this is all having upon his family saying that all families go through bad patches. Kripa feels it has all been blown out of proportion by his sister-in-law. He has also not found time to make an appointment with his GP to progress the counselling.
- Kripa is not observed with the children and little further information about him as a parent is ascertained.

- Milli is aware of Kripa's affair as he told her about it on their first meeting. She feels that this demonstrates that Kripa has mixed feelings about his wife and children. She puts this information in the core assessment record, even though Roshni is unaware of this, without thinking about the impact this could have.

Family and environmental factors

- Roshni has started to express how she has felt isolated and alone with her two children over the last four years and misses the social contact she used to have when she was working. Her closest relationship is with her sister but this has been undermined by Asha's increasing frustration that she continues to live with Kripa. Kripa has also argued with Badra and won't let the children visit their aunt any longer. (family's social integration)
- Family income appears sufficient but there are some credit card debts in Kripa's name. Roshni says she has little understanding of the family finance and that this is Kripa's responsibility.
- The house does require some significant structural work on the roof, which Kripa says they can't afford. This has been worrying Roshni. (housing)
- Kripa's job involves long hours and periods away from the home. This puts pressure on Roshni who says she sometimes feels like a single mother. Kripa is often tired and bad tempered at the end of the day. (employment)
- The children and Roshni's main social contact is with staff at the nursery school. (community resources)

Ajay

Child's developmental needs

- Ajay is in good health but his speech development seems slightly delayed. Though not yet significant enough to require specialist support, it may indicate Ajay has been affected by his family's situation. Roshni acknowledges that she has not been as focused on Ajay as a baby as she was with Maya. She reports not communicating as much with him and finding it hard to express her love for him although all his basic care needs are attended to. Ajay's distress when Roshni puts him down or leaves the room is very evident. (health, emotional and behavioural development)
- His relationship with his father seems to be distant as Roshni reports that Ajay does not respond to Kripa's inconsistent efforts to comfort him. (family and social relationships)

Parenting capacity - Roshni

- Roshni is the main carer for the children. She understands what Ajay needs and appears to try hard to meet those needs. Yasmin however has formed a view that the marital situation is sapping Roshni's ability to think and act independently and is reducing the child focus she normally displays. This is having a greater impact upon Ajay. (basic care, emotional warmth, stimulation, guidance and boundaries)

- Roshni can see that the situation between Kripa and herself is having a negative impact upon Ajay but is unable to acknowledge the extent of the impact on his emotional well-being. There is also an ongoing risk that Ajay could be physically harmed during the incidents of violence between his parents. (safety and stability)

Parenting capacity - Kripa

As in Maya's assessment – see previously

Family and environmental factors

As in Maya's assessment – see previously

Analysis

If the situation continues, Milli considers that the children are at ongoing risk of harm and this leads her to conclude that a child protection conference is necessary. Though she can be a capable parent, Roshni's parenting capacity has been adversely affected by the domestic violence and she is not able to protect her children from witnessing acts of violence. Yasmin is of the view that the family need to be given goals and expectations and support to achieve them. She thinks this will need to be framed by a child protection plan until either the domestic violence stops or Roshni and Kripa separate. As she sees no evidence of capacity or motivation to change in Kripa she consequently believes Roshni needs to be supported to separate from him.

Milli also concludes that with the right support Roshni can meet her children's needs. However, although Roshni has acknowledged that Kripa's behaviour is having an adverse impact upon her children, she has not reached the point of taking proactive action to protect the children. Roshni has cooperated with agencies and says she will make any necessary changes but Milli remains concerned that Kripa has barely engaged with the assessment. He has not done or said anything to indicate he is motivated to change his behaviour, i.e. seeking advice from his GP, alcohol advice or changing his work pattern. Kripa's ongoing blocking of the children's contact with Asha removes a protective factor from the family and is further evidence of his unwillingness to effect change within his family.

Milli is also concerned about the family finances but does not feel that she has gathered enough information to understand the impact this issue is having on the family's functioning. Her manager is concerned that the issues of alcohol and work stress have not been addressed fully in the assessment and wants the child protection conference to consider the need for further assessment of this area. The GP has not yet provided Milli with any information for the assessment despite attempts by Milli to gather information from her.

Milli's manager asks her to share the core assessment, as it has been completed thus far in the Report to the Child Protection Conference, with both parents and further explore the areas of finance and alcohol/work stress before making any final recommendations about the plan for the children.

Finding only Roshni at home, Milli briefly summarises the core assessment as completed thus far and leaves a copy of the Report to the Case Conference for Roshni and Kripa to read. That evening a further violent episode occurs and Roshni receives stab wounds to her breast and hands. Maya runs to Asha's house and Asha contacts the police. They arrest Kripa, who is found wandering the streets, very drunk. Roshni is taken to hospital where she remains for two days. The children are cared for by Asha. Both children are highly distressed and unable to settle. Ajay has been refusing to eat and Maya is waking repeatedly during the night crying.

Should Milli have put the information relating the affair in the report?

Milli should not have included the information about Kripa's affair in the report without discussing this first with Kripa and giving him an opportunity to tell Roshni first. To inform Roshni, without Kripa's consent, Milli would have to consider the information to be a key factor in determining whether Roshni and Kripa can adequately parent their children. Milli should have gone through the report with the couple verbally before leaving them a copy to read in their own time.

Child protection conference

Purpose

The initial child protection conference brings together family members, the child who is the subject of the conference (where appropriate), and those professionals most involved with the child and family, following s47 enquiries. Its purpose is:

- to bring together and analyse, in an inter-agency setting, the information that has been obtained about the child's developmental needs, and the parents' or carers' capacity to respond to these needs to ensure the child's safety and promote the child's health and development within the context of their wider family and environment

- to consider the evidence presented to the conference and taking in to account the child's present situation and information about his or her family history and present and past family functioning, make judgments about the likelihood of the child suffering significant harm in future, and decide whether the child is continuing to, or is likely to, suffer significant harm; and
- to decide what future action is required in order to safeguard and promote the welfare of the child, including the child becoming the subject of a child protection plan, what the planned developmental outcomes are for the child and how best to intervene to achieve these.

(*Working Together to Safeguard Children*, DCSF 2010: 161)

Attendance

Those attending conferences should be there because they have a significant contribution to make, arising from professional expertise, knowledge of the child or family or both. The LA social work manager should consider whether to seek advice from, or have present, a medical professional who can present the medical information in a manner which can be understood by conference attendees and enable such information to be evaluated from a sound evidence base. There should be sufficient expertise available – through personal representation and written reports – to enable the conference to make an informed decision about what action is necessary to safeguard and promote the welfare of the child, and to make realistic and workable proposals for taking action forward. At the same time, a conference that is larger than it needs to be can inhibit discussion and intimidate the child and family members. (*Working Together to Safeguard Children*, DCSF 2010: 162)

Case Study Exercise

List the strengths and difficulties within the family situation that should be considered by the conference in this case.

In most local authorities the chair will be independent of the management of the case. The chair will meet separately with Roshni and Kripa to explain how the meeting will work and what outcome the meeting needs to achieve. Roshni is not yet ready to be in the same room as Kripa and the chair has to establish a process by which both can participate in the meeting separately. The conference considers the following strengths and difficulties in the family situation:

Strengths

- Roshni's usual good standard of care for both children
- Roshni's willingness to engage, particularly with universal services

- Asha's willingness to provide ongoing support and protection
- Maya and Ajay's good attendance at nursery/baby group
- Good enough home conditions
- Roshni's acknowledgement that their arguments and the violence is having an adverse impact upon both children

Difficulties

- Kripa's refusal to fully engage with the assessment process
- Both parents, but in particular Kripa's, reluctance to accept the extent to which their arguments and his violence are harming the children
- Kripa's lack of involvement in caring for the children
- Kripa's affair and his alcohol consumption, which he has yet to acknowledge as problematic
- The escalation of violence to the point where weapons are now being used
- Both parents' denial of violence to other professionals during earlier assessments
- Roshni's indecision about whether she wants to continue her marriage to Kripa
- Decline of contact with Asha (sister), a protective factor
- Lack of clarity about the state of family finances and whether this is a source of stress

What recommendation would you make to the child protection conference about the need for the children to be made subject to a child protection plan?

Case Study Exercise

Episode 4 – Planning

The conference decides that the children are at risk of significant harm should Kripa return to the family home and therefore need to be the subject of a child protection plan. A plan is agreed, as shown in Case Study Table 2.1.

Episode 5 – Intervention

The police have charged Kripa with actual bodily harm and have taken forensic evidence from the home. They also have medical evidence relating to Roshni's injuries. Kripa has bail conditions not to return to the family home and is staying with his parents. After a week Roshni wishes to withdraw the charges against Kripa but the Crown Prosecution Service goes ahead with the prosecution, with her as a hostile witness. Despite this, Roshni is stating to Yasmin that she is worried about the violence and the impact it has had on the children and does not want Kripa to return home yet. Problematically, Roshni is refusing to meet with Milli due to the information about Kripa's affair being included in the core assessment record.

Milli's manager invites Roshni in to meet with her, and suggests that she bring Yasmin with her. Roshni states she is annoyed that she was not told sooner about the affair and feels Kripa's violence towards her that night was as a result of the report. Milli's manager agrees that the matter should have been handled differently and that Milli is deeply upset and sorry about her actions. Milli's manager says that Milli wishes to apologise and would like to continue to work with Roshni as she feels they do know each other well and did have a good relationship. On hearing this Roshni agrees to continue to work with Milli and says that she hopes she has learnt from the matter.

Kripa pleads guilty, receives a community sentence with conditions to attend anger management sessions. He wants to return to the family home. As a result of missing three weeks of work and the conviction for ABH, Kripa loses his job. Though Roshni is clearly saying that she is thinking about having another go at making the marriage work, she has not as yet let him back in the house. Kripa is not cooperating with proposed assessments and consequently has not seen either of his children since the child protection conference. Milli seeks legal advice, as she is very concerned about Roshni's ambivalence and the prospect of Kripa returning to the family home.

Legal services suggest the threshold for proceedings may have been met with the last incident. However, as the children have only just been made the subject of a child protection plan and Kripa is due to start an anger management programme, time needs to be given to see whether the combination of the plan and the programme make a difference. Milli's manager reflects on Roshni's current ambivalence about her relationship with Kripa and the need for her to have more time to benefit from the support she is receiving to enable her to move on. Roshni says that she does not want Kripa to return home but has not told the police, so this is not part of his sentencing conditions. Milli and her manager decide to inform Kripa that if he returns home prior to completing his anger management sessions, they will remove the children. Kripa's solicitor demands that social services seek and fund alternative accommodation for him. The local authority housing service is refusing to house Kripa as he still owns his own house and has been staying with his parents in their three-bedroomed home.

In supervision Milli and her manager discuss what changes need to be made to the plan for the children. They agree the following

- Roshni's financial situation should also be reviewed to ensure she understands her situation and is able to make informed plans for the future. The Asian women's domestic violence project may be able to provide the benefits advice as well as counselling and emotional support. Roshni will be reminded that should she allow Kripa to return home that this could lead to the removal of his children and the initiation of care proceedings.

Case Study 2 Table 2.1   Child protection plan – Maya and Ajay

Intervention	Desired outcome/s	By whom	By when
Kripa to remain out of the family home and arrangements for his contact with the children to be organised by the children's social worker	Safety of the children	Milli Tucker Kripa	One week
Roshni not to have contact with Kripa without the prior agreement with the children's social worker. Should contact take place without this agreement then consideration of legal intervention to be taken by social services	Safety of the children	Milli Tucker Roshni and Kripa	Immediately
An assessment of Kripa's parenting to be undertaken through assessment interviews and observed contacts	An understanding of Kripa's parenting capacity and motivation to change	Milli Tucker Kripa	6 weeks
Further assessment to be undertaken in relation to Kripa • the impact of work related stress • the extent and impact of his alcohol use • family finances as a source of stress	A fuller understanding of the factors negatively impacting on Kripa's ability to parent and family functioning	Milli Tucker Kripa	6 weeks
Social worker to undertake key worker role and visit children on a fortnightly basis and to talk to Maya on her own	Ongoing monitoring of plan and ensuring the safety and well-being of the children	Milli Tucker	One week and then ongoing
Domestic violence services to be put in place for Roshni, including culturally appropriate support and advice from the police	Empowering Roshni to make appropriate decisions for herself and the children	Milli Tucker	Two weeks
Social worker and police to develop a safety plan for Roshni should Kripa turn up at the home	Safety of Roshni and the children	Milli Tucker Police DV Liaison Officer	Immediately
Asha to have regular contact with Roshni and the children	Family support for Roshni and the children	Asha and Roshni	One week and then ongoing
Maya to continue to attend nursery and Roshni and Ajay, the carer and baby group	Children continue to make developmental progress	Roshni	One week and then ongoing
Health visitor to monitor Ajay's development	Ajay continues to make developmental progress particularly in relation to his speech	Health Visitor	Ongoing

Case Study 2 Table 2.1   (Continued)

Intervention	Desired outcome/s	By whom	By when
Yasmin to continue to provide parenting and emotional support to Roshni	Roshni appropriately supported	Yasmin Handa	One week and then ongoing
Core Group to meet monthly. To consist of • Milli • Roshni • Yasmin • Health visitor • Nursery teacher • Domestic Violence support service rep	Refinement of plan as necessary and monitoring of implementation of plan	Milli Tucker	Two weeks and then ongoing

- Kripa is to be asked again to cooperate with the required assessments and to be advised that if he attempts to return home prior to the completion of the assessment and the anger management programme that this could lead to the removal of his children and the initiation of care proceedings. The intervention with Kripa needs to be done in conjunction with the probation service.
- A letter will be sent to Kripa's solicitors refuting responsibility for his accommodation costs.

Roshni gets a part-time job in a local hairdressers, with the help of the nursery's employment support service, and starts her counselling with the Asian women's project. She makes some friends in her new job and her growing confidence is apparent. Her salary when combined with working family tax credit is just about managing to pay the mortgage. Kripa has a number of debts, which are secured on the home, and the citizen's advice service is advising Roshni about this. Maya and Ajay have continued to attend nursery and there has been a noticeable change in both children's behaviour and demeanour since Kripa left the family home. Yasmin is able to point this out to Roshni who recognises the difference Kripa's absence is making.

Kripa has requested unsupervised contact with the children but this is refused because he is still declining to meet with Milli in order to undertake the parenting assessment. Kripa has been attending probation appointments and the probation office has agreed to contact Milli should they believe Kripa to be visiting or seeing the children. Kripa has not engaged with the alcohol service and has failed to see his GP.

Roshni admits to the domestic abuse project that Kripa was drunk most of the time when at home. She is becoming very scared about what he might do next, as she thinks he is going to be thrown out of his parent's home due to his drinking. Kripa has been contacting her by phone and asking her to meet with him. Roshni is close to deciding that she no longer wants Kripa back and she agrees to discuss this at the next core group meeting. At this meeting it is agreed that Yasmin will support Roshni to seek legal advice about how she can keep the family home and stop Kripa returning. After receiving the legal advice, she plans to serve Kripa with notice for divorce. Roshni states that the fact she had had culturally appropriate support had helped her take charge of her life again. This included having an Asian solicitor. Due to increasing concerns about her safety, she plans to go and visit her extended family when Kripa is due to receive the letter giving him notice of divorce proceedings.

On receiving the letter Kripa goes to the family home and pours petrol into the letterbox and then attempts to light it. Asha sees this and calls the police. Kripa is arrested and remanded to prison.

> Consider the interventions put in place to ensure the children's safety and well-being. Which were the most effective?

When evaluating effectiveness consider:

- How the social worker focused on the needs of the children
- How the social worker was supportive of the parents while at the same time challenged their views and behaviours
- The impact of locally available family support services
- The impact of culturally appropriate services for Roshni, particularly with regard to domestic violence
- Whether Roshni and Maya think their lives have improved. If so, what do they think has made the difference?

Episode 6 – Review

Kripa receives a two-year prison sentence. The review child protection conference takes place after three months. The conference participants agree that as Kripa is in prison and Roshni has filed for divorce the children no longer need to be the subject of a child protection plan. Ajay is a noticeably happier child and his communication skills are now in line with the other areas of his development. Maya says she wants her daddy to visit her only on her birthday and only if he brings a present. She says she likes her mummy's new job as the ladies give her biscuits when she visits and mummy has learnt to dance since she has been working.

There is, however, an ongoing need for a multidisciplinary plan with a lead professional in place to ensure that the right support is in place when Kripa is released from prison. Yasmin is nominated again as the lead professional and social service involvement ceases at this point.

Consider the rationale for withdrawing social work involvement. Do you agree with it and, if not, what was left to be undertaken by a social worker?

In conclusion

The outcome of this intervention remains unclear in the long term as no one knows what will happen when Kripa is released from prison. However, Roshni has taken steps to emotionally and legally separate from Kripa and this has clearly been positive for both herself and her children. She is once again a capable parent and there is evidence that the children's emotional distress has begun to subside. It is reasonable to say that, up to this point at least, the interventions put into place have been successful.

Case Study 3

Charlie

Background

Lisa is a 27-year old British-born woman of African Carribbean descent. She attended college to study for A levels but dropped out and has only worked occasionally as a shop assistant. She became pregnant with Charlie when she was 20. The father is Michael, whom she met in a nightclub. The couple are not married and Michael's name is not on Charlie's birth certificate. Michael is a white British man who is now 30. He left school without qualifications and has not had any legitimate employment. He has a significant criminal record, including robbery, crimes of violence and drug offences. When Charlie was three, Michael received a five-year prison sentence for dealing in cocaine. Seven months before Michael's arrest, Charlie had been made the subject of a child protection plan by a multidisciplinary child protection conference after the children's centre he attended expressed concerns that he was being neglected. The social work assessment, completed as part of a s47 enquiry, indicated that both Michael and Lisa were heroin addicts, leading chaotic lives, and that Charlie was both inadequately cared for and supervised.

After Michael's arrest and subsequent imprisonment, Lisa was more receptive to engaging with the support services available through the National Health Service to reduce her drug dependency. As a consequence she began to parent Charlie more appropriately and the need for a child protection plan ended. The involvement of social services subsequently ceased and Lisa continued to be well supported by the children's centre. Michael was released from prison when Charlie was seven years old and recommenced his relationship with Lisa. She, in turn, started to use heroin once again. Charlie was now attending primary school and staff there knew nothing about his parents' history of drug misuse or Michael's recent release from prison. His class teacher recognised Charlie's attention-seeking behaviour and occasional temper outbursts but this was managed in class. She had recently, however, observed the deterioration in his appearance, concentration and attendance and had spoken to the head teacher, who was a designated lead within the school for child protection issues, about this. They had agreed that their concerns needed to be raised with Lisa and had arranged to meet with her in school.

(Continued)

(Continued)

Lisa's father died when she was five years old. Her mother, Sheila, lives in a neighbouring town but finds travelling difficult due to her physical disabilities, so she only sees Charlie at birthdays and Christmas. Sheila's other daughter, Anna, coincidentally lives in the same town as Michael's parents, approximately 40 miles away. Michael has one sister, Maggie, living in the same town as Lisa and him. She is well known to the police and to social services. Both her children are looked after by the local authority due to her substance misuse.

Key issues in this case

Substance misuse

Impact of substance misuse

Use of illegal drugs affects people in different ways and causes different kinds of problems. The effects of drug use and its impact on individuals and their lifestyle will vary according to:

- the individual's physical and psychological state
- the nature of the drug(s) used and how they are obtained
- the pattern and degree of drug use
- the method of administration (e.g. injection)
- the circumstances in which the drug is used
- whether a drug is used in combination with other drugs, or with alcohol

(Scottish Government: 2003: 8–9)

We estimate that there are between 200,000 and 300,000 children in England and Wales where one or both parents have serious drug problems. This represents about 2-3% of children under the age of 16 ... Parental problem drug use can and often does compromise children's health and development at every stage from conception onwards. (Home Office 2003: 10)

When a parent consistently places the purchase and use of drugs over their child's welfare and/or fails to meet the child's physical or emotional needs, the outlook for the child's heath and development is poor (p. 60) (Home Office 2003: 60)

Police protection powers

Under s46 of the Children Act 1989, where a police officer has reasonable cause to believe that a child would otherwise be likely to suffer significant harm, they may remove the child to suitable accommodation and keep him or her there or take reasonable steps to ensure that the child's removal from any hospital, or other place in which the child is then being accommodated is prevented. No child may be kept in police protection for more than 72 hours.

Emergency Protection Order

Under s44 of the Children Act 1989 an Emergency Protection Order (EPO) can be granted by a court if there is reasonable cause to believe that the child is likely to suffer significant harm if he is not removed to accommodation provided by or on behalf of the applicant, or if he does not remain in the place in which he is then being accommodated (by implication, a safe place). In the first instance an EPO may be granted for up to 8 days. The courts may extend the duration of the EPO only once and for a maximum period of 7 days.

Care Order

Under s31 of the Children Act 1989 a court can grant a Care Order if satisfied that the threshold conditions are met. These are:

- the child concerned is suffering significant harm, or is likely to suffer significant harm and
- the harm or likelihood of harm is attributable to:
  - o the care given to the child, or likely to be given to him if the order were not made, not being what it would be reasonable to expect a parent to give him; or
  - o the child is beyond parental control.

If satisfied, and once the welfare checklist has been applied, the court must make whichever order (or no order) is most consistent with the welfare interests of the child. In doing this, the court will have as its paramount consideration the welfare of the child. The local authority designated by the care order is responsible for looking after the child. It must provide accommodation for him/her and maintain him/her; safeguard and promote his/her welfare; and give effect to or act in accordance with the other welfare responsibilities set out in the Act and regulations arising from the Act.

Public law outline

Applications for Care Order need to undertaken in accordance with the public law outline (PLO), which came into force on 1 April 2008, as guidance for the case management of care proceedings. This reduced the court process to four stages, ensured that timetables are focused around the needs of the child and determined that there should be earlier identification of the key issues through assessment. It also ensured that free pre-proceedings legal advice is made available to parents with the aim of narrowing or resolving the issues in the case.

Kinship care

Numbers of children living in kinship care arrangements

The number of children living in kinship care is significant (approximately 200,000 in England and Wales) and increasing. Yet kinship care is largely invisible at key national policy and funding levels.

Kinship care contributes to placement stability, user satisfaction and identity

Kinship care makes a major contribution in securing placement stability. Along with greater user (i.e. child) satisfaction, compared with their previous placements, 'contributing to placement stability' appears to be one of the strongest and recurring themes in the research to date. Kinship care also makes a strong contribution to sustaining a child's sense of identity, and provides security and attachment.

Kinship care relationships are more complex than non-relative care relationships

There is evidence that inter- and intra-family relationships are more complicated and stress-prone in family and friends foster care arrangements than in stranger foster care arrangements. This is because of family history in the former. A commitment to working with family networks is vital. According to the evidence a commitment to, and awareness of, family and friends networks, family systems and systemic interventions are required to undertake good practice in kinship care.

Kinship carers – support needs and services

The largest group of kinship carers are grandparents, and the majority of all kinship carers are female (e.g. aunts, female friends). Kinship carers are often older, and much less well off financially than non-relative foster carers. They have a range of health, social work, education, emotional and housing and financial needs, which are largely unmet and require multi-agency input. There are major service, cultural and cross-generational competences, and training consequences that flow from kinship carers unmet needs.

(Office of the Children's Commissioner 2006: 4)

Outcomes for looked after children

- In 2006, only 12% of children in care achieved 5 A*–C grades at GCSE (or equivalent) compared to 59% of all children;
- Their health is poorer than that of other children. 45% of children in care are assessed as having a mental health disorder compared with around 10% of the general population;
- Over 50% of children in care responding to *Care Matters* said that they had difficulties accessing positive activities;

- 9.6% of children in care aged 10 or over, were cautioned or convicted for an offence during the year – almost three times the rate for all children of this age; and
- 30% of care leavers aged 19 were not in education, employment or training (NEET)

Outcomes for looked after children are generally poor when compared with the 0–19 population as a whole and placement costs often exceed the allocated budget. This has led many local authorities to adopt policies that are about deflecting the need for children to become looked after and, where this is unavoidable, to promote alternative community-based placements such as those with family and friends through Residence Orders or Special Guardianship Orders or with adoptive parents through Adoption Orders. Where children continue to be cared for in residential homes or by long term foster carers, maximising educational achievement and securing placement stability are evidenced by research as key in producing better outcomes for looked after children (*Care Matters: Time for Change*, DfES, 2007: 5/6)

Episode 1 – Threshold for service and consent

The police raid Lisa's flat, on a Saturday night, after a tip-off from a neighbour about drug dealing. The police find three young men in the front room smoking crack. Lisa is almost unconscious in the bedroom and Michael is with her. In the bedroom is £250,000 worth of heroin and crack cocaine. A large sum of money and a number of knives are also found in Lisa's wardrobe. Charlie is found asleep in his bedroom. His room is poorly decorated and there is no light bulb. He has been using a potty in the room as he has been told he is not allowed out of the room. There is little food in the flat.

The police call social services as they have arrested Lisa, Michael and the other adults. They have taken Charlie into police protection. The emergency duty social worker places Charlie with short term task centred foster carers. Gary Wordsworth, an experienced white/British social worker, is allocated the case on Monday.

As both parents have been placed on remand, it is evident that, in the short term at least, Charlie needs to be cared for by the local authority. However, once the Police Protection expires, the local authority can only continue caring for Charlie with Lisa's consent or under the auspices of an Emergency Protection Order or an Interim Care Order, both of which can only be granted by a court. Michael does not have parental responsibility for Charlie.

Gary attempts to visit Lisa in prison to ask her about her wishes for Charlie whilst she is detained. Lisa refuses to meet with Gary and her solicitor is unable to provide any view from Lisa. As a result, Gary and his manager agree that they need to apply for an Emergency Protection Order in order to secure a legal basis for continuing to care for Charlie. The Emergency

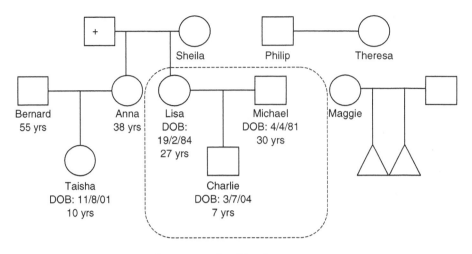

Case Study 3 Figure 3.1   Genogram for Charlie

Protection Order is granted and Gary then agrees with his manager that the next step will be an application for an Interim Care Order in respect of Charlie. This is in the expectation that both of his parents are likely to remain on remand and then receive prison sentences.

The emergency duty social worker had completed the Contact and Referral record/s and had started the Initial Assessment record. Gary therefore has to:

- Complete the Initial Assessment followed by a Core Assessment relevant to a child age 5-10 years within 35 days
- Draw up a Placement Plan within 5 working days of the start of the placement
- Establish a Care Plan including the plan for permanence for Charlie within 10 days of the start of the placement detailing how the placement will contribute to meeting his needs
- Commence the Chronology and draw up a genogram and ecomap

Together with legal section, he will draw up a letter of notification of care proceedings, which will be sent to both Lisa and Michael.

> The notification to the parents should, in its written version and where the urgency of the safeguarding concerns about the child permits its use, take the form of a 'Letter Before Proceedings'… It should include:
>
> a summary of the local authority's concerns about the actual or likely harm to the child and the evidence on which these concerns are based;
>
> information about what the local authority has done to safeguard and promote the child's welfare, what needs to be addressed, what support will be provided and what the outcome will be if the problems are not addressed;

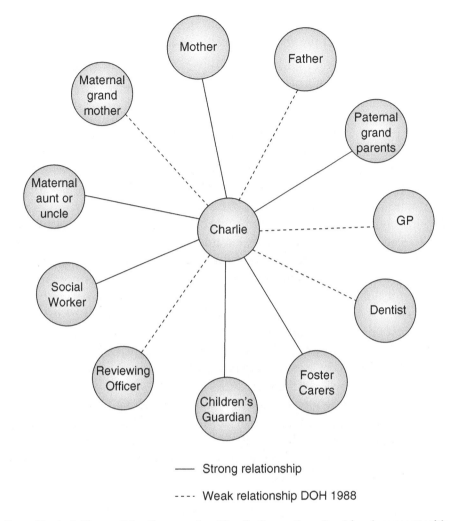

— Strong relationship

---- Weak relationship DOH 1988

Case Study 3 Figure 3.2   Ecomap for Charlie 3 months after his placement with foster carers

information about how to obtain legal help (on a non–means–tested basis) and advice (including, in particular, details of local solicitors who provide a legal aid service in public law Children Act 1989 cases) together with encouragement to seek such advice as soon as possible.

(DCSF 2008c: 5)

Gary will then need to prepare for a Looked After Child Review, due 28 days after the placement commences. This meeting will review the plan for the child and will be chaired by an Independent Reviewing Officer (IRO).

A health assessment, a personal education plan and a contact plan will need to be in place by the time the review meeting takes place.

Episode 2 – Assessment

Charlie was naturally very distressed by the manner in which he was separated from his parents and the fact that they are both now in prison. A neglected child with poor self-care skills, he finds it difficult to allow an adult to help him or express care for him. The foster carers are white/British, who know little of his African Caribbean heritage. He was initially highly rejecting of them, appearing angry and anxious, but did begin to build relationships with the other children within the home. On placement, school reported that he is slow to learn and below average in his attainment. He has also displayed difficulties in concentrating and is easily stressed by slightly challenging circumstances. This manifests itself in two ways: he either demands attention from the teacher and clings to her, or becomes angry and rejecting of those around him.

The courts expect a core assessment to have been completed by the child's social worker prior to the initiation of care proceedings. Though a court would accept in these circumstances that would have not been possible, it would still expect a completed core assessment to be available at the earliest opportunity. This case study however will also focus on the specialist assessments that courts require.

The court grants an interim care order and appoints a Children's Guardian, Marion Fish, an experienced social worker, to represent Charlie's interests during the court proceedings. All parties to the proceedings, including Charlie, have their own legal representation. The judge requires that the following areas are assessed in order to inform the court's decision making:

- An assessment of Lisa's parenting capacity, paying particular attention to the impact of Lisa's substance misuse, her relationship with Michael and the priority it takes over parenting Charlie, and her wishes and feelings in relation to the future care of Charlie
- An assessment of Michael's commitment to be an active parent to Charlie, paying particular attention to the impact of Michael's substance misuse, the quality of his relationship with Charlie, and his wishes and feelings in relation to the future care of Charlie
- Assessments of potential alternative kinship carers for Charlie
- Assessment of Charlie's wishes and feelings

> **What aspects of Lisa's drug use would need to be considered as part of her assessment?**

- Her substance misuse history, including the impact her relationship with Michael has on her drug use

- Her choice of drugs and extent of drug use
- How she funds her drug use
- Her attitude to her drug use and motivation to change
- Her engagement with drug use services, past and present
- The impact of her drug use upon her ability to parent, her understanding of this and what she does to reduce its impact
- Her long-term wishes in relation to her drug use. This will involve an assessment of whether she is prepared to end her relationship with Michael in order to resume Charlie's care
- How others view her drug use and describe its impact on her parenting
- Who she would want to care for Charlie should she receive a prison sentence and whether this should be a temporary or permanent arrangement

---

Who could be considered as kinship carers?

- Sheila (maternal grandmother)
- Anna and Bernard (maternal aunt and uncle)
- Theresa and Philip (paternal grandparents)
- Maggie (paternal aunt)

What would need to be assessed in order to establish the kinship carer's suitability to care for Charlie?

- Ability to provide an adequate level of care for Charlie over the course of his life. This would include an assessment of the quality of their parenting and the outcome of their parenting to date would need to be fully considered.
- Ability to manage the relationship between Lisa, Michael and Charlie in a way that keeps Charlie safe but also maximises his relationship with his parents and grandparents.

How would Charlie's wishes and feelings be assessed?

It should take place over a clear timeframe and involve discussion with:

- Charlie
- Lisa
- Michael
- Charlie's foster carers
- School staff

The assessment will involve life story work and developing wish lists with Charlie, as well as securing the views of others about Charlie's current needs and wishes. Direct observation of Charlie in a variety of settings will also be important, in order to assess his attachments, relationships and emotional and physical development.

Outcome of core assessment

Gary's core assessment establishes:

Child's developmental needs

- Charlie is small for his age and has poor dental health. (health)
- Educational attainment has been impeded by poor concentration and inability to manage new requests or change. (education)
- Charlie struggles to adapt to change and cannot always maintain appropriate self control. (emotional and behavioural development)
- Charlie has identity issues, particularly about his multiple heritage, which Michael has always viewed negatively. He has always wanted more acknowledgement from and time with his father. (identity)
- Charlie has an ambivalent relationship with his mother and to an even greater extent with his father. Relationships with his extended family are not strong or well developed. (family and social relationships)
- Charlie has a poor sense of personal hygiene. (social presentation)
- Charlie has little ability in relation to self care skills and has to be prompted about and assisted with most areas. (self care skills)

Parenting capacity - Lisa

- Lisa did not always meet Charlie's basic care needs in relation to food, toileting, warmth and personal hygiene. Charlie's bedroom was basic, dirty and full of litter. He did, however, have access to a TV and consol games. (basic care)
- Charlie was exposed to harm in a number of ways – Lisa did not always provide adequate supervision, protection from hazards, ensure sufficient sleep, provide enough food at regular intervals, and he was exposed to unsafe, volatile adults. (ensuring safety)
- Lisa is not always attuned to Charlie's needs. She praised and encouraged him when not under the influence of drugs but when using heroin was inconsistent and unresponsive. (emotional warmth)
- The flat was basic, with little evidence of anything, besides a TV and consol games, that would stimulate a seven-year-old. (stimulation)
- Lisa was capable of providing her son with boundaries and positive discipline but again this was inconsistent dependent on her drug-induced state. (guidance and boundaries)
- Charlie has an insecure attachment with his mother and father. (stability)
- Lisa prioritised her wish to have Michael in her life over Charlie's need to be parented safely and appropriately. (basic care and ensuring safety)

Parenting capacity - Michael

* It was clear that though he was present in Charlie's life, Michael had never parented him. Charlie's relationship with him was characterised by ambivalence. There was little prospect of Michael ever caring for Charlie. Michael did, however, expect his relationship with Lisa to continue and assessment of Lisa and Michael as a couple had to be undertaken.

Family and environmental factors

* Lisa has no significant support from her family and only sees her mother on an occasional basis. The basis of her friendship network is substance misuse. Michael's sister, Maggie, is a frequent visitor at the flat and is fond of Charlie but her overriding interest is in crack cocaine. The community support Lisa received from staff at Charlie's children centre ended when Charlie started primary school.

Drug use assessment

The assessment is undertaken by a clinical psychologist who specialises in addiction and substance misuse. It concludes that though Lisa did have some insight into the impact the drug use had on her parenting, she was reluctant to acknowledge the consequences for Charlie's health, development and emotional well-being. The psychologist questioned Lisa's ability to prioritise Charlie over her substance misuse and her relationship with Michael. Given her overriding commitment to Michael and her earlier relapse into drug addiction, she was deemed at high risk of a further relapse on release from prison.

The assessment of Michael indicated that he had no insight into nor interest in the impact on Charlie of his substance misuse. Whilst in prison Michael had tested positive to cannabis.

Kinship assessments

Charlie's maternal grandmother, Shelia, his paternal grandparents, Theresa and Philip, and his maternal aunt, Anna, and her husband, Bernard, are all potential kinship carers for Charlie. Given that Michael's sister, Maggie, had had her own children removed, she was quickly ruled out as a potential carer for Charlie. Gary's manager wanted the kinship care arrangements to be secured, if possible under private law arrangements, in order to avoid Charlie continuing to be looked after by the local authority. This means that the assessments would not need to be undertaken under the fostering regulations.

Gary's manager wants the kinship assessments to consider:

* Ability of the family member to provide good enough basic parenting for the child
* The wider family and environmental factors that could impact upon their ability as carers
* The ability of the family member to provide long-term care for Charlie into adulthood and to understand the impact on Charlie's health, development and attachments of his mother's parenting
* The family member's understanding of Lisa's problems and whether they understand her potential role in Charlie's future as well as the potential risk of Lisa disrupting or challenging the placement
* The family member's understanding of Michael's problems and the challenges he may pose to the placement
* The family member's understanding of Charlie's needs in relation to his history, identity and attachment difficulties

What private law orders could be used to secure Charlie's future with kinship carers?

* Residence Order
* Special Guardianship Order
* Adoption Order

Are there any alternatives to kinship care, which could be considered?

* Charlie could remain looked after by the local authority under a Care Order and live with either kinship foster carers or registered long-term foster carers
* Charlie could remain looked after and then be returned to his mother's care under a Care Order (placement with parent) or under a Supervision Order
* Charlie could be placed for adoption with approved adopters not previously known to Charlie and become the subject of an Adoption Order

Assessment of Sheila

Contact is established between Charlie and Sheila. An assessment plan is drawn up by Gary. This involves five assessment meetings and an observed contact visit.

Sheila does not manage to attend the prearranged contact visit due to her ill health. She is disabled by osteoarthritis and Gary concludes that this would make it very difficult for her to care for Charlie. Sheila is also very optimistic about her daughter's ability to become drug free and says that as soon as she is out of prison she would want to return Charlie to her care. Charlie says he does not want to live with Sheila because he does not know her that well and is worried he would have to care for her because she is disabled. Gary shares this concern. Gary ceases the assessment after three visits and shares his views with Sheila. Reluctantly she agrees she could not look after Charlie long term, but is anxious that if he goes to live with a member of Michael's family that she will lose contact with him. If she can't look after Charlie herself then she would want her daughter, Anna, to do so. Gary reassures her that willingness to maintain Charlie's contact with her will form part of his assessment of Charlie's paternal grandparents.

Assessment of Theresa and Philip

An assessment plan is drawn up by Gary but the assessment is brought to a swift conclusion, after the first visit, when Theresa expresses serious doubts about the viability of caring for Charlie. She acknowledges that she and her husband never managed to exert parental control over Michael and Maggie and she feels that, now they are older, they would find it even more difficult with Charlie. Theresa and Philip are anxious to have regular contact with Charlie, which Gary then sets up.

Assessment of Anna and Bernard

Anna lives with her husband, Bernard, and daughter, Taisha, who is 10 years old, in their own home. Anna has not seen Charlie since he was born but has always sent a Christmas card and birthday present. Charlie wants to see his aunt and contact is arranged for twice a month on a Sunday. Gary asks the local authority where Anna lives to undertake a special guardianship assessment of Anna and her family and the case is allocated to Amie Khan, a social worker based in the Family Placements Service, with three years' post qualification experience.

This assessment concludes that Anna and her husband provide Taisha with a good standard of parenting and have a well-developed understanding of the needs of children. Criminal Records Bureau (CRB) checks and character references about the adults are obtained. A report from their daughter's school is requested. These references highlight that Bernard and Anna have a strong support network and are viewed as a loving, stable family. They present as committed to maintaining contact with Lisa and other family members as appropriate. They are willing to facilitate contact between Charlie and his father, though they very much disapprove of Michael's drug use and see him as having had a disastrous influence over Lisa. They also recognise the potential for Charlie to be disappointed, hurt or damaged by his mother should she fail to remain drug free. Anna's experience of her sister's behaviour has given them a good understanding of the impact drug misuse can have on family dynamics. She does not think Lisa is strong enough to become drug free and does not think Charlie should have any unsupervised contact with his mother.

Anna and her husband are both British and of African Caribbean descent. They are able to talk about black identity and the need for children to understand their heritage and be equipped to deal with racism. They understand that Charlie has a dual heritage background but believe he will be better cared for in a black or dual heritage family, than a white family. They are concerned that Charlie is currently in a white foster home, which they don't think can meet his identity needs. They are committed to Charlie understanding both his mother's and father's culture.

Taisha is interviewed on her own by the social worker. She expresses concern that she may have to share her computer and is worried that they won't be able to go on holiday, due to the cost of taking both her and Charlie. However, she also says that she likes Charlie and thinks her mum and dad are being very kind in asking Charlie to live with them. She thinks he is 'all right' for a seven-year-old boy but is naturally worried about sharing her parents for the first time. She is a confident and mature child whose school report shows her to be both popular and achieving.

Medicals are carried out on both adults. This reveals that Anna had cancer three years ago, now in remission, and was treated for depression at the end of the treatment. Anna is 38 and Bernard is 55 years old; the doctor comments that the care of a seven-year-old emotionally damaged boy may be too demanding for them in the long term. The CRB check reveals that 20 years ago Bernard received a suspended prison sentence for assault.

Though Lisa is prepared to agree to Charlie living with Anna and Bernard while she is in prison, she is adamant that she will be resuming care of him on her release. She is therefore opposed to the court granting Anna and Bernard any order that would give them any parental responsibility. Michael is clear that on release from prison he expects to resume his relationship with Lisa and to have Charlie come home to them. He seems to expect that life will go on as it did before and does not acknowledge any need for change

Case Study Exercise

Write a closing analytical statement about Anna's family and their suitability to care for Charlie. Identify both strengths and areas of difficulty.

The outcome of the kinship assessments will need to be reflected in the statement for the Family Court proceedings. This will outline:

- The benefits of Charlie living with a family member and not being subject to a Care Order
- Anna and Bernard's commitment to Charlie evidenced by their willingness to get to know him and understand his physical and emotional needs
- Anna and Bernard's experience of bringing up their own daughter, which so far they have done successfully
- Anna and Bernard's local support networks
- The benefits of being cared for by a black family
- Anna and Bernard's experience of having a family member affected by drug misuse and how this has affected the family
- Their ability to safely manage the contact Charlie will need with his mother and father on their release from prison and to promote contact with his grandparents
- The benefits to Charlie of living with a family with a child, having had the experience of a placement with other children. He will also potentially get support in integrating into school by having an older child to support him
- Issues relating to Anna's previous ill health and Bernard's age. If they become ill again or find Charlie's energy too demanding, caring for Charlie may present challenges for them. Charlie is a young boy who will need to be cared for over the next 10 years at least
- The context of the offence committed by Bernard, his attitude to that offence and his attitude to acts of violence in general

> How could any areas of difficulty this assessment has identified be resolved or mitigated against?

- Issues arising from the distance they live from Charlie's place of birth. Charlie will have to move school and make new friends

This transition will need careful planning with regard to building up the time Charlie spends with Anna, Bernard and Taisha. His new family will need to be fully informed about Charlie's history, current needs and lifestyle. His foster carers need to be fully involved in the preparations for his move and should remain in contact with him. His new school will need full information from his existing school and a new personal education plan (PEP) should be in place before he starts his new school.

- Age and health of the carers

It will be important here to secure relevant information from health professionals. Anna and Bernard's support networks should be clarified and how this could assist them in their care of Charlie evaluated.

- Bernard's criminal conviction

Bernard needs to convince Amie that he no longer approves of acts of violence as a means of problem resolution and explain this attitudinal change.

The assessment of Charlie's wishes and feelings

Gary considers it important to build a picture of Charlie's wishes and feelings from a number of sources. As well as talking to Charlie, he also plans to talk to those who know Charlie well. From these other sources he wants to find out how easy Charlie will find it to articulate his wishes, his feelings and how far his loyalty to his parents, particularly to his mother, might get in the way of this. He will also try to establish what Charlie has already said to those he trusts. Gary knows that Charlie needs to understand his situation and to be given enough time to think about what he wants. He also wants Charlie to understand that he is not responsible for the situation he is in and though his views are important and will be fully taken into account, in the end, the adults responsible for him will decide where he will live.

Gary therefore plans the following activity in order to establish Charlie's wishes and feelings:

- Five sessions of life story work with Charlie
- Development of a wish list with Charlie about his future and what he wants from anyone who cares for him
- A discussion with Charlie's foster carers
- A discussion with Lisa and Michael
- Observation of contact between Charlie and Anna, Charlie and Lisa, Charlie and Michael

Both his foster carers and teacher think Charlie is capable of giving his opinion about his future. He has told his foster carers that he is sad that his mother is in prison and wished she did not use drugs. He has talked at length about how frightened he was when she was under the influence of drugs but was too scared to tell anyone. He has said he wants her to get better so he can live with her again. He expresses little interest in his father and says that he doesn't want to see him very often. On Mother's Day Charlie bought cards for both his foster mother and Lisa and made his own 'Aunt Day' card for Anna.

The five life story sessions gave Charlie an opportunity to talk about his understanding of his life so far. He had some understanding of what had happened and why, but clearly felt abandoned by his parents, particularly by his mother. He wanted to draw and photograph his life so far and took lots of pride in the book that resulted from the activity. He started to ask about his future at the end of the fourth session, which led into Charlie writing a wish list for his future at the end of the book. This included living in a nice house, having lots of nice food, doing okay at school, learning to play football really well and seeing his mum, aunt, grandparents and perhaps his father sometimes.

The court process was explained to Charlie using a storybook produced by the British Association for Adoption and Fostering (BAAF). Charlie was asked about where and with whom he would like to live. He said that he would like to live with his aunt and uncle until his mother was released from prison and then he would want to live with her again. He would be older then and could help her live a better life.

> What other techniques or tools could be used to establish Charlie's wishes and feelings?

Charlie could have:

* written a letter to the judge telling him what he wants for the future
* drawn a genogram of his family identifying those whom he likes and trusts and those he doesn't
* drawn an ecomap showing whom he feels close to
* drawn a picture of everyone who is special to him and described why each person was special
* used a special computer program to develop his life story book and talk about his desired future

Episode 3 – Intervention

Since being in care Charlie has been supported through a care plan established to ensure all his identified needs are met. This considers such issues as his physical and emotional health, educational attainment, his social development and his need for contact with the significant adults in his life. Given everyone was supporting the idea that Charlie move to live with his aunt and uncle, the care plan had ensured that Charlie had been spending more time with them, particularly at weekends and during school holidays, in order to build a relationship with them.

This care plan is regularly reviewed by an Independent Reviewing Officer at statutory meetings, to which all significant adults and professionals in Charlie's life are invited. At a minimum these meetings are convened 20 days after a child is accommodated, 3 months after that and then 6-monthly thereafter. Once a child has been looked after for 6 months, assessment and progress records should be completed and routinely updated.

The court ultimately decides that Charlie should be subject to a Special Guardianship Order in favour of Anna and Bernard. This was in spite of Lisa's objections. She had wanted Charlie to live with her sister without the benefit of an order, so that she could resume his care on release from prison. Charlie's Guardian had argued that this was too risky to contemplate given the high risk that on her release from prison Lisa would resume the lifestyle that led to Charlie's removal from her care. Without Anna and Bernard's agreement to Charlie moving back to his mother's care, Lisa will now have to apply to the court, which again will subject her lifestyle to scrutiny. Face-to-face contact is agreed to take place with his mother four times a year, with telephone and letter contact on birthdays and Christmas. Face-to-face contact with his father was agreed twice a year. Contact with his grandparents would be mutually agreed between them and Anna and Bernard. A review meeting is then held to consider how best to support Charlie's move to his new home.

Episode 4 – Review

Charlie's last review was attended by Gary, Charlie's teacher, foster carers and Anna and Bernard. Charlie did not attend because he didn't like hearing all these people talk about him. Gary met with him before the review to secure his views and Charlie also spoke to the Independent Reviewing Officer after the review, who talked to him about the outcome.

Case Study Exercise

> Suggest other ways that could have been used to encourage Charlie to participate in his LAC Review

Charlie could:

- write down the good things in his life and things he would like to change
- talk to his foster carers and ask them to represent his views
- speak to the reviewing officer before the meeting to explain what he wants
- provide a drawing or poem about his life to the group
- be asked about whom he thinks should attend, and perhaps the meeting could be split in half with Charlie's meeting first and then the meeting with everyone else

Charlie has been living with his foster carer and their children for over 13 months and now, overall, has a positive relationship with them. They help him realise that he needs to attend this meeting so that he understands how the move to his aunt and uncle's will happen. His teacher expresses concern about another big upheaval in his life that would involve Charlie in moving to a new home, city and school, all at the same time. Anna and Bernard are aware of this and want to minimise the disruption Charlie experiences. The following plan is agreed.

Charlie will:

- spend the next three weekends with Anna and Bernard
- move at the end of the school term – three weeks away. This will be facilitated by his foster carers
- be visited by his foster carers and their children during the second week of the school holidays
- have the summer holidays to settle in to his new home and before he will start at his new school

Gary will:

- request that his old school transfer his school records to his new school and provide his new school with relevant information about him. With the new school he will plan Charlie's introductions and develop a personal education plan
- notify Charlie's current GP of the need to transfer his medical records to his new GP. If Charlie is taking any medication or undertaking any medical treatment this should be carefully explained to Anna and Bernard. It would be advisable to get this provided in writing
- ensure that his foster carers provide written information about Charlie's weekly routine including bedtimes, favourite food, worries, behaviours and how to respond to, and manage, his emotions and behaviours
- arrange a small celebration event to support Charlie's departure from his foster carers and his arrival at Anna and Bernard's home
- discuss with Anna and Bernard the need for a special guardianship support plan
- establish a new contact plan that will ensure that Charlie sees both his parents and grandparents and has some ongoing contact with his foster carers

Anna and Bernard will:

- prepare their house and family and friends for Charlie's arrival
- apply for a place for Charlie at Taisha's school
- register Charlie with their GP
- write to Lisa to tell her that they will provide a good home for Charlie and will help maintain the contact agreement reached in court

His class teacher will:

- ensure his school records are up to date and make arrangements for their transfer to his new school

Gary establishes a Special Guardianship Support Plan, which is reviewed after a year. Responsibility for reviewing this plan has moved to a different team and it is Moira Davis, a social worker with one year's experience, who visits to undertake the review. Charlie still has some behavioural problems but he is making steady progress in school and has taken up football. He says that he feels safe living with Anna and Bernard but still misses his mother. He also says he is worried that his mum will want him back when she is released from prison and expresses torn loyalties. He is reassured that his mum can't just take him back and Moira asks Anna to show Charlie the court order and explain again to Charlie what the order means.

Anna and Bernard report they found it difficult to adjust to Charlie's energy and found his behaviour difficult to manage at times. Through discussion with both Gary and then Moira they have some understanding of what Charlie has experienced and how his behaviour is his way of coping with his earlier experiences. They are helped to adopt behaviour that promotes their attachment to Charlie and his attachment to them. Through football he has made some new friends and this has helped Charlie settle into the local area. Anna and Bernard are also careful to be consistent and reliable in their care of Charlie. Taisha says that she likes Charlie, though she doesn't always like the way he behaves but overall is pleased to have a little brother to boss around. Anna and Bernard ask for more help with managing the logistics of the four contact arrangements, which they find very demanding. They also want help funding for more activities after school and holiday activities for Charlie. Bernard has been forced to retire due to ill health and this has affected the family income.

Moira reassesses the family income and recommends they apply for additional benefits. She agrees to ask her manager for an annual lump sum payment of £300 to pay for out of school activities for Charlie. This will be reviewed every year.

Episode 5 – Responding to changing circumstances

When Lisa is released from prison on a licence she keeps phoning Anna and Bernard, demanding Charlie back. She also stayed with Michael's parents for a week, during which she turned up at their house uninvited, demanding to see Charlie. Bernard refused to let her in. This has upset Charlie and made Anna, in particular, angry as well as upset. Lisa was due to have face-to-face contact with Charlie last month but Anna did not want to talk to Lisa and so no arrangements were made.

What actions could Moira take now to resolve the contact issues?

Moira helps Anna understand that, though she is angry with Lisa, that this can't come between Charlie's need to have an ongoing relationship with his mother. She asks Anna and Bernard what would make contact easier and what arrangements they would feel able to support. In an attempt to become drug free Lisa has moved in with her mother and Anna and Bernard agree that Charlie could visit for the day during the weekend every eight weeks. If this goes OK then they will consider an overnight stay. They also agree that Lisa can ring Charlie twice a week.

Moira visits Lisa who remains convinced that Charlie would want to live with her again, if Anna hadn't turned him against her. Moira explains the actual position to Lisa and that if she wants a positive relationship with Charlie, she and her sister need to cooperate about contact. She puts Anna's proposal to her. Lisa is reluctant to accept what Moira is saying but does understand that Anna has the legal entitlement to care for Charlie and so agrees the new contact plan. All parties agree to work to the new contact arrangement for 4 months when Moira agrees to visit again to see how it is working in practice.

Initially the plan works and Charlie begins to have some overnight stays at his grandmother's house. The contact plan falls apart, however, when Lisa moves out when Michael is released from prison and resumes her heroin habit once again. Anna refuses face-to-face contact while Lisa is drug dependent and only allows telephone and letter contact. There are times when Lisa calls at the house and causes a scene and this does upset her son. However, he continues to feel safe and secure with Anna and Bernard and overall continues to progress and enjoy his life in their care.

In conclusion

Charlie was fortunate in that he had extended family members willing, able and capable of caring for him. He also had minimal changes in social workers and when change happened he experienced a good handover in relation to written reports and joint visits. Moira was therefore well briefed at the point she undertook casework responsibility and Charlie and his carers had confidence that his new social worker understood the issues they were grappling with. The situation with his mother has ongoing complications but with the right support he and his aunt and uncle cope with those complications and get on with the other aspects of their lives. Overall it is clear that in this case social work has positively intervened in Charlie's life and effected a good outcome.

Glossary of Legislation Concerned with Safeguarding Children

Children Act 1989

This was designed to improve the balance between the rights and responsibilities of the state and parents and between the need to protect children and the need to enable parents to challenge state intervention in the upbringing of their children. It encouraged working in partnership with parents and providing them with support at an early stage. This would help keep the use of care proceedings to a minimum. The Act also emphasises that the welfare of the child is paramount and that their views should be taken into account when formulating plans. Key provisions are as follows:

Section 17 of the Children Act 1989 provides the following definition of a Child In Need:

> A child is taken to be in need if:
>
>> The child is unlikely to achieve or maintain or to have an opportunity of achieving or maintaining a reasonable standard of health or development without the provision for him of services by a local authority
>
>> The child's health or development is likely to be significantly impaired or further impaired without the provision for him of such services; or
>
>> The child is disabled

In **s17(11)** health is further defined as encompassing both physical and mental health, and development as encompassing physical, intellectual, emotional, social or behavioural development. A child is defined as disabled where s/he is blind, deaf, dumb or suffers from a mental disorder or is substantially and permanently handicapped by illness, injury or congenital deformity or such other disability as may be described.

(It should be noted, however, that this is an outdated medical definition and that the Disability Discrimination Act 1995 (DDA) has subsequently defined a disabled person as someone who has a physical or mental impairment that has a substantial and long-term adverse effect on his or her ability to carry out normal day-to-day activities. This definition needs to be considered in the context of the current social model of disability.)

Section 31(92)(a) introduced the criterion that had to be satisfied to warrant state intervention: 'that the child concerned is suffering, or is likely to suffer significant harm'. Harm is defined as 'ill treatment or the impairment of health or development' (**s31(9)**) and the judgement as to whether harm is significant is informed by comparing the child's health and development with that which could be reasonably expected of a similar child (**s31(10)**).

Section 47(1) laid a specific duty on the local authority where they

Have reasonable cause to suspect that a child who lives, or is found in their area, is suffering, or is likely to suffer, significant harm, the authority should make, or cause to be made such enquiries as they consider necessary to enable them to decide whether they should take any action to safeguard or promote the child's welfare.

Section 47(3) specified that

The enquiries shall, in particular, be directed towards establishing whether the authority should make any application to the court, or exercise any of their powers under the Act, with respect to the child.

Sex Offenders Act 1997

This requires sex offenders convicted or cautioned on or after 1 September 1997 to notify the police of their names and addresses and of any subsequent changes.

Crime and Disorder Act 1998

This reformed juvenile justice by establishing the Youth Justice Board and multi-agency Youth Offending Teams, introducing new measures to help prevent youth crime, e.g. Child Safety Orders as well as new options for dealing with young offenders, e.g. reprimands and final warnings and reparation orders. It also sought to force parents to exert their parental responsibility through Parenting Orders.

Protection of Children Act 1999

This aimed to prevent paedophiles from working with children. It requires childcare organisations in England and Wales to inform the Department of Health about anyone known to them who is suspected of harming children or putting them at risk. It made it mandatory for employers to check this list (administered by the Criminal Records Bureau) when employing someone in a post involving the care of children, and also made it an offence to employ anyone on this list.

Care Standards Act 2000

Strongly influenced by the Waterhouse Report *Lost in Care* (2000), this reformed the regulatory system for care services in England and Wales. Standards were established for the arrangements for looking after children away from their home in a range of settings, including residential care, fostering and adoptive placements, childminding and day care, boarding schools and further education colleges that accommodate children. The responsibility for inspection was given to the new Care Standards Commission with the exception of childminding and day care, which was given to Ofsted, the schools inspection service. (All inspection responsibilities with regard to children's social services are now located with Ofsted.) This Act also provides the legislative base for the General Social Care Council established in 2001.

Children (Leaving Care) Act 2000

This defined eligibility for care leaving services and strengthened the provision to be made available in relation to: accommodation, education, training and employment for young people requiring support leaving the public care system. It also obliged local authorities to appoint a personal adviser for each young person who would draw up an appropriate Pathway Plan that should ensure appropriate support for the young person to embark upon adult life.

Criminal Justice and Court Services Act 2000

This imposed a statutory duty on the police and the probation service to work together to protect the public from sexual and violent offenders through Multi Agency Public Protection Arrangements (MAPPAs). This created formal arrangements by which the risks posed by sexual and violent offenders on their release from prison could be assessed and managed.

Adoption and Children Act 2002

This followed on from the Prime Minister's Review of Adoption 2000. It replaced the Adoption Act 1976 and brought adoption law in line with both the Children Act 1989 and the United Nations Convention on the Rights of the Child (UNCRC). Article 21 of the latter requires party States to 'recognise and/or permit the system of adoption to ensure that the best interests of the child shall be the paramount consideration'. It aimed to maximise the use of adoption as a means of achieving permanence for a wide range of children and to increase the pool of available adopters. Its new provisions include a legal obligation upon local authorities to provide adoption support services, new orders relating to special guardianship and placements and advocacy rights for looked after children. This also amended the Children Act 1989 by including a provision that made clear that the harm a child may be at risk of suffering includes 'any impairment of the child's health or development as a result of witnessing the ill-treatment of another person, such as domestic violence'. Ill-treatment is broader than physical violence and includes sexual abuse and forms of ill-treatment which are not physical, such as seeing a parent being harassed or intimidated by another person.

Education Act 2002

This included provision (s75) requiring school governing bodies, local education authorities and further education institutions to make arrangements to safeguard and promote the welfare of children.

Sexual Offences Act 2003

This was introduced to update the legislation relating to offences against children. It includes the offences of grooming, abuse of position of trust and trafficking and covers offences committed by British citizens whilst abroad. It also updated the **Sex Offenders Act 1997** to strengthen the monitoring of offenders on the sex offenders register.

Children Act 2004

This aimed to progress the Every Child Matters five outcomes framework and introduced the following duties and responsibilities:

- A duty on local authorities to make arrangements to promote cooperation between agencies in order to improve children's well-being, supported by a new power to pool resources to support the new arrangements
- A duty for the key agencies that work with children to put into place arrangements to safeguard and promote the welfare of children and young people
- The replacement of non-statutory Area Child Protection Committees with statutory Local Safeguarding Children Boards
- A duty on local authorities to put into place a lead member and director of children services responsible for, as a minimum, children's social care services and local education authority (LEA) services so creating Children's Services Authorities
- The appointment of a new Children's Commissioner for England
- A duty on local authorities to draw up, with relevant partner agencies, a single Children and Young People's Plan to replace a range of statutory planning previously required
- The establishment of a National Index containing basic information about all children and young people to enable practitioners to identify who else is involved with the child and whether any concerns have been recorded
- The establishment of an integrated inspection framework for children's services leading to the Care Standards Commission with Ofsted then assuming responsibility for the inspection of all social care services for children, both fieldwork and provider
- Provisions relating to private fostering, fostering allowances and education support for looked after children

Domestic Violence, Crime and Victims Act 2004

This closed a legal loophole by creating a new offence of causing or allowing the death of a child or vulnerable adult. The offence established a new criminal responsibility for members of a household where they know that a child or vulnerable adult is at significant risk of serious harm.

Serious Organised Crime and Police Act 2005

This set up the framework for the Child Exploitation and Online Protection (CEOP) Centre to be created. It also included provisions for improving the vetting system to stop adults who pose a risk from working with children (s163).

Safeguarding Vulnerable Groups Act 2006

The 2004 Bichard Inquiry looked into vetting procedures following the murders of Jessica Chapman and Holly Wells in Soham. It recommended the establishment of a new centralised vetting and barring scheme for people working with children. This piece of legislation was the government's response to the recommendations of that Inquiry and it established a new Independent Safeguarding Authority (ISA) designed to help prevent unsuitable people from working with children and vulnerable adults. Its role is to assess every person who wants to work or volunteer with vulnerable people. Potential employees and volunteers will need to apply to register with the ISA. In 2011, the Coalition government undertook a review of the vetting and barring scheme and decided to reduce the scope of the scheme and to integrate the ISA with the Criminal Records Bureau.

Children and Young Persons Act 2008

The purpose of the Act is to extend the statutory framework for children in care in England and Wales and to ensure that such young people receive high quality care and services which are focused on and tailored to their needs. The 2008 Act endeavours to improve the stability of placements and improve the educational experience and attainment of young people in local authority care or those about to leave care.

Glossary of Acronyms and Terms

ACAS Advisory, Conciliation and Arbitration Service – an independent body that aims to improve organisations and working life through better employment relations

ACMD Advisory Council on the Misuse of Drugs – independent expert body that advises government on drug-related issues in the UK

ACPC Area Child Protection Committee – non-statutory predecessor to the statutory Safeguarding Children Board

ADSS Association of Directors of Social Services – now two associations, one for adult services and the other for children's services – ADASS and ADCS

APIR Assessment, Planning, Intervention and Review – a process that frames social work activity when responding to a request for a service for a child/young person

ASD Autism Spectrum Disorder – covers a range of diagnoses associated with autism – a difference in cognitive development that impacts upon social interaction, social communication and social imagination

ASWP Advanced Social Work Professional – proposed by the CWDC as the advanced stage of the social work career pathway that recognises excellence in practice

ASYE Assessed and Supported Year in Employment – proposed by the Social Work Task Force as the final stage in becoming a social worker

BAAF British Association for Adoption and Fostering – charity that supports, campaigns and advises on issues relating to fostering and adoption

BASW British Association of Social Workers – professional association for social workers

CAF Common Assessment Framework – a framework for assessing children with additional needs

CAFCASS Children and Family Court Advisory Service – public body responsible for promoting the welfare of children subject to public and private law proceedings

CEOP Centre	Child Exploitation and Online Protection Centre – organisation that aims to eradicate the sexual abuse of children – has a particular focus on trafficking, building intelligence about adult sex offenders and Internet safety
Child protection	Activity to protect specific children suffering or likely to suffer from significant harm
Child Protection Conference Chair	Person responsible for chairing initial and review conferences – usually independent and with no involvement in managing the case
Children's Guardian	A professionally qualified social worker, employed by CAFCASS, who represents the child in public law proceedings and offers an independent view of what should happen in the child's life
Children's Trust	Arrangements, outlined in the Children Act 2004, by which services for children in a local authority area are organised into a trust with the aim of jointly improving outcomes for children/ young people
CIN	Child in Need as defined by the Children Act 1989
CPD	Continuous Professional Development, which can be achieved through training, reading, participation in active research, mentoring, co-working, post-qualifying courses etc.
CRB	Criminal Records Bureau – an executive agency of the Home Office that provides data about criminal records to employers relating to individuals working with children or vulnerable adults
CSA	Children Services Authority – a legal entity, defined in the Children Act 2004, that combines education and social care services for children/young people
CWDC	Children's Workforce Development Council – one of six bodies that make up Skills for Care and Development responsible for promoting workforce development and reform. The government intends to withdraw its funding and the legal status of CWDC as a non-departmental public body in 2012
DCSF	Department for Children, Schools and Families – predecessor to DfE
DDA	Disability Discrimination Act 1995 – aims to protect disabled people and prevent disability discrimination – much of this Act has been replaced by the provisions of the Disability and Equality Act 2010
DfE	Department for Education
DfES	Department for Education and Skills – predecessor to DCSF
DH	Department of Health

DV/DA	Domestic violence/domestic abuse
EBP/EIP	Evidence-based practice/evidence-informed practice
ECM	Every Child Matters – Labour government initiative aimed at improving outcomes for children
EPD	Early Professional Development – CWDC pilot programme that concerned the second and third years of social work practice
EPO	Emergency Protection Order – defined by the Children Act 1989
ESCR	Electronic Social Care Record – brings together all information recorded about a service user in one place on a computer-based system
GSCC	General Social Care Council – sets standards of conduct and practice for *social care* workers and their employers in England, and maintains the Social Care Register. Will cease to exist in 2012 with its functions transferred to the Health Professions Council
GP	General Practitioner
HPC	Health Professions Council – regulatory body responsible for setting and maintaining standards of 17 health professions – due to be renamed and to take over the functions of the GSCC
ICS	Integrated Children's System – aims to provide a conceptual framework, method of practice and business process to support practitioners and managers in undertaking the key tasks of assessment, planning and intervention and review in accordance with legislation
Inter-agency working	More than one agency working together in a planned and formal way towards agreed goals and objectives for the child/young person
IRO	Independent Reviewing Officer – person responsible for reviewing the care plans of Looked After Children, as required by the Adoption and Children Act 2002 and the Children and Young Persons Act 2008
ISA	Independent Safeguarding Authority – body set up as required by the Safeguarding Vulnerable Groups Act 2006, passed as a result of the Bichard Inquiry – responsible for preventing unsuitable people working with children and vulnerable adults
LA	Local authority – an elected body responsible for ensuring the delivery of local public services
LAC	Looked after child – child in the care of the local authority
LEA	Local education authority – body responsible for ensuring that appropriate education provision is available in a local authority area
LSCB	Local Safeguarding Children Board – a statutory board made up of a local authority and their statutory partners to make sure that key agencies work together to safeguard and promote the welfare of children

MAPPA	Multi Agency Public Protection Arrangements – introduced by the Criminal Justice and Courts Services Act 2000 to manage registered sex offenders, violent and other types of sexual offenders, and offenders who pose a serious risk of harm to the public
MIND	Leading mental health charity
Multi-agency working	More than one agency working with a child/young person but not necessarily delivering a joint service
NEET	Not in education, employment or training. Usually refers to 16–25 year old young people
NSPCC	National Society for the Prevention of Cruelty to Children – campaigning charity that is seeking to end cruelty to children
Ofsted	Organisation responsible for the inspection of a range of children's services, including social care, early years settings and schools
NQSW	Newly Qualified Social Worker – CWDC pilot programme for the first year of social work practice
Parental responsibility	Areas in which a parent can exercise legal responsibility for a child as defined by the Children Act 1989
PLO	Public Law Outline – issued by the Ministry of Justice to provide guidance on case management in public law proceedings
PPR	Person Posing a Risk – a person whose history indicates that she/he could pose a risk to a child/young person
PRTL	Post Registration Training and Learning – record of achievement must evidence 15 days of study, training, courses, seminars, reading, teaching or other activities that could reasonably be expected to advance the social worker's professional development. It must be completed every 3 years as required by the GSCC for re-registration purposes
RIP	Research in Practice – a charity that brings together the Dartington Hall Trust, Sheffield University and the ADCS to promote evidence-informed social work practice
Safeguarding	Protecting children from harm and promoting their welfare
SCIE	Social Care Institute for Excellence – government-funded charity that seeks to identify and spread knowledge about good practice to the social care workforce
SCR	Serious Case Review – considers the learning from the involvement of agencies and professionals when a child is seriously injured or dies as a consequence of abuse or neglect – required by Chapter 8 of *Working Together to Safeguard Children* (DCSF 2010)
SENCO	Special educational needs co-ordinator in schools
SSI	Social Services Inspectorate – one of the predecessors in children's social care of Ofsted

UNCRC   United Nations Convention on the Rights of the Child – international legally binding instrument that defines the rights of all those under the age of 18 years of age

YOS   Youth Offending Service – multi-agency teams with a statutory responsibility for responding to the needs of young offenders and those on the edge of offending behaviour

References

ACAS (Advisory, Conciliation and Arbitration Service) (2010) *The Recruitment Process'.* Available at www.acas.org.uk/index.aspx?articleid=748 (accessed 17 January 2010).

Adoption and Children Act 2002. London: The Stationery Office.

ADSS (Association of Directors of Social Services) (2003) *Response of the Association of Directors of Social Services (ADSS) to the Green Paper 'Every Child Matters'.* Available at www.adass.org.uk/publications/consresp/2003/greenfin.pdf (accessed 15 December 2007).

Aldgate, J. and Seden, J. (2006) 'Direct work with children', in J. Aldgate, D. Jones, W. Rose and C. Jeffery (eds), *The Developing World of the Child.* London: Jessica Kingsley Publishers.

Aldgate, J. and Tunstill, J. (1995) *Making Sense of Section 17: Implementing Services for Children in Need within the 1989 Children Act.* London: The Stationery Office.

Audit Commission (1994) *Seen but Not Heard: Coordinating Community Child Health and Social Services for Children in Need within the 1989 Children Act.* London: HMSO.

Baldwin, N. and Walker, L. (2005) 'Assessment', in R. Adams and L. Dominelli (eds), *Social Work Futures: Crossing Boundaries, Transforming Practice.* Basingstoke: Palgrave Macmillan.

Barker, R. L. (2003) *The Social Work Dictionary*, 5th edn. Washington, DC: NASW Press.

Barrett, M. and Hodgson, R. (2006) *Firm Foundations.* Dartington: Research in Practice.

BASW (2011) *Code of Ethics for Social Work.* Available at www.basw.co.uk/about/code-of-ethics/ (accessed 20 April 2011).

Bens, I. (1998) *Team Launch! Strategies for New Team Start-ups.* Sarasota, FL: Participative Dynamics.

Bichard, M. (2004) *The Bichard Inquiry Report.* London: Stationery Office.

Booth, T. and Booth, W. (1996) 'Parental competence and parents with learning difficulties', *Child and Family Social Work*, 1 (2): 81–6.

Booth, T. and Booth, W. (1998) *Growing Up with Parents Who Have Learning Difficulties.* London: Routledge.

Brechin, A. and Sidell, M. (2000) 'Ways of knowing', in R. Gomm and C. Davis (eds), *Using Evidence in Social Care.* London: Sage Publications.

Brofenbrenner, U. (1979) *The Ecology of Human Development.* Cambridge, MA: Harvard University Press.

Calder, M. (2003) 'The assessment framework: A critique and reformulation', in M. Calder and S. Hackett (eds), *Assessment in Child Care: Using and Developing Frameworks for Practice.* Lyme Regis: Russell House Publishing.

Calder, M. (ed.) (2008) *The Carrot or the Stick? Towards Effective Practice with Involuntary Clients in Safeguarding Children Work.* Lyme Regis: Russell House Publishing.

Calder, M. and Hackett, S. (eds) (2003) *Assessment in Child Care: Using and Developing Frameworks for Practice.* Lyme Regis: Russell House Publishing.

Carpenter, J., McLaughlin, H., Patsios, D., Blewett, J., Platt, D., Scholar, H., Tunstill, J., Wood, M. and Shardlow, S. (2010) *Newly Qualified Social Worker Programme Evaluation of the First Year: 2008–2009*. Leeds: CWDC. Available at www.cwdcouncil.org.uk/assets/0001/1070/NQSW_Y1_Evaluation_full_colour.pdf (accessed 23 January 2011).

CHANGE (2010) *Supporting Parents with Learning Disabilities: Good Practice Guidance: Easy Read*. Available at www.changepeople.co.uk/productDetails.php?id=2110&type=4 (accessed 6 January 2011).

Children Act 1989. London: HMSO.

Children Act 2004. London: HMSO.

Children and Young Persons Act 2008. London: The Stationery Office.

Cleaver, H. and Walker, S. (2004) 'From policy to practice: the implementation of a new framework for social work assessments of children and families', *Child and Family Social Work*, 9 (1): 81–90.

Cleaver, H., Unell, I. and Aldgate, J. (1999) *Children's Needs – Parenting Capacity: The impact of parental mental illness, problem alcohol and drug use and domestic violence on children's development*. London: The Stationery Office.

Cleaver, H. and Walker, S. with Meadows, P. (2004) *Assessing Children's Needs: The Impact of the Assessment Framework*. London: Jessica Kingsley Publishers.

Clifford, D. and Burke, B. (2004) 'Moral and professional dilemmas in long term assessment of children and families', *Journal of Social Work*, 4: 305–21.

Corby, B. (2006) *Child Abuse: Towards a Knowledge Base*. Maidenhead: Open University Press.

Cottrell, S. (2005) *Critical Thinking Skills*. Basingstoke: Palgrave Macmillan.

Cox, A. and Bentovim, A. (2000) 'The Family Pack of Questionnaires and Scales', in Department of Health et al., *Framework for the Assessment of Children in Need and their Families*. London: The Stationery Office.

Cunningham, G. (2004) 'Supervision and governance', in D. Statham (ed.), *Managing Front Line Practice in Social Care*. London: Jessica Kingsley Publishers.

CWDC (Children's Workforce Development Council) (2006) *CWDC Induction Standards for Use in Children's Social Care*. Leeds: CWDC. Available at www.cwdcouncil.org.uk/social-care/induction (accessed 17 January 2010).

CWDC (Children's Workforce Development Council) (2009) *The Common Assessment Framework for Children and Young People: A Guide for Practitioners*. Leeds: CWDC. Available at www.cwdcouncil.org.uk/assets/0000/9081/CAF_Practitioner_Guide.pdf (accessed 2 March 2011).

CWDC (Children's Workforce Development Council) (2010) *CWDC Social Work Programme*. Available at www.cwdcouncil.org.uk/social-work/programme (accessed 17 January 2010).

CWDC (Children's Workforce Development Council) (2011) *Newly Qualified Social Worker & Early Professional Development Programmes*. Available at www.cwdcouncil.org.uk/social-work/nqsw-epd (accessed 2 March 2011).

Dalzell, R. and Sawyer, E. (2007) *Putting Analysis into Assessment: Undertaking Assessments of Children in Need*. London: National Children's Bureau.

Daniel, P. and Ivatts, J. (1998) *Children and Social Policy*. London: Macmillan.

Davies, M. (1994) *The Essential Social Worker: An Introduction to Professional Practice in the 1990s*. Farnham: Ashgate.

Dennis, J. (2005) *Ringing the Changes: The impact of Guidance on the Use of Sections 17 and 20 of the Children Act 1989 to Support Unaccompanied Asylum-seeking Children.* London: Refugee Council. Available at www.refugeecouncil.org.uk/OneStopCMS/Core/CrawlerResource Server.aspx?resource=063A9362-8227-4445-AA30-CCE982B3D36A&mode=link&guid= 6157b27655574ed4b8fb03f1a2de4fb7 (accessed 20 January 2011).

DCSF (Department for Children, Schools and Families and Communities and Local Government) (2008a) *Information Sharing: Guidance for Practitioners and Managers.* Nottingham: DCSF Publications. Available at www.education.gov.uk/publications.

DCSF (2008b) *Integrated Children's System Evaluation: Summary of Key Findings. Research Brief.* Available at www.education.gov.uk/publications/standard/publicationDetail/ Page1/DCSF-RBX-02-08.

DCSF (2008c) *The Children Act 1989 Guidance and Regulations Volume 1 Court Orders.* London: The Stationery Office.

DCSF (Department for Children, Schools and Families) (2009) www.dcsf.gov.uk/every-childmatters/safeguardingandsocialcare/integratedchildrenssytem/abouttheintegrated childrenssystem/about (accessed 17 January 2010).

DCSF (Department for Children, Schools and Families) (2010) *Working Together to Safeguard Children.* Nottingham: DCSF Publications. Available at www.education.gov. uk/publications.

DfES (Department for Education and Skills) (2003) *Every Child Matters – Summary.* Nottingham: DfES Publications. Available at www.education.gov.uk/consultations/ downloadableDocs/EveryChildMattersSummary.pdf (accessed 3 March 2011).

DfES (Department for Education and Skills) (2004a) *Every Child Matters: Change for Children.* Nottingham: DfES Publications. Available at www.education.gov.uk/publications.

DfES (Department for Education and Skills) (2004b) *Every Child Matters: Next Steps.* Nottingham: DfES Publications. Available at www.education.gov.uk/publications.

DfES (Department for Education and Skills) (2007) *Care Matters: Time for Change.* Cm 7137. London: The Stationery Office. Available at www.education.gov.uk/publications.

DH (Department of Health) (1985) *The Pink Book: Social Work Decisions in Child Care.* London. The Stationery Office.

DH (Department of Health) (1988) *Protecting Children: A Guide for Social Workers Undertaking a Comprehensive Assessment.* London: The Stationery Office.

DH (Department of Health) (1991a) *Patterns and Outcomes in Child Placement.* London. The Stationery Office.

DH (Department of Health) (1991b) *Child Abuse: A Study of Inquiry Reports 1980–1989.* London: The Stationery Office.

DH (Department of Health) (1995) *Child Protection: Messages from Research.* London: The Stationery Office.

DH (Department of Health) (1998) *Modernising Social Services.* Cm 4169. London: The Stationery Office.

DH (Department of Health) (1999) *Working Together to Safeguard Children.* London: The Stationery Office.

DH (Department of Health) (2000) *A Quality Strategy for Social Care.* London: Department of Health. Available at www.dh.gov.uk/en/Publicationsandstatistics/Publications/ PublicationsPolicyAndGuidance/DH_4009379 (accessed 6 February 2011).

DH (Department of Health) (2002) *Fair Access to Care Services – Guidance on Eligibility Criteria for Adult Social Care.* Local Authority Circular LAC (2002)13. Available at www.

dh.gov.uk/en/Publicationsandstatistics/Publications/PublicationsPolicyAndGuidance/DH_4009653 (accessed 6 February 2011).

DH (Department of Health) (2003) *Guidance on Accommodating Children in Need and their Families*. Local Government Circular LAC (2003)13. Available at www.dh.gov.uk/en/Publicationsandstatistics/Lettersandcirculars/Localauthoritysocialservicesletters/DH_4003946 (accessed 20 January 2011).

DH (Department of Health) (2005) *Responding to Domestic Abuse: Handbook for Health Professionals*. London: The Stationery Office.

DH (Department of Health) (2010) *Prioritising Need in the Context of Putting People First. A Whole System Approach to Eligibility for Social Care Guidance on Eligibility Criteria for Adult Social Care*. London: The Stationery Office.

DH et al. (Department of Health, Department for Education and Employment and the Home Office) (2000) *Framework for the Assessment of Children in Need and their Families: Practice Guidance*. London. Stationery Office. Available at http://www.dh.gov.uk/en/Publicationsandstatistics/Publications/PublicationsPolicyAndGuidance/DH_4008144.

DH and DfES (Department of Health and the Department for Education and Skills) (2004) *National Service Framework for Children, Young People and Maternity Services: Core Standards*. London: DH Publications. Available at www.dh.gov.uk/en/Publicationsandstatistics/Publications/PublicationsPolicyAndGuidance/DH_4089099.

DH and DfES (Department of Health and the Department for Education and Skills) (2007) *Good Practice Guidance on Working with Parents with a Learning Difficulty*. London: DH Publications.

DH (Department of Health) and the Home Office (1991) *Working Together under the Children Act 1989: A Guide to Arrangements for Inter-agency Co-operation for the Protection of Children from Abuse*. London: HMSO.

DHSS (Department of Health and Social Security) (1982) *Child Abuse: A Study of Inquiry Reports 1973–1981*. London: HMSO.

DSS (Department of Social Security) (1995) *Households below Average Income: A Statistical Analysis 1979–1992/3 and revised edition*. London: HMSO.

De Shazer, S. (1985) *Keys to Solution in Brief Therapy*. London: Norton.

Disability and Equality Act 2010. London: The Stationery Office.

Egan, G. (1994) *The Skilled Helper*. Monterey, CA: Brooks/Cole Publishers.

Fahlberg, V. (1994) *A Child's Journey Through Placement*. London: BAAF.

Fawcett, M. (2009) *Learning Through Child Observation*. London: Jessica Kingsley Publishers.

Fook, J. (2002) *Social Work: Critical Thinking and Practice*. London: Sage Publications.

Fook, J. and Gardner, F. (2007) *Practising Critical Reflection: A Resource Handbook*. Maidenhead: Open University Press.

Fox Harding, L. (1997) *Perspectives in Child Care Policy*. London: Longman.

Franklin, B. and Parton, N. (1991) *Social Work, the Media and Public Relations*. London: Routledge.

General Social Care Council (2000) *Quality Assuring for Child Care Social Work*. London: GSCC.

Gerhardt, S. (2004) *Why Love Matters: How Affection Shapes a Baby's Brain*. Hove: Routledge.

Gilchrist, E., Johnson, R., Takriti, R., Weston, S., Beech, A. and Kebbell, M. (2003) *Domestic Violence Offenders: Characteristics and Offending Related Needs*. London: Home Office.

Haringey Local Safeguarding Children Board (2009) *Serious Case Review Baby Peter.* Available at www.haringeylscb.org/executive_summary_peter_final.pdf.

Harris, N. (1987) 'Defensive social work', *British Journal of Social Work*, 17(1): 61–69.

Helm, D. (2010) *Making Sense of Child and Family Assessment: How to Interpret Children's Needs.* London: Jessica Kingsley Publishers.

Hester, M. and Pearson, C. (1998) 'From periphery to centre: domestic violence in work with abused children'. Cited in Department of Health (1999) *Working Together to Safeguard Children.* London: The Stationery Office.

Hill, M. (2000) *Understanding Social Policy.* Oxford: Blackwell.

HM Treasury (2003) *Every Child Matters.* Cm. 5860. London: The Stationery Office.

Hoare, L., Stranger, C., Adams, K. et al. (1998) *Someone Else's Children: Inspection of Planning and Decision Making for Children Looked After and the Safety of Children Looked After.* London: Department of Health.

Hobsbawm, E. (1994) *The Age of Extremes: The Short Twentieth Century 1914–1991.* London: Michael Joseph.

Holland, S. (2010) 'Engaging children and their parents in the assessment process', in J. Horwath (ed.), *The Child's World: The Comprehensive Guide to Assessing Children in Need.* London: Jessica Kingsley Publishers.

Holland, S. (2011) *Child and Family Assessment in Social Work Practice*, 2nd edition. London: Sage Publications.

Hollows, A. (2003) 'Making professional judgements in the framework for assessment of children in need and their families', in M. Calder and S. Hackett (eds), *Assessment in Child Care: Using and Developing Frameworks for Practice.* Lyme Regis: Russell House Publishing.

Home Office (1998) *Supporting Families: A Consultation Document.* London: The Stationery Office.

Home Office (2003) *Hidden Harm: Responding to the Needs of Children of Problem Drug Users.* Available at www.drugmisuse.isdscotland.org/publications/local/hharm_summary. pdf (accessed 3 October 2009).

Home Office UK Border Agency (2010) *Immigration Rules.* Available at www.ukba. homeoffice.gov.uk/policyandlaw/immigrationlaw/immigrationrules/ (accessed 15 January 2011).

Horwath, J. (ed.) (2010) *The Child's World: The Comprehensive Guide to Assessing Children in Need.* London: Jessica Kingsley Publishers.

Howe, D. (2003) 'Assessments using an attachment perspective', in C. Calder and S. Hackett (eds), *Assessment in Child Care: Using and Developing Frameworks for Practice.* Lyme Regis: Russell House Publishing Ltd.

Howe, D. (2009) *A Brief Introduction to Social Work Theory.* Basingstoke: Palgrave Macmillan.

Howe, D. (2010) 'Attachment: Implications for assessing children's needs and parenting capacity', in J. Horwath (ed.), *The Child's World: The Comprehensive Guide to Assessing Children in Need.* London: Jessica Kingsley Publishers.

Howes, N. (2010) 'Here to listen', in J. Horwath (ed.), *The Child's World: The Comprehensive Guide to Assessing Children in Need.* London: Jessica Kingsley Publishers.

Humphreys, C. and Stanley, N. (eds) (2006) *Domestic Violence and Child Protection: Directions for Good Practice.* London: Jessica Kingsley Publishers.

Iwaniec, D. (2006) *The Emotionally Abused and Neglected Child: Identification, Assessment and Intervention. A Practice Handbook.* Chichester: John Wiley and Sons.

Jack, G. and Jack, D. (2000) 'Ecological social work: The application of a systems model of development in context', in P. Stepney and D. Ford (eds), *Social Work Models, Methods and Theory*. Lyme Regis: Russell House Publishing Ltd.

Joint Chief Inspectors Report (2002) *Safeguarding Children: The second joint Chief Inspectors' Report on Arrangements to Safeguard Children*. London: The Stationery Office.

Kadushin, A. (1976) *Supervision in Social Work*. New York: Columbia University Press.

Laming Report (2003) *The Victoria Climbié Inquiry*. Report of an Inquiry by Lord Laming. Cm. 5730. London: The Stationery Office.

Lefevre, M. (2008) 'Assessment and decision-making in child protection: relationship-based considerations', in M. Calder (ed.), *The Carrot or the Stick? Towards Effective Practice with Involuntary Clients in Safeguarding Children Work*. Lyme Regis: Russell House Publishing.

Leicestershire and Rutland Local Safeguarding Board. Available at www.lrlscb.org (accessed 6 February 2011).

Lewis, J. and Glennerster, H. (1996) *Implementing the New Community Care*. Milton Keynes: Open University Press.

Lishman, J. (1994) 'Communication in social work', in British Association of Social Workers (BASW), *Practical Social Work*. Basingstoke: Palgrave Macmillan.

Littlechild, B. (2005) 'The nature and effects of violence against child-protection social workers: Providing effective support', *British Journal of Social Work*, 35 (3): 387–401.

Lymbery, M. and Butler, S. (2004) *Social Work Ideals and Practice Realities*. Basingstoke: Palgrave Macmillan.

Maclean, M. (2002) 'The Green Paper Supporting Families 1998', in A. Carling, S. Duncan and R. Edwards (eds), *Analysing Families: Morality and Rationality in Policy and Practice*. London: Routledge.

Marsh, P. and Fisher, M. (2005) *Developing the Evidence Base for Social Work and Social Care Practice*. Social Care Institute for Excellence. Available at www.scie.org.uk/publications/reports/report10.asp (accessed 4 July 2011).

McCracken, D.G. (1988) *The Long Interview*. Beverly Hills, CA: Sage Publications.

Middleton, L. (1999) *Disabled Children Challenging Social Exclusion*. Oxford: Blackwell Science.

Milner, J. and O'Bryne, P. (2009) *Assessment in Social Work*. Basingstoke: Palgrave Macmillan.

Morgan, R. (2006) *About Social Workers: A Children's Views Report*. Available at www.rights4me.org (accessed 3 February 2011).

Morris, J. and Wates, M. (2007) *Working Together to Support Disabled Parents*. SCIE Guide 19. London: Social Care Institute for Excellence. Available at www.scie.org.uk/publications/guides/guide19/index.asp (accessed 6 January 2011).

Morris, K. (2002) 'Family-based social work', in R. Adams, L. Dominelli and M. Payne (eds), *Critical Practice in Social Work*. Basingstoke: Palgrave Macmillan.

Morrison, T. (2000) *Supervision in Social Care*. Brighton: Pavilion.

Morrison, T. (2010) 'Assessing parental motivation for change', in J. Horworth (ed.) *The Child's World: The Comprehensive Guide to Assessing Children in Need*. London: Jessica Kingsley.

Munro, E. (2005) 'A systems approach to investigating child abuse deaths', *British Journal of Social Work*, 35: 531–46.

Munro, E. (2008) *Effective Child Protection*. London: Sage Publications.

Munro, E. (2010) *The Munro Review of Child Protection – Part One: A Systems Analysis*. London: DfE. Available at www.education.gov.uk/munroreview/ (accessed 21 January 2011).

Munro, E. (2011) *The Munro Review of Child Protection Interim Report: The Child's Journey*. London: DfE. Available at www.education.gov.uk/munroreview/ (accessed 3 March 2011).

Myers, S. (2008) *Solution-focused Approaches*. Lyme Regis: Russell House Publishing.

Newman, T. and Roberts, H. (1997) 'Assessing social work effectiveness in child care practice: the contribution of randomized controlled trials', *Child: Health, Care and Development*, 23 (4): 287–96.

Office of the Children's Commissioner (2006) *Kinship Care – Submission Children in Care Green Paper Team*. Available at www.childrenscommissioner.gov.uk/force_download.php?... assets%2Fcp%2Fpublication%2F94%2FKinship_Care (accessed 20 September 2009).

Packman, J. and Jordan, B. (1991) 'The Children Act: Looking forward, looking back', *British Journal of Social Work,* 21: 315–27.

Parton, N. (1999) 'Ideology, politics and policy', in O. Stevenson (ed.), *Child Welfare in the UK*. Oxford: Blackwell.

Parton, N. (2006) *Safeguarding Childhood: Early Intervention and Surveillance in a Late Modern Society*. Basingstoke: Palgrave Macmillan.

Parton, N. and Thomas, T. (1983) 'Child abuse and citizenship', in B. Jordan and N. Parton (eds), *The Political Dimensions of Social Work*. Oxford: Blackwell.

Payne, M. (2005) *Modern Social Work Theory*. Basingstoke: Palgrave Macmillan.

Postle, K. (2002) 'Working between the idea and the reality: ambiguities and tensions in care managers' work', *British Journal of Social Work*, 32: 335–51.

Prochaska, J. and Di Clemente, C. (1982) 'Trans-theoretical therapy: towards a more integrative model of change', *Psychotherapy: Theory, Research and Practice*, 19 (3): 276–88.

Prochaska, J. and Norcross, J. (2009) *Systems of Psychotherapy: A Transtheoretical Analysis*. Belmont, CA: Wadsworth Publishing Co.

Raynes, B. (2003) 'A stepwise process of assessment', in H. Calder and S. Hackett (eds), *Assessment in Child Care. Using and Developing Frameworks for Practice*. Lyme Regis: Russell House Publishing.

Reder, P. and Duncan, S. (1999) *Lost Innocents: A Follow-up Study of Fatal Child Abuse*. London: Routledge.

Reder, P., Duncan, S. and Gray, M. (1993) *Beyond Blame: Child Abuse Tragedies Revisited*. London: Routledge.

Rees, J. (2009) *Life Story Books for Adopted Children: A Family Friendly Approach*. London: Jessica Kingsley Publishers.

Rogers, C. (1980) *A Way of Being*. New York: Routledge.

Ross, C. (1997) *Something to Draw On. Activities and Interventions Using an Art Therapy Approach*. London: Jessica Kingsley Publishers.

Rowe, J. and Lambert, L. (1973) *Children Who Wait*. London: Association of British Adoption Agencies.

SCIE (Social Care Institute for Excellence) (2005) SCIE Research Briefing 14: 'Helping parents with learning disabilities in their role as parents'. www.scie.org.uk/publications/briefings/briefing14/index.asp (accessed 2 March 2011).

Scottish Government (2003) *Good Practice Guidance for Working with Children and Families affected by Substance Misuse: Getting Our Priorities Right.* Edinburgh: The Scottish Government. Available at www.scotland.gov.uk/Publications/2003/02/16469/18726 (accessed 20 October 2009).

Scourfield, J. (2001a) 'Constructing women in child protection work', *Child and Family Social Work*, 6: 77–87.

Scourfield, J. (2001b) 'Constructing men in child protection work', *Men and Masculinities*, 4 (1): 70–89.

Searing, H. (2003) 'The continuing relevance of casework ideas to long-term child protection work', *Child & Family Social Work*, 8 (4): 311–20.

Seden, J. (2007) *Assessing the Needs of Children and Their Families.* Children and Young People Rights to Action Research Briefing 15. Department for Education and Skills/Research in Practice. Available at www.rip.org.uk/publications/researchbriefings.asp (accessed 20 November 2010)

Seebohm Report (1968) *Report by the Committee on Local Authority and Allied Social Services.* Cmnd 3703. London: The Stationery Office.

Sheffield Area Child Protection Committee (2005) *Serious Case Review Executive Summary in respect of the 'W' Children.*

Sheffield City Council Practice Guidance (2010) *Assessing and Supporting Learning Disabled Parents.* Sheffield: SCC.

Sibeon, R. (1990) 'Comments on the structure and form of social work knowledge', *Social Work and Social Sciences Review*, 1 (1): 29–44.

Social Work Reform Board (2010) *Building a Safe and Confident Future: One Year On. Detailed Proposals from the Social Work Reform Board.* Available at www.education.gov.uk/publications/standard/publicationDetail/Page1/DFE-00602-2010 (accessed 2 March 2011).

Social Work Task Force (2009) *Facing Up to the Task: Interim Report of the Social Work Taskforce.* Available at www.education.gov.uk/publications/standard/publicationdetail/page1/DCSF-00752-2009 (accessed 2 March 2011).

Spratt, T. and Callan, J. (2004) 'Parent's views on social work interventions in child welfare cases', *British Journal of Social Work*, 34: 199–244.

Statham, D. (2004) 'Research and the management of practice', in D. Statham (ed.), *Managing Front Line Practice in Social Care.* London: Jessica Kingsley Publishers.

Stepney, P. and Ford, D. (2000) *Social Work Models, Methods and Theories: A Framework for Practice.* Lyme Regis: Russell House Publishing.

Stevenson, O. (1999) 'Social work with children and families', in O. Stevenson (ed.), *Child Welfare in the UK.* Oxford: Blackwell.

Stevenson, O. (2004) 'The future of social work', in M. Lymbery and S. Butler (eds), *Social Work Ideals and Practice Realities.* Basingstoke: Palgrave Macmillan.

Thompson, N. (2005) *Understanding Social Work: Preparing for Practice.* Basingstoke: Palgrave Macmillan.

Trevithick, P. (2005) *Social Work Skills*, 2nd edn. Berkshire: Open University Press.

Trinder, L. (2000) 'A critical appraisal of evidence-based practice', in L. Trinder and S. Reynolds (eds), *Evidence-Based Practice: A Critical Appraisal.* Oxford: Blackwell.

Turney, D. (2009) *Analysis and Critical Thinking in Assessment Literature Review.* Dartington: Research in Practice.

UN High Commissioner for Refugees (1994) *Refugee Children: Guidelines on Protection and Care*. Available at www.unhcr.org/refworld/docid/3ae6b3470.html (accessed 17 January 2011).

Utting, W., Baines, C., Stuart, M. et al. (1997) *People Like Us: The Report of the Review of the Safeguards for Children Living Away from Home*. London: The Stationery Office.

Walter, I., Nutley, S., Percy-Smith, J., McNeish, D. and Frost, S. (2004) *Improving the Use of Research in Social Care Practice*. SCIE Knowledge Review 07. London: Social Care Institute for Excellence. Available at www.scie.org.uk/publications/knowledge reviews/kr07.pdf (accessed 6 February 2011).

Warner, N. (1992) *Choosing with Care – The Report of the Committee of Inquiry into the Selection, Development and Management of Staff in Children's Homes*. London: HMSO.

Waterhouse, R. (2000) *Lost in Care, Report of the Tribunal of Inquiry into the Abuse of Children in Care in the Former County Council Areas of Gwynedd and Clwyd Since 1974*. London: Stationery Office.

Watson, D. and West, J. (2006) *Social Work Process and Practice*. Basingstoke: Palgrave Macmillan.

Webb, S. (2001) 'Some considerations on the validity of evidence based practice', *British Journal of Social Work*, 31(1): 57–79.

White, S. and Featherstone, B. (2005) 'Communicating misunderstandings: multi agency work as social work practice', *Child and Family Social Work*, 10 (3): 207–16.

Women's Aid (2011) *Domestic Violence: General*. Available at www.womensaid.org.uk/domestic_violence_topic.asp?section=0001000100220041&sectionTitle=Domestic+violence+%28general%29 (accessed 1 February 2011).

Young, J. (1999) *The Exclusive Society: Social Exclusion, Crime and Difference in Late Modernity*. London: Sage Publications.

Index

NOTE: Page numbers in italic type refer to figures and tables.